THATCHER'S SPY

Willie Carlin was born and raised in Derry. Joining the British Army in 1965, he was recruited by MI5 in 1974, and later the Force Research Unit, to infiltrate Sinn Féin. Over the next 11 years, he built up close contacts with Martin McGuinness and Mitchel McLaughlin, becoming one of Britain's most valuable long-term agents in Northern Ireland. His cover was blown by a former handler in 1985, and he and his family were extracted to a new life with new identities. He continues to live outside Ireland to this day.

THATCHER'S SPY

MY LIFE AS AN MI5 AGENT INSIDE SINN FÉIN

WILLIE CARLIN

MERRION
PRESS

First published in 2019 by
Merrion Press
An imprint of Irish Academic Press
10 George's Street
Newbridge
Co. Kildare
Ireland
www.merrionpress.ie

9781785372858 (Paper)
9781785372865 (Kindle)
9781785372872 (Epub)
9781785372889 (PDF)

British Library Cataloguing in Publication Data
An entry can be found on request

Library of Congress Cataloging in Publication Data
An entry can be found on request

Typeset in Sabon LT Std 12/17 pt

Cover front: The Molostock/Shutterstock.com;
Malivan_Iuliia/Shutterstock.com.
Cover back: Gareth McCormack/Alamy Stock Photo.

CONTENTS

ACKNOWLEDGEMENTS

To Liam Clarke, my dear friend, who sadly passed away before this book was published. Liam was the *Sunday Times* journalist who befriended me and helped join the dots of my life as a spy. I miss him dearly.

Hugh Jordan of the *Sunday World* is a journalist and a friend who has worked tirelessly over many years to keep my story in the public eye.

My thanks to Henry McDonald of the *Observer* who worked endlessly on my raw manuscript and reshaped it into the book it is today.

To Neil McKay of the *Herald*, simply the best journalist I've ever met.

Jennifer O'Leary from BBC NI's Spotlight team is a reporter whose courage I greatly admire.

Bernie from the Kenova Inquiry team.

Aaron Edwards. A colleague from Sandhurst.

Imran Khan, my lawyer and friend, who has always been there for me and my family.

To Conor Graham, Publisher with Merrion Press, for believing in me and risking his entire business in order to publish this book.

Finally to my friends in Ayrshire, Scotland.

This book is dedicated to all those men, women and children of Derry who lost their lives during the Troubles, and to all those who strove for peace, either openly or behind the scenes.

PROLOGUE

'YOU'LL BE DEAD BY THE MORNING'

By the mid-1980s my star was rising inside Sinn Féin. I was well regarded as a republican activist in Derry and was known to have the ear of leading republicans like Mitchel McLaughlin and Martin McGuinness. But there was another side to this story, for since 1974 I had led a double life, part Sinn Féin activist and part undercover secret agent for the British government, and to MI5 I was simply known as 'agent 007'. This would all end abruptly when I was warned one day that if I didn't leave Northern Ireland I would be 'dead by the morning'. Before you dismiss the end of my covert life as a highly placed agent inside the Irish republican movement as a pale imitation of the spy fiction of Ian Fleming or John le Carré, please read on.

It was thanks to a fellow spy, codenamed 'Stakeknife', and with a little help from one of British history's most controversial prime ministers that I was spared interrogation, torture and a bullet in the brain. I really was within hours of summary execution by the IRA were it not for Margaret Thatcher and, more crucially, the Provisional's spy catcher supreme, who, unknown to Martin McGuinness and the rest of the IRA leadership, was also a highly placed British agent operating at the heart of their organisation. Were it not for him I would have ended up dumped on the side of a lonely border road or in the back of an alley in Derry, my bloodied corpse left like a dog as a warning to others, killed for treachery by my old friends and comrades.

The end arrived innocuously enough in March 1985. I was watching the television news at home in the Waterside in Derry, when I received a telephone call through from my handler, 'Ginger', who was stationed at Ebrington, a military-security barracks built in the nineteenth century overlooking the River Foyle. There was an unusual urgency in his voice as he told me to get to the base as quickly as possible. I could tell something was off when he offered to pick me up at the end of my street, not at our usual secret rendezvous point. As I entered the intelligence briefing room I was met by another British military intelligence officer, 'Karen', who looked at me gravely. 'The Boss wants a word, Willie,' she said, as a medium-sized stocky man with black hair, wearing a blue V-neck jumper and grey trousers, entered the room.

The casually dressed spymaster looked at me seriously and bluntly laid out the situation, 'Right Willie, I'm not going to beat about the bush, but I have to tell you. Your cover's been blown.' He went on to stress that my relationship with British military intelligence had not been compromised. However, it was my previous role working for MI5 from the mid-1970s that had been exposed. 'We have intercepted an order from the IRA to lift and interrogate you. It's our information that you will probably be taken away in about eight hours' time,' the head of the military intelligence unit continued. 'Willie, you'll be dead by the morning, so I'm pulling you out of here tonight.'

I was speechless as he carried on with his 'orders'.

'What I want you to do is go home now, tell your wife and give her the choice of coming with you. But you must emphasise to her that her life will be in danger if you disappear on your own. I can have you and your family out of here in a couple of hours and I'll take you all up to Belfast tonight where you'll be safe, but we must move fast because I don't know who else knows or who might move against you.'

Then he informed me that Margaret Thatcher herself was personally aware of the situation and was furious I had been unmasked as a traitor (in the Provisional IRA's eyes), and that my reports of the political intrigue and machinations within Sinn Féin had been carefully read over the last few years by the Prime Minister herself in 10 Downing Street, 'You can be sure of one thing though, the Prime Minister already knows and is said to be livid, so you can bet she will be asking questions. You don't have to worry about being abandoned, you'll be well looked after.'

Just before my exposure I had been rising up the ranks of Sinn Féin in Derry and was getting ever closer to Martin McGuinness, then the IRA's chief of staff as well as one of the party's key strategists, and later Deputy First Minister of Northern Ireland. My briefings to my handlers in Ebrington included information on McGuinness's internal battles with even more hardline republicans, as well as his thoughts, ranging from participation in elections to his hostility to the extension into Scotland of the IRA's English bombing campaign. Some of the secret political intelligence I had provided was mulled over and analysed by the Prime Minister, as well as her Cabinet ministers; it gave them a unique insight into the evolution of Sinn Féin and, critically, McGuinness's own thinking.

As the Troubles raged in Northern Ireland, the wider world in the mid-1980s was gridlocked by the new Cold War. The Soviet Union, with its massive nuclear arsenal, still posed an existential threat to the West. Meanwhile, Ronald Reagan fuelled paranoia not only in Moscow but on the streets of western European cities with his 'Star Wars' program to militarise space alongside his deployment of cruise missiles in the UK and West Germany. The secret spy war against the Soviets continued apace, which included KGB spies covertly working for the British and Americans while disgruntled MI5 officers offered up secrets of their own to the USSR. One such traitor on the British side was Michael Bettaney, or as I had once known him, 'Ben'.

After I was recruited as an MI5 agent following my discharge from the British Army in the early 1970s, Ben had been my handler. In 1980, Bettaney was moved at my request from the north of Ireland to work in the security service's Soviet counter-espionage agency, based at Gower Street in London. His critics later claimed that Bettaney was driven by alcoholism and anger after being passed over for promotion; his supporters on the British far left, who befriended him when he was eventually imprisoned, allege that the working class, Oxford-educated linguist was an idealist and only volunteered to help the KGB for ideological reasons. Whatever the truth about his motives, Bettaney was compromised thanks to one of the security service's most valuable assets inside the KGB – Oleg Gordievsky. Bettaney had been trying to contact the senior KGB chief in the USSR's London embassy, but his information was passed to another officer, Arkady Guk, who didn't take any notice of his request and instead forwarded it to Oleg Gordievsky – the deputy head of the KBG in London – who was in fact an agent for MI6. It wasn't long before Bettaney was trapped and caught. This Cold War drama set off a chain reaction which resulted in our flight out of Derry with the threat of death hanging over me and my family.

After being found guilty of spying for the Soviets, in 1983 Bettaney was sentenced to twenty-three years in jail. While in Swaleside prison he befriended IRA prisoners, including one of its most important leaders, Belfast man Brian Keenan, who had established links with Libyan dictator Colonel Gaddafi and the Assad regime in Syria. An ironic friendship built up between Bettaney and members of the IRA's England department during their incarceration; after all, Bettaney had been badly injured in an IRA car bomb while working for MI5 in Belfast in 1976. What he had to tell the IRA inmates, and in particular Keenan, was sensational. After prison staff left Keenan alone with Bettaney at mass, the ex-British spook revealed to the IRA veteran that a highly placed informer had become one of Martin McGuinness's most trusted allies, and this agent had been in place within Derry Sinn Féin since 1974.

At first, when the information reached Belfast, the IRA thought it was a wind-up. But when they discovered who Bettaney really was they began to pump him for information. The Boss made it clear that the IRA had worked out that Bettaney had identified me, Willie Carlin, as the informer at McGuinness's side, and the IRA's 'Nutting Squad' (also nicknamed 'The Head-Hunters') had been dispatched from Belfast to lift me and take me away to a certain death. Astonished and horrified by this news, I asked the spymaster how he knew the 'Nutting Squad' was on my tail, but I would only get an answer to that conundrum once I was safely spirited out of Northern Ireland.

As I travelled back home with Ginger on the night of the revelation that my undercover career was over he had some stern advice, pleading with me to get the family ready for a rapid exit out of Derry. Ginger promised that undercover security teams would flood the area at the time of our late-night departure, to ensure our safety, but we could not bring anything with us bar a few suitcases. We would be unable to ship our furniture over to a new location in England once we were resettled, and it would have to be a quick, clean break from the city where generations of my family had grown up.

Fortunately, I had a cover story for my beloved wife Mary, which, like most really good cover stories, was based on fact. Prior to being summoned to Ebrington, the IRA's Derry Brigade had informed me that the loyalist Ulster Volunteer Force (UVF), which had an armed unit on the mainly Protestant Waterside of the city, were stalking me for a planned assassination. I truthfully told Mary that we had to get out now because the UVF were coming to kill me, though at the time I could not bring myself to reveal everything about my fourteen-year undercover stint in the republican movement – first as an MI5 agent and then in Military Intelligence.

I looked around our living room at all the things Mary had struggled over the years to buy. I was heartbroken. We had a lovely home and now it was all going to be taken away from us. In a way Mary had more to lose than I did. I wasn't that involved with my family, though I loved them very much, but she was the lynchpin of her mum and dad's life. Mary fretted grievously about what would happen to her elderly mother and father once we left Derry; she visited them every day, did their shopping, organised their bills, looked after their pensions and often made meals for them. How they would survive without her and how she would cope not ever seeing them again played on my mind as we dressed the children and tried to get ready in time for Ginger's call. Mary even rinsed the dishes and ran the cleaner over the carpet in the living room. My son Mark was not convinced about our story that we were all going on a holiday, though Michael was okay about it. As for my daughter Maria, she was only five and didn't really understand. But she loved her 'nanny' and I wasn't sure how she'd adjust, never seeing her again.

It seemed to take ages for the phone to ring as we sat there in the dark, looking out of the window, but at 2.20am Ginger called and within minutes the Carlin family were in two cars, heading out of our street. We spent the next four hours in Ebrington before being whisked away to Belfast and then put up in the Palace Barracks near Holywood, which is still home to British Army regiments in the north and latterly has become the regional HQ of MI5. After a week in the military base we were taken to RAF Aldergrove where to my astonishment Margaret Thatcher's ministerial jet was waiting to fly us to England. The Prime Minister had ordered that the plane she travelled on to world summits, conferences and other important engagements all over the planet was 'loaned' to the Carlins for the day.

At the bottom of the six steps leading up to the doorway of Thatcher's plane, a female RAF Sergeant and an officer saluted as Mary, my children and I boarded. I remember wondering what our 'meeters and greeters' must have thought when they saw this ordinary family from Derry approach Mrs Thatcher's jet carrying one bulging, battered suitcase and two black bin liners stuffed with clothes. As we entered the aircraft, I recall the distinct whiff of lemon freshener in the air, as well as the plush blue carpet beneath our feet. The seats were of white leather, with blue RAF cloths on the headrests. My children had never been on a plane before, which prompted my daughter Maria to exclaim, 'Whoa!' as the jet tore down the runway and soared into the air. After the plane reached cruising altitude my son Michael bounded out of his seat and made for the toilets. When he returned he elbowed his brother Mark in the side and boasted, 'Mark! I just did a pee in Maggie Thatcher's toilet. You should go and try it. It flushes itself when you put the seat down!' Michael then kept asking me why Maggie's loo was 'tin' and not white; he didn't know that it was stainless steel.

About half an hour into the flight the RAF crew came around with tea and biscuits. I stared down at the blue carpet where Mrs Thatcher and her ministers had walked so many times before and was struck by the absurdity of it all. What the hell was I doing on her private jet? And what would the future have in store for us now that we were going into permanent exile? But there was another question that still burned in the back of my brain: How did the Boss, Karen, Ginger and the rest of the team know that I had come perilously close to execution at the hands of arguably the IRA's most ruthless unit – its internal security team.

As we came in to land at RAF Northholt, some of Ginger's words echoed around my head. He had uttered them as he drove me back to the house to tell Mary that we had to leave Derry for good, 'You'll look back on this moment and thank God for our man in Belfast because he just saved your life.'

The identity of the mysterious 'man in Belfast', who tipped off his own handlers that Willie Carlin was about to be picked up, questioned, beaten, psychologically tortured and then shot dead, would haunt me in exile for many years. But for now that was at the end of my time as a spy, an undercover life that began with a calling.

CHAPTER 1

FROM HOLY ORDERS
TO BATTLE ORDERS

Prior to my decision to follow my father's footsteps into the British Army I had another calling, and this one was from God. Just before leaving primary school in Derry I went to see the biblical epic *King of Kings* at the Rialto Cinema on Market Street. Moved and mesmerised by Jeffrey Hunter's portrayal of Jesus, my best friend Michael Stewart and I talked about becoming priests. Shortly after Easter, we spoke to our parents about the priesthood and later were sent to a religious retreat across the border in Donegal, which was part of a special weekend for boys in their mid-teens thinking of entering Holy Orders. Although impressed by the selfless frugality of the monks at the Doon Well and Ards Monastery, the desire to become a priest had wore off by my final year in 'big school'. In contrast, Michael entered the seminary in his early twenties, and eventually served in Nottingham and Derry before tragically dying at a young age from an undetected brain tumour.

I often wonder where my life might have taken me if I had trodden the same path as Michael and ended up in some Derry parish, or even in an isolated mission in a far-flung place on the other side of the world. But by my late teens there was a calling towards another life in uniform – the colours of the Queen's Royal Irish Hussars.

Although born into a devout Derry Catholic family, it was
not unusual for a family like mine to have strong, historic
connections to the British military. At the time of my birth on
30 July 1948, my father Tommy Carlin was working at the local
Royal Navy base, HMS *Sea Eagle*, on the Waterside. During the
Second World War, Derry was an important naval installation
for the British and later the American navies during the Battle of
the Atlantic. German U-boats were scuttled in the Foyle after the
defeat of the Third Reich, and the city was filled with tales of the
Yanks who were based in Derry during the 1940s. Our history
classes in primary school were full of stories of bad Nazis and the
bold Americans who were sent to save us. There was never any
mention of the IRA, the English, or the Troubles of the 1920s,
and I knew where an exotic place called Burma was because I
would tell my classmates and my teachers that this was where
my daddy had been stationed during the war.

Tommy Carlin spent the post-war years working with the
Royal Navy, this time as a civilian worker at HMS *Sea Eagle*,
where he also played in the Navy's football team – the Sea Eagle
Rovers. I remember one afternoon watching his team play on
the big sports ground at Clooney Park West on Waterside. After
their 1-0 defeat, he and the rest of the Rovers retired to a place
overlooking the Foyle called Ebrington Barracks on their way
back to *Sea Eagle*. It was the first time I walked through the
gateway of the nineteenth-century barracks and little did I know
that this place was going to play a key role in my later life as a
secret agent.

I finally left school at the tender age of fifteen in the summer
of 1962, and within 72 hours of being out in the big bad world
of work I got my first job. The Birmingham Sound Reproducers
(BSR) factory manufactured record players and was situated

in what we called the 'new road' that backed onto Bligh's lane. I was almost immediately sent to work in the paint shop section of the plant where I learnt how to spray paint amid the deafening noise of the machinery and the endless banter of the older men on the production line. Although I was earning about a half-crown per week I didn't like the job and was a bit spooked (given my priestly leanings and continued devout faith) at the filthy language on the shop floor; sometimes even fights broke out between grown men on the line. In fact, the only time I saw peaceful unity in the paint shop was when the news broke more than a year later that President John F. Kennedy had been shot dead in Dallas. To Derry Catholics, Kennedy was a cult hero, given his religion and proud Irish ancestry, and in many Catholic homes in the city images of him hung beside portraits of the Sacred Heart and Our Lady. Two days after his assassination the whole BSR factory downed tools, including myself, and we marched to Derry's Catholic Cathedral for a memorial mass in JFK's honour.

By the summer of 1965, I had become disillusioned with working at BSR and spoke to my father about trying again for the priesthood. When I was dissuaded against it I returned heavy-hearted to the factory gates to find the entire plant was on strike. The stoppage was a result of Derry workers going on a fact-finding tour of BSR's factory in Birmingham, where they heard a rumour that its mainly female workforce earned more than us. The bitterness over the strike resulted in poor industrial relations and led to a series of one-day strikes and walk-outs. Eventually, the owners closed the factory, moved out of Derry and left 1,500 men and boys on the dole.

During the summer I befriended Davy McMenamy, the first Protestant lad I ever knew. We had met at BSR the previous

Christmas and hit it off straight away. We hung out in some of the city's dance halls and even attended dances in the Memorial Hall on Derry's Walls, the social club run by the staunchly loyalist Apprentice Boys. There was no open sectarianism on the dance floor, though. Back then the only fights in the Memorial Hall were usually between two boys fighting over a girl. I drank my first ever beer with Davy at Butlin's holiday camp across the border in County Meath in the Irish Republic.

Davy and I talked about what might happen once BSR shut up shop in Derry. My father had often told stories of his life in the army and he agreed to chat to us about the military. One night, Davy came over to our home and Dad regaled us with tales of drills and marches as if he was trying to put us off. However, he did suggest that a much better option for us would be an armoured regiment, where we would get to drive around in armoured cars and even tanks. My older brother Robert joined in the conversation and soon all three of us were hooked. Just after my seventeenth birthday, we visited the Army Recruitment Office on Derry's Strand Road. There we met with Sergeant Derek Dunseith, the brother of the legendary Radio Ulster presenter, the late David Dunseith. After we had filled in our application forms my father signed the enlistment papers and off I went to England to join the Queen's Royal Irish Hussars.

Within weeks of meeting Sergeant Dunseith at the recruiting office on the Strand Road, and after a medical examination in Omagh, Robert and I were on our way to the Royal Armoured Corps Training Headquarters at Catterick Camp in Yorkshire. The train left Derry at 5.40pm and my father chatted to us in the station as we waited to depart. It was one of those awkward Irish conversations between a father and his sons, peppered with banalities like 'Don't forget to phone' and 'Have you got your ferry ticket?' Then he said what all Irish parents say to their sons who, deep down, they don't really want to leave, and my father was no exception. He was very proud that Robert and I were following in his footsteps and joining the army, but at the same time he was very sad that we were leaving him. He kept saying, 'Sure, it won't be long before you're back'. Soon, a whistle blew and we boarded the train. Within minutes we were waving goodbye to my father as the train pulled out of the station and we headed for Belfast.

That night I was so excited on the ferry that I couldn't sleep. I'd never seen a big ship before, let alone been on one, and we spent hours wandering around in awe of this machine. There were people in the bar, experienced travellers, who knew of the turbulent crossing that lay ahead, and their way of coping with it was to get drunk and fall asleep where they sat. By 4am, as the ferry rocked from side to side in the storm, I was uncontrollably sick. As the ship arrived at Heysham ferry terminal the next morning, still pale and ill we caught the train to Richmond. On arrival at Catterick, Robert and I were met at the guardroom by a Corporal who was passing his Sunday doing the crossword. We were a day early and none of the new recruits were expected until the next day. He directed us to Headquarters, where we were met by a Corporal of the Household Cavalry who showed us to our room. There were twelve beds in the room and we could choose any two we liked. After unpacking, Robert and I decided to go for a walk around the camp. Apart from the odd person in civvies we never actually saw any soldiers. We found a phone box and, as arranged, rang home to Leenan Gardens in Creggan where my father and mother were waiting to take the call.

The next four weeks for intake 65-9 (the ninth intake of the year) was full of kit inspections, locker checks, marching, running, and doing punishment press-ups because someone had done something wrong. A typical evening was spent listening to the radio whilst shining boots, polishing buckles or ironing kit. We were woken every morning at half past five to prepare for room inspection. Each of us had jobs to do: cleaning the Blanco room, the washrooms, the showers, the ironing room, the stairs and landing and our own room, which had to be polished and bumpered every morning. If the morning inspection went well, we were straight on parade for a day's training. If it didn't, we were cleaning again until 10am. By the end of the first week, most of us had sussed out that all the shouting and roaring and throwing of kit around the room was obviously an exercise, by our instructors, to break us and make sure that only the best got through basic training. During this time I realised two things about myself: I was very fit – probably due to running from Creggan to the Long Tower school and back twice a day for ten years – and I didn't like the English. There was something arrogant about them. Not just our instructors, but most of the lads in the intake were pushy and always thought they knew what they were talking about.

By mid-October, what was left of the intake was preparing to 'pass out' and looking forward to a weekend's leave. The kit inspections didn't happen as often, the block we lived in was immaculate, the locker inspections usually went well every day and we were a tight-knit group when it came to combat training or marching. Most of the lads in our intake had made it through because they were either determined or had the guts to sustain the daily attacks which were, in the main, well-meant and designed to change us from being civilians to soldiers.

After four weeks we had completed our GMT (General Military Training) and were rehearsing for the 'passing out' parade with the regimental band. The parade itself was a memorable experience; a day of celebration with most of the lads' parents sitting watching us as we did our stuff on the parade ground. I was very proud as my name, 24056669 Trooper Carlin, was called out and I marched forward to receive the cap badge of my regiment: 'The Queen's Royal Irish Hussars'.

Just as we were preparing to go home after the parade, my brother Robert informed me that he had failed his physical and was to be back-squatted for two weeks on our return from leave. Everyone in the intake was given leave on Friday afternoon until eight o'clock Monday morning. All of them were home by Friday night, except for Robert and I. By the skin of our teeth we made it to Heysham and the Friday night sailing of the Belfast ferry, and after an overnight journey and a two-hour train journey to Derry we got home just after 11am. Sadly, because there were no sailings from Belfast to Heysham on a Sunday, we had to leave Derry again that same Saturday night at 5.40. This gave us just fourteen hours at home, with barely enough time to have a chat about our experience and get something to eat.

We must have been the only soldiers in the British Army ever to take our kit home to show our parents how well polished it all was. During that day, the topic of Robert having to stay back came up. My father spoke to me in the kitchen, 'Wullie, would you mind very much if I got in touch with the Colonel at Catterick and asked if you could stay behind with Robert? I could put it to him that both of you want to go to Germany together because the truth is, Wullie, I don't think Robert will make it through on his own.' I was shocked because I was looking forward to joining the regiment as soon as possible. That evening, as we waited by the train in the Waterside station, my father asked me again. I was still divided between what he was asking and going to Germany. In the end I agreed to stay with Robert.

The next few weeks in Catterick were really the making of me. I was in a new squad that was learning some of the things Robert and I already knew. When it came to marching or kit inspections we were models for the other lads in the room. Suddenly, the English weren't so cocky. Often they would ask me for help, which I gladly gave. In the end, the time passed quickly enough and Robert and I made it through. We were now qualified drivers of Saladin armoured cars and Ferret Scout cars – the same military vehicles that would become commonplace on the streets of our own home town a few years later as the Troubles erupted.

After a week's leave in Derry we flew from Manchester to Hanover on a BOAC jet. This again was a new experience; I'd never been on an aeroplane before. Indeed, I'd never been to an airport before. I'll never forget the feeling in my stomach as the plane hurtled down the runway and took off. I was scared shitless as my stomach came up to the back of my throat but I just sat there smiling, as most people do, during the experience. Later that evening we arrived in Wolfenbuttle, just east of Hanover, by minibus and entered the world of the Queen's Royal Irish Hussars.

***

Life in the regiment was totally different from training. There were no kit inspections, civilian cleaners cleaned the washrooms and toilets, there were no more than three people to a room, there was no shouting or roaring at the men, and most of the soldiers had forgotten how to march. The weeks went from Monday to

Friday, preparing vehicles, servicing them, going for short drives around Wolfenbuttle and back again. No one worked after 5pm and Wednesday afternoons were reserved for Egyptian PT (lying in bed). I didn't enjoy Egyptian PT at all; instead I went for a run every Wednesday with Bob Kelly, a Lance Corporal from Dublin. He was the regiment's top cross-country runner and he soon told the captain of the team how good I was.

In 1966, telephone communication – or indeed any communication – was radically different from today. To speak to my parents from Germany I would first have to write a letter to them giving details of the exact time I would be ringing the call box in Leenan Gardens. Then three days before the call was to be made it had to be booked through the WVS (Women's Voluntary Service). The day before the call I would be notified of the time of the call (usually the time requested), and on the night of the call the WVS would phone London for a connection to Belfast, who would then connect to Derry. When the operator in Derry came on the line, the number of the telephone box in Leenan Gardens would be given and when my father answered he would be told to stand by for an international call from Germany. Once the connection was made, I was sent to the phone booth along the corridor to pick up the receiver. Calls were not allowed to last any longer than fifteen minutes and the time seemed to fly by before the operator from London would inform me that my time was up.

By 1967, I had been promoted to Lance Corporal and had settled in well. We had been on several exercises and won troop competitions against other regiments. The big main exercise each year was known as the FTX (Field Training eXercise) – a NATO operation which involved four weeks in the field. This was great if you were keen, enthusiastic and single, as I was, but not so good if you were experienced, married and enjoyed the social life that being a soldier in West Germany brought. During one of the exercises, I was involved in what was called an international Cold War incident. Third troop, 'A' Squadron, led by Lieutenant Sutcliffe, were scrambled and called out for a reconnaissance patrol along the River Elbe, which straddled the border between West Germany and East Germany. An East German survey ship had tied up on the west side of the river – on our side of the border – and the crew had mutinied and taken the captain and the other officers captive. They were now threatening to blow up the ship if their demands were not met, and as I sat in the driver's seat of the scout car, peering through the periscope, activity on the ship heightened and gunfire was heard.

I was shaking and tried to stay calm as I watched from the edge of a wood just a few hundred yards from the riverbank and the ship. Just then, a helicopter appeared overhead with a spotlight directed at the vessel. By now my knees were trembling and I put my right hand down to steady them. I could feel the sweat running down my neck and my hands were clammy as I gripped the metal steering wheel inside the cab. I had visions of being blown up or shot in the opening salvo of the Third World War as it spread along the Iron Curtain. Corporal Frankie Shivers, my commander, was advised over the radio to load up the Browning machine gun with live rounds. I heard him say, 'If we open fire on this ship we could start World War Three.' There were a further four hours of intense activity over the radio network; things were getting worse and I just sat there, frozen to the seat. All I could think of was to say a decade of the Rosary and pray that we could get out of this wood, away from the river and back to the safety of our camp.

At the other end of the woods sat another scout car manned by a commander and driven by another young Irishman just like me. Trooper Hughie McCabe was married, a Catholic from Belfast who was also not enjoying defending our gracious Queen and the German border. He and I passed the hours away chatting on the internal network about all sorts of things, we even sang songs over the net, much to the amusement of our commanders. Watching the ship we saw people come and go from the cabins until eventually things seemed to quieten down. Just before daybreak, Corporal Shivers and Lieutenant Sutcliffe were ordered to stand down. We were later told that the East German sailors had been overpowered and the ship returned to its captain. Back in the squad room we were hailed as heroes and the Colonel himself came from headquarters to congratulate us personally.

After the exercise was over, life in the camp returned to normal with lots of dos in the mess, and, for me, baby-sitting various NCOs. Tony Bamford, who had joined the army in 1966, was posted to our regiment and had become a frequent visitor to my room. As time passed we became friends, often going to the cinema or to the mess together. Tony was going on leave for the whole of August; he and his girlfriend, Mary, were to be engaged. I had also planned to be on leave for the last two weeks in August and the first two weeks in September.

Tony and I arranged to meet up when I got to Derry, and I invited him to a party at my aunt Vera's. Tony had been writing to Mary on and off for over a year and had dated her while he was on leave. He also phoned her regularly. I spoke with her one night as Tony introduced me over the phone. She sounded like a nice girl and I was pleased for him. At this time, my brother Robert was in 'B' Squadron and drove three-ton trucks, so I rarely saw him. He had gained in confidence and had friends of his own, so for the first time I travelled to Derry on leave on my own. My mother didn't know that I was coming and Tony brought her the message that I would be phoning her at the phone box in Leenan Gardens at 7pm that night. I arrived in Derry at lunchtime and was picked up by my uncle George, then spending the afternoon at Vera's. Just before 7pm, as my mother and father waited for the phone to ring, I walked up behind them and put my arms round my mother. 'Hello Mammy,' I said giving her a hug. My father had seen me coming, but stayed silent. There were tears and lots more hugs. Suddenly, I didn't feel like a soldier any more, I just felt like a wee boy who had come home. Life was boring in Creggan; most of the people that I knew were busy working or mixing with new friends and I spent most of the days helping my mother around the house.

Before my return to Germany from leave I met up with Tony and Mary. We spent the afternoon sitting in the Waterside park, listening to Tony Blackburn on Mary's transistor radio. She was a lovely girl, full of fun and energy, and she said she would write to me too as I didn't have a girlfriend or a pen friend. A few months later, back in Paderborn, Germany, Tony told me that he and Mary had sort of drifted apart and they didn't communicate anymore, which probably explained why she had never written to me. However, that Christmas Day a backlog of Christmas mail was brought into my room. There were some letters from my mother and father, cards from my brothers Tommy and Dickie and my sister Doreen, together with other cards from various aunts and uncles. There was one particular card that simply said, 'Season's Greetings' and underneath was written 'Remember me, Mary McGonagle', and her address. At the bottom in brackets, Mary had added, 'Please write to me'. I spent the rest of Christmas Day writing to Mary, and by the time I had finished had used nearly a full writing pad. I posted my letter on the first available delivery, hoping she would receive it by the New Year. Within weeks, I had received a letter back from Mary and had spoken to her on the phone. We continued to write over the spring of 1968, and I went home again on leave in June.

* * *

The regiment was posted to Bovington in Dorset, where the Royal Armoured Corps had its headquarters. At the time the centre was mainly staffed by civilians, but a recent change in emphasis by the Ministry of Defence meant that a regiment would now be in charge. The Queen's Royal Irish Hussars were the first armoured corps regiment to run Bovington and we were all to be in place by September 1968. Of course, living in the UK meant being able to get home easier, and Mary and I had talked about my coming to Derry more often and how she might be able to travel to England and visit me. It was during one such leave that Mary and I made love for the first time. I was a virgin, and I discovered that Mary was too. It was one of those fumbling love sessions that you read about, except that I was twenty and she was nineteen – the products of a good Catholic upbringing.

After I returned to Bovington, I settled down into a new way of life. I was now a Lcpl (Lance Corporal) clerk in the orderly room and was on a camp with men and women – the women being from the WRAC. During a phone call to Mary one evening, I asked her if we could get engaged. She said yes, and within weeks we were engaged to be married. The ring (from H Samuels in Ferryquay Street) was £10.17.06 and we celebrated by having two suppers in a nearby chip shop as we discussed how to tell our parents. We decided upon a ceremony on 19 July the following year and spent the next nine months saving to get married, since we had decided that we should pay for everything ourselves. Mary and I phoned each other nearly every night.

By May 1969, Mary was telling me of marches in the Creggan and Bogside and she had joined an organisation called 'The Civil Rights Association'. Ivan Cooper, one of her bosses at Kelly's Factory, was one of the leaders, together with a young man called John Hume. She told me about being charged and batoned by the 'B' Specials, who I had never heard of, and started to send me copies of the *Derry Journal* so I could read about it for myself.

On 1 July 1969 I asked the Colonel for permission to marry. As a soldier in the British Army, his permission was needed and a document had to be provided to give to the priest. Put simply, I was a number, a soldier, whose life belonged to the Ministry of Defence and, being under twenty-one, they had to be sure that I knew what I was doing and had thought things through. After a little grilling on both sides, permission was granted and I travelled home with my brother Robert and Nelson Bennett. Nelson was a Protestant and the Colonel's staff-car driver. He and I had become friendly as he waited around the orderly room to pick up the Colonel. I had asked him, as he was going on leave as well, if he fancied coming to Derry and being my groomsman. He agreed and all three of us set off for Derry, equipped with our ceremonial uniforms.

In Derry things were quite tense, but I visited Mary every night as we prepared for our wedding. Although we had saved enough money, there were still things that we made ourselves – like flowers for the guests. We had real flowers for our parents, our immediate family and the bridesmaids but for the rest of the guests we made paper flowers, which was quite common in Derry in the 60s. We would spend an hour or so each night making paper flowers using two toilet rolls, white for the men and pink for the ladies. Four pieces of toilet roll were folded into eight, bound around a pipe-cleaner, opened up layer by layer and then pared off with scissors to form the shape of a flower. A piece of real fern was attached to the rear, and silver paper was wrapped around the pipe-cleaner. The flower itself was sprayed with perfume.

On the morning of Saturday 19 July, Robert, Nelson and I, fully dressed in our 'blues' with lanyards, chainmail and spurs, posed for photographs at the back of our house in Creggan. All of the neighbours wished us well as we boarded the wedding car and headed off, down through the city centre and over to St Columb's Chapel on the Waterside. I remember travelling through the Guildhall Square and seeing all the RUC Land Rovers and a large crowd shouting at them. Soon I was waiting at the altar with Mary, her bridesmaid Ria and her flower girls, Linda and Elaine, by my side. Father Jimmy Doherty, a trendy young priest, performed the marriage ceremony.

Our wedding reception was held in the Woodleigh Hotel on the Derry side. As we celebrated at our reception, only a few hundred yards away the RUC and the 'B' Specials were attacking a small civil rights march. There were rumours amongst our guests that the army might have to be brought in to save the Catholics from the bigoted and sectarian 'B' Specials. Mary and I left the reception for our honeymoon just before 4pm. Her cousin Anthony, who had a car, drove us to Butlins in Mosney, County Meath. One night during the honeymoon there was a report on the news that a rioter had been shot dead by the RUC in Belfast. It was being said that he was possibly a terrorist because he had been aiming a rifle at an RUC patrol near a block of flats. Sadly, this turned out not to be the case; the victim was none other than Trooper Hughie McCabe, the young soldier who had defended the German border with me on the banks of the River Elbe. He was mistaken for a gunman whilst home on leave and had been shot by an RUC man who said he was on the roof of a block of flats brandishing a rifle. Sometime later, the Queen's Royal Irish Hussars held an internal board of inquiry which found that Trooper McCabe had been mistaken for a gunman and his death was possibly an 'error of judgement' at the height of intense rioting. His family was later paid compensation for the mistake, but the RUC man who killed Hughie was never cautioned, admonished or punished for his 'error of judgement'.

After our honeymoon I returned to Bovington, where a Colonel Biddy advised me of a house that I could have for £2.10s a week. It was twenty minutes from the camp in a town called Wareham in Dorset, and by September Mary and I had moved into our first new home at Tarrant's Lodge in Wareham. It was one of the nicest places we had ever seen; the neighbours were kind, there was a supermarket on the corner, and the minibus picked me up at the door every morning. The problem was, it arrived at 6.30am and I didn't get home again until 7.30 each night. Thinking back, it must have been terrible for Mary. She usually had the housework completed by 10am and must have been terribly bored for the rest of the day. We spent only a short time in Wareham, and by the end of October Mary and I had moved to a married quarters in Dorchester. By the spring, Mary was heavily pregnant and was booked into a private clinic in Dorchester – all paid for by the army. To show how naive we both were, our local GP, Doctor Burns, visited us one evening with diagrams on how the baby would be born; Mary didn't know and I had no idea either. He was amazed at our innocence and was very sympathetic. Towards the end of March he called in to see Mary nearly every other day. The regiment broke up for Easter leave on Holy Thursday, and I had sensibly booked two weeks' leave because our baby was due any day. On 28 March 1970, at 5.40pm on Easter Saturday, our son, Mark William Carlin, was born weighing 8 lb 7 oz.

By September 1971, the regiment had served its time in Bovington and we were posted to the city of Paderborn. Mary and I were allocated a married quarters on Von Stauffenberg Strasse near Elsen, about five miles from the camp. It was during this posting that the Troubles in Northern Ireland was becoming clear in our minds. By now the situation in Derry was getting very, very serious. The IRA was becoming active and youths were being beaten and shot at by the British Army. Gunmen were on the streets and law and order was breaking down. It was at this time that we learned the very sad news that 14-year-old Annette McGavigan, a distant cousin of mine who we had met back home a few weeks earlier, had been shot dead by the British Army.

We didn't have a TV in the flat because it was all in German, though we did have BFBS (British Forces Broadcasting Service) radio, and it was reported that Annette had been rioting. I was shocked and outraged at first, then very confused when my brother phoned to say Annette had been deliberately shot whilst collecting pebbles for a montage she was putting together as part of a school project. I thought that the army had been sent to Northern Ireland to bring about law and order. Most of us assumed this meant sorting out the 'B' Specials and bringing them to book for some of their atrocities. There were now fights in the camp between the Irish and the English, but these were mostly drunken rows and never really amounted to anything.

* * *

On arriving home one evening, Mary informed me that she was pregnant again. We had been trying for another baby for a while and we celebrated with a party on the Saturday night. In the early 1970s, parties in Germany were a way of releasing energy as most of the exercises were by now fairly low-key and we weren't away from home as often. The estate we lived in had been built for the army by the West German government, almost to order, and had been taken over, equipped and furnished by the quartermaster's office. It was a mini 'land of plenty' in those days; a married soldier was given everything from the bed and bedding, all furniture, fixtures and fittings, right down to an egg timer.

At the end of January 1972, the reality of the events back home shook us to the core. It was reported on the BFBS network that some rioters and several gunmen had been shot dead by the army in Derry. I didn't know what to think until I learned more about what was increasingly becoming known as Bloody Sunday, when British soldiers shot twenty-eight unarmed civilians during a protest march against internment by the Northern Ireland Civil Rights Association (NICRA). Thirteen people were killed on the day and another man died four months later as a result of his injuries. Many were shot while running from the soldiers and some while trying to help the wounded. Later, in the summer of 1972, on 8 June to be precise, Mary gave birth to our daughter Sharon at the British Military Hospital in Rinteln.

Two weeks later, Mary, Mark, Sharon and I left Germany for the last time. I had volunteered and applied for a posting at Bovington Camp in Dorset. That meant a Sergeant's pay with the acting rank of Sergeant, only this time to the Junior Leader's Regiment Royal Armoured Corps. Though the posting didn't commence until September, I had to take six weeks' leave prior to it – something I wasn't prepared to give up. Of course, Mary was delighted and she looked forward to going home with Sharon and Mark; because in those days Germany felt like the other side of the world. After a two-day drive all the way from Germany, we arrived in Derry. Mary's mum and dad now lived on Violet Street, having sold their house on Riverview Terrace. Sharon was the apple of everyone's eye, and a photograph was quickly arranged with Mary's granny, her mother, Mary and Sharon showing four generations in the family. We hardly saw Sharon, such was the queue to look after her.

I was warned that to visit the Derry side was dangerous and we were definitely not to take our car. Shortly after 8pm one summer evening, Mary and I walked across the bridge, up Carlisle Road, through Ferryquay Gate, heading for my brother Dickie's flat in Pump Street. We were suddenly confronted by hundreds of youths, men and women running towards us. Bottles were being thrown and shots fired; we had walked straight into a riot. I grabbed Mary and pushed her into a doorway in front of Woolworth's and we both got on our knees and crouched down as young men and women ran past us, some of them charging towards the Derry Walls, some up Pump Street, while others ran straight down Carlisle Road. Some of the youths wore masks and turned to engage the army with stones and bottles; others threw petrol bombs. Mary and I were right in the firing line and I decided that we should probably make a run for it, towards the soldiers, and identify ourselves so as not to be confused as rioters. Another couple who had sought safety beside us in the doorway also ran towards the soldiers, trying to explain to one soldier that they were simply trying to make their way home. Instead, the soldier in question beat both of them to the ground. Outraged, I ran out and was almost hit by a petrol bomb that exploded at my feet. I managed to jump over it and pulled Mary by the hand towards two soldiers who were standing on the corner near 'The Diamond', the shopping centre in the commercial heart of the city.

I shouted at the Corporal and complained about his colleague's abuse of the young couple, who now lay bloody and battered outside Austin's Store. He told me to 'fuck off!' and when I produced my MOD90 (military identity card) and ordered him to give me his name and number his colleague drew a baton and smashed me over the head with it and I fell to the ground; a 'Brit' was beating a fellow Brit because he assumed I was a republican rioter! The next thing I remember was Mary dragging me to the doorway of Austin's. We eventually made our way back to the Waterside, where Mary's father took me to the hospital. I received six stitches to my head and was told I was very lucky. Even after all these years I still bear the mark of that baton. The RUC, who were at the hospital most of the night taking the names and addresses of anyone admitted in order to connect them with the rioting, took my name and address, and before I knew it, I was to be charged with rioting.

I couldn't phone anyone at the regiment, as they were all on leave, but went to the RUC station on Spencer Road the next day to make a statement. I met with an inspector who, despite expressing sympathy, told me I shouldn't have been in the area and that being a soldier made it all the more serious. I was to be reported to the military police at Ebrington Barracks, who would pass on their report to my commanding officer at Bovington. I spent the next two weeks reading and hearing all about the British Army in Derry, the RUC, the thirteen people that had been murdered on Bloody Sunday, the IRA, a guy called Martin McGuinness, and Sinn Féin.

It was at this time that I discovered that Jim Wray, my classmate and friend, had been one of those murdered by the Parachute Regiment on Bloody Sunday. I felt sick for days, but worse still was when I found out that Seamus Cusack, my friend from Melmore, had also been shot dead in 1971. People were quite adamant that he had not been armed, was not a member of any organisation and had in fact been murdered. It all seemed insane to me; Derry had gone mad. I couldn't wait to get out of the city and away to my new posting.

Back at Bovington, just before the intake returned for autumn 1972, a letter arrived from the military police at Ebrington Barracks addressed to the commanding officer. The chief clerk in the base called me to his office, closed the door and smiled, 'Look what I got.' As chief clerk it was his duty to open all mail addressed to the colonel. I pulled my chair closer to his desk as he opened the envelope. He read the letter, which had two documents attached to it, put it down and stared at me looking pensive. 'I think you're in trouble,' he said. It was the report of my alleged rioting in Derry.

I explained to him what had actually happened and he went off to have a word with the colonel. This wasn't a very good start to my new job, particularly as I hadn't even met the colonel yet. As it happened, Colonel Green from the Royal Tank Regiment turned out to be very understanding and told me to forget about it and that he would have a word. In the time I served there it was Colonel Green who took me under his wing, mentored me and taught me how to respond to the trials and tribulations of being his assistant.

* * *

Mary was a great manager of our finances, and she was able to save enough for us to go back to Derry for Christmas. In early December we did some seasonal shopping and bought a large truck with bricks in it for Mark and a fluffy little teddy bear for Sharon. She was a little young for Christmas, but we promised one another that next year when she better understood the festival she would have a bigger present. Sharon was a lovely, happy baby, and had both of us wrapped around her little finger. Indeed, one night when she was a little restless Mary asked me to fetch the teddy bear to settle her down. But I refused, saying that 'it will only spoil Christmas Day for her'.

On the morning of 16 December 1972, the day we were due to set off for Derry, tragedy struck our family. We had packed our cases and loaded the car the night before, ready for an early start. It was frosty that night but the house was warm and we all slept well. I rose first and went down to make Sharon a bottle while Mary got Mark and Sharon out of bed and dressed. I was standing by the cooker when I heard an almighty scream from upstairs. I dropped the kettle and ran to see what had happened. As I reached the doorway of Sharon's little room, Mary was screaming at the top of her voice and shaking uncontrollably. I grabbed her by the waist to stop her. 'Mary, for God's sake what's wrong?' She turned and, with tears streaming down her face, pointed towards Sharon's cot. I stepped past her and walked over to where my baby lay. I touched Sharon's cold face and lifted her into my arms. She wasn't breathing, so I laid her on the floor, tilted her head back and began giving her mouth to mouth resuscitation. Mary knelt beside me, rubbing the back of Sharon's small, cold hand and whispering encouraging words, 'That's it, Willie! She's moving! Keep going!' After five minutes or so I knew in my heart what Mary didn't want to believe. Sharon was dead. I lifted her tubby little body and carried her down the stairs.

'Mary,' I said, 'run down the lane to John Sawyer's house and ask them to phone a doctor'. Mary ran out of the front door and I could hear her screaming, 'Please, somebody help us. Please help us.' After a minute I checked Sharon's pulse again but there was no sign of life. I lifted her onto the sofa and covered her with a baby blanket. She looked as though she was asleep. I burst into tears, dropped to my knees beside her, and, holding her tiny limp hand, began shouting at the Sacred Heart picture that hung above the fireplace, 'No! Please God. No!' Mary arrived back with Margaret Sawyer, John's wife, who was a nurse at the local hospital. She pushed past me, went straight over to the sofa and checked Sharon for any signs of life. After checking the lifeless body, Margaret came over and put her arms around us saying, 'I'm so sorry.' Mary burst into tears and dropped to her knees shouting, 'Oh God, no! Please don't do this to me!'

A few minutes later the doctor arrived and began examining Sharon. With a big sigh he stood up. 'I'm afraid the baby is dead,' he said. Mary collapsed onto the floor again, in a near faint, and when she came around she began screaming. The doctor asked me to hold her while he gave her an injection to sedate her, and after a few minutes Mary was fast asleep.

'Daddy, are we nearly ready?' said Mark, tugging at my sleeve. Poor Mark, with all that was happening I had forgotten all about him. I lifted him onto my lap and tried to explain what had happened, but at two years of age he just didn't understand. He walked over to the sofa, where he was used to seeing Sharon lie, bent down and kissed her saying, 'There now, there now.' I burst into tears.

Sometime later two police officers from Dorchester arrived and immediately started asking questions. Who discovered the baby's body? Where was I at the time? When was the last time I saw her alive? When was she last fed? Who fed her? Have you still got the bottle? Where is the box with the baby food? On and on they went. I was cracking up and by this time Mary was awake and sobbing. Just then Sergeant Crabb, the local bobby, arrived and beckoned his two colleagues to the door. He had a quiet word with them and that was the last that we ever saw of them, although Sergeant Crabb walked us through the same questions, just for the record. Before he left, we asked Sergeant Crabb if he could contact the local police in Derry to deliver the sad news to Mary's parents. The undertakers in High Street arrived later in a black Ford van and prepared Sharon's body in the kitchen. Within minutes the undertakers were gone and we three were alone again. Mark had tears in his eyes and I held him. He was too young to say very much but he knew it was bad. I burst into tears, I just wanted to die. I felt so useless. How could God do this to us? I struggled through the rest of the day and managed to get Mary down to the phone box to call her mum. It was one of the most heart-breaking calls I've ever witnessed.

Mary was unable to go to the funeral and couldn't bear the thought of seeing Sharon being buried in the cold December ground. At the funeral parlour, the clerk gave me some wreaths, one from Colonel Green and his wife, another from Del Wennel, one from Jock and Steph, and one from Sergeant Crabb.

Sharon's small white coffin was lifted into the back of a black car normally used for weddings. I sat beside the coffin and we drove the short distance to the cemetery, just outside Dorchester. It was a very cold frosty morning, and it was at times like this that I realised the value of having your family and friends around you. Instead, here I was in England in a graveyard in the middle of nowhere, standing over a muddy hole in the ground. Beside me stood the old gravedigger and the local priest, Irishman Father Flynn, who was also padre to the local prison. The three of us gathered to celebrate the short life of Sharon Carlin. I felt so ashamed, she deserved better than this. I held back tears as the priest began his oration, white smoke from his breath rising into the frosty morning air as he prayed. The old gravedigger stood beside him, leaning on a shovel with his head bowed and his cap in his hand. The sound of crows echoed around the cemetery. 'There always seems to be bloody crows at funerals,' I thought. Within minutes the ceremony was nearing its end and we began lowering Sharon's small white coffin into the ground. After a few more prayers the priest shook my hand and hobbled off to his car.

I stood there, staring down at the silver cross on the coffin lid. When the first lump of muddy earth hit the casket I fell to my knees, sobbing like a baby. Until then I had been fairly strong, but the sound and sight of the earth on the coffin's lid was just too much. The gravedigger helped me to my feet, my knees covered in mud, and I knew he wanted me to leave. I picked a tiny red rose from one of the wreaths and dropped it into the grave, then I turned, still sobbing, and walked back towards the black car where the driver was waiting.

By lunchtime, Mary, Mark and I were in the car heading home to Ireland. Back in Derry, we were supported through our trauma with the help of Mary's mum and dad. The neighbours were just brilliant, as Derry people normally are at times of bereavement. We decided that Mary should stay with her family for a few weeks, as it was obvious she could never go back to the house in Winfrith. I had phoned Colonel Green, who understood our situation and was arranging for us to be allocated a married quarters in the camp itself, where we would be less isolated. I travelled alone back to England, signed for the new house and drove to the old house in Winfrith.

Everything was how we had left it. Sharon's pram sat in the hallway and the airing cupboard was full of her baby-grows and pink dresses. Upstairs, her cot sat as it was left that awful morning, though the blanket she used to cling to whilst going to sleep lay on the floor, where it had fallen in the panic. Her frilly pillow lay on the cot mattress and I was overcome with emotion as I picked it up and held it to my face. I could smell Sharon's aroma and I started to cry as I breathed in her baby smell. As I stood over her chest of drawers I was overcome with emotion at the sight of the small golden teddy bear, the very same present Mary had wanted to give her all those weeks ago. I had insisted she shouldn't get it until Christmas Day and I slid down the wall sobbing my heart out. Had I listened to Mary we could have seen the joy on her little face; I felt so guilty.

In between tears I managed to pack everything and move our bits and pieces to the new married quarters. Before leaving Dorchester I drove to the cemetery and placed the teddy bear on Sharon's grave, which still had the wreaths on it. I bent down and took the cards off the flowers, put them in my pocket and stood there talking to Sharon for a few minutes. I said a little prayer and promised her that I would come back soon. I didn't know then that it would be twenty-three years before I would see her again. The next day I picked up the formal death certificate. I sat and looked at the line that read: 'Cause of Death INFANCY SYNDROME'. I didn't know what it meant, though nowadays most parents know that 'Sudden Infancy Syndrome' means cot death.

Thinking back, I realise that Mary and I were blessed with friends like Margaret Sawyer and Sergeant Bob Crabb. By late 1973, Mary, Mark and I were settled in our new quarters on Gaza Road. Mary had friends and neighbours from the regiment, and everyone advised us to have another baby as soon as we could. By August that year Mary received the good news that she was pregnant again. The baby was due in April 1974 and she was delighted. Of course, we were hoping for a little girl. Even though things were getting better with our new house, our new friends and a better quality of life, Mary was yearning for home and just wanted us to go back to Derry so that she could be with her family.

* * *

One night around New Year, Mary and I discussed the possibility of going back to live in Derry. The Troubles were at their height and Derry didn't look like the sort of place an ex-British soldier would be welcome. Mark was nearly five and it was time for him to go to school, and we knew the army school wasn't that good. Not because the Education Corps was incompetent, but families move around a lot in the services and sometimes the interruptions put the child back months. After weeks of discussion I promised that I would write to my sister Doreen and my father and ask their advice, since my family was closer to republicanism than Mary's and they would know whether it was safe for me to return or not. My brother Robert had left the army after six years and settled down in Derry without any problem. Deep inside I knew they would tell me I was mad and that to come back would endanger my life, and I also knew that if Mary was aware of this she might change her outlook. By early January 1974 I had received a reply from Doreen, and it wasn't what I expected. I would be safe enough and no one would touch me so long as I was genuinely coming home and had discharge papers. She went on to tell me that she had spoken to her friend 'Paul', who knew Mary very well. He had heard about Sharon's death and couldn't foresee any problem.

I was now under great pressure to leave the army, but I decided to share my thoughts and feelings with Colonel Green. 'You would be mad to leave at this point in your career,' was his response. 'Besides, you'll be in great danger if you return to Ireland.' After further discussion I agreed that he could check out the real security situation in Derry through a friend of his in the Intelligence Corps, a decision that would change my life, and ultimately Mary's, forever.

CHAPTER 2

BACK HOME IN DERRY

T.E. Lawrence, better known as Lawrence of Arabia, was one of the famous old boys of Bovington Camp. His Dorset retreat at Clouds Hill cottage was located just behind the barracks, and I had often visited the place because of my interest in the legendary British spy and Arabist – whom Peter O'Toole immortalised on film in David Lean's epic biopic of his extraordinary life. Lawrence had rented the cottage in 1923 after returning from the Middle East, and he was killed nearby in a motorcycle accident twelve years later. It was here in this most apposite of spots, inside his beloved country hideaway, that I was recruited by MI5.

My commanding officer, Colonel Green, was aware of my wish to leave the army and return to war-torn Derry. He had passed on this request to a friend of his who called himself Captain Thorpe. It was Captain Thorpe who suggested we meet for coffee at Lawrence's cottage, ostensibly to discuss what to do with the rest of my life once I left the regiment.

Two days after his call I sat in my car watching the junction where we'd agreed to meet. Right on cue a green military Morris Countryman arrived driven by a tall man in army uniform. He motioned me to join him and Captain Thorpe drove to a remote area at the back of Clouds Hill, where we waited on the open road. A black Mercedes pulled in behind us and the captain asked me to get out and meet the driver. A man in civilian clothes emerged from the Mercedes and introduced himself as 'Alan', removing his black leather gloves. He was very well-dressed and spoke with a very soft English accent. He led me away from Captain Thorpe, as if he wanted our conversation to be private and out of earshot.

'I'm not in the army so you don't have to call me Sir,' he said. We walked and talked and he told me that his organisation had a special project on the back burner that they were now seeking to activate. He informed me that they had trawled the Officer Training College at Sandhurst looking for 'the right person with the right credentials' without success. My file had ended up in his office for an entirely different reason and had been brought to his attention. He told me his boss was surprised to find someone with my record and background serving in the British Army. They had checked my file at the Ministry of Defence, my confidential reports, qualifications, my personal skills, and agreed that I might be a right 'fit'. For what? I wondered.

He then said something that left me perplexed. Alan referred to the letter from Derry which stated that a certain 'Paul' had made it clear to my family that even as a former British soldier I would still be safe to return home to Derry. 'The person referred to in this letter as "Paul" is Paul Fleming, from a well-known republican family in the Waterside, Londonderry.' Alan was remarkably well informed about who was who and the rising stars of the republican movement in Derry. Nonetheless, he went on to describe how bad the intelligence was in the area, particularly political intelligence. 'Despite what you might read in the papers or hear in the mess, the republican movement in Londonderry is not Communist or Marxist. There is no "Danny the Red". In your city, ever since the Para's fucked up on Bloody Sunday, they've had more recruits join their ranks than the entire Infantry Corps of the British Army.' Alan stressed that the organisation was still open for infiltration, adding these chilling words, 'Which is where you come in.'

I protested, 'There must be some mistake. I'm only a clerk from Bovington Camp.'

'No you're not,' he said, 'you're a nationalist from Creggan Estate. Your family has already been affected by the Troubles and I'm not just referring to your sister. Your brother's niece, Annette McGavigan, was shot dead by British troops in very dubious circumstances. So, listen to me Willie, we're not looking for an SAS type. Besides, there will be an operation run by the army which targets the IRA. But understand this, that's not what we want you to do. On the contrary, we would prefer you didn't get involved with the gunmen. We're interested in the "politics" of the Troubles, to run alongside another initiative which should be up and running by November.'

We'd been talking for over twenty minutes when I stopped him. 'Look. Who are "we"? I mean, who are you?'

He explained that his name was Alan Rees-Morgan and then said, 'Let's just say we're the agency who advises the Minister of Defence and the Prime Minister', who, he added incidentally, 'won't be around for much longer. There are a lot of changes coming here on the mainland. There could be a Labour government by next week and they'll want to try to resolve the situation, which we believe will have a negative effect on the unionists.' He continued, 'Our estimation is that the Troubles are going to get worse, with more rioting, more divisions and more opportunities for someone like you to get involved locally.'

I was in a state of shock. He gave me his phone number and asked me not to tell anyone else about our conversation. He said he would give me a few weeks to think about it and reminded me that my role (if I accepted it) would be strictly to do with politics and that in no way was I to get involved with the IRA or any other paramilitary organisation. 'Leave that to others,' he said. 'Don't get involved. And if you do come across personnel or details of an action, you must not pass it over, we're not interested. Keep it to yourself. Remember, my policy is that the best way to keep that kind of secret is to tell no one. Okay?'

Alan got into his car and drove off, leaving me standing on my own a few hundred yards from Captain Thorpe's car. 'How did you get on?' he asked, as I got into the passenger seat.

'I don't know,' I replied. 'I've either just been blackmailed or wound up big time.'

'Look William,' said Captain Thorpe, 'that gentleman comes direct from London. He's the real McCoy. His organisation doesn't officially exist. They're a secret and they are interested in recruiting you. You must be very special because they normally recruit from Oxford or Cambridge. I've been in the Intelligence Corps for fourteen years and only ever met two of them. If I were you I would jump at whatever he offered.'

'Well, he didn't offer me anything. Just gave me information about the situation in Northern Ireland.'

'I don't want to know!' the captain interrupted, raising his left palm outwards towards my face. 'Just phone him and give him your answer. Don't tell anyone about this meeting, especially Colonel Green and definitely not your wife'.

It wasn't long before I was back at my desk trying to get my head around what had just happened. Over the next two weeks I tried to figure out what to do.

As Alan had predicted, Prime Minister Edward Heath resigned on 4 March 1974 and was replaced with a Labour government making all sorts of noises about Northern Ireland, including pulling the troops out – much to the anger of the unionists who were threatening to bring down the Northern Ireland Executive. Alan had been right so far and in the end I phoned the number he had given me. He called back but declined another meeting, saying, 'If you're interested, I'll tell you the next step, if not we forget about it. No hard feelings.' I sat and thought. On the one hand I didn't want to leave the army, on the other hand Mary desperately wanted to go home. This whole exercise sounded like an undercover mission, the kind of thing you only read about in spy novels or saw at the cinema.

'You see, Alan,' I said, 'it's all a bit scary and to be honest, whilst I'd love to say yes, I'm a bit afraid.'

'Look, Willie, I'm not going to lie to you. What we want you to do is very, very dangerous. You could get killed. It's a very volatile situation over there but we think that between your confidence, your connections in Derry and our guidance we might be able to make a difference. Let me make it clear to you. You'll have to live the life. You'll have to try to become a republican – one of them. You won't be armed and the army won't know about you, nor will the RUC. You'll be on your own. You will get occasional financial assistance and your salary will be put aside for you should you survive. If we find out that your life is in danger, we'll pull you out. However, if you're caught, the government will deny all knowledge of you because they don't know about this project. You will in fact be a secret.'

The proposal from this man, whom I didn't know, was for me to go to live in Derry, unarmed with no backup, and spy for the intelligence service. I could be killed, and no one would ever acknowledge my existence in a city at war. By 1974, the year of our return home, there had been 3,208 shootings and 1,113 bombs across Northern Ireland with 220 dead including 13 in Derry. 'If I agree,' I asked, 'when do you want me to start?'

'As soon as your baby is born,' he answered.

* * *

On 1 April 1974 our son Michael was born. Mary was a little disappointed that we didn't have a little girl, but she was over the moon about us leaving the army and returning to Derry. She came out of hospital the next day and on 3 April 1974 we were on the motorway heading for Ireland and a new life. I didn't tell Mary the real reason for my change of heart because as much as she wanted to return to Derry even she would never have agreed with what I was about to do. I had just given up a brilliant career, and here I was driving my wife, my 4-year-old son Mark, and a 3-day-old baby to Derry and into real danger. Worse still, all I had was a phone number in London and the word of someone I didn't even know. I was supposedly a paid employee of the Ministry of Defence, but in some nebulous, unspecified secret role.

In early May 1974, Mary and I were allocated a house at Rose Court in Gobnascale, a small nationalist housing estate in the mainly Protestant Waterside. Compared to nearby Irish Street it was a fairly newish estate with about 500 families. I've read that 'Gobnascale' is an old Irish word for 'Hill of Stories', and during my time living there on that hill there would be many stories to tell. It was a bit scary at first, as night after night the republican youth of the estate rioted at the junction of our street and the Trench Road just a few yards from the house. On two separate occasions we had our main window shot in by plastic bullets when the RUC fired at rioters, who often took refuge in our garden. I was living next door to the Breens, a republican family, and four doors away from the very same Paul Fleming who had given my sister the green light, presumably from the IRA, that I was safe to return.

Things were mostly quiet on the little housing estate of Gobnascale, but that all changed one morning just a few weeks after we arrived. 'Dolly' Shotter, as she is still known, was a young woman in her twenties married to a local man. She was known as Dolly because of her good looks, her long blonde hair, and her love of country music and Dolly Parton. She lived at the time with her husband and her father-in-law, Alfie, in a little bungalow at the edge of Strabane Old Road and Corrody Road. The Nash family and the Shotters gave support to the local IRA volunteers, more out of fear than any belief in what they claimed to represent. Unlike the Derry side there were no senior IRA men in the area, and most of the volunteers on the Waterside were still in their mid-teens. With access to guns and explosives they were dangerous to be around, with no telling what they would get up to or who they would hurt in the process.

Two such volunteers were Paul Fleming (the young man who Alan Rees-Morgan had spoken about back at Clouds Hill), who lived adjacent to me in Rose Court, and young Liam Duffy, whose father was a member of the Peace Movement. Liam's father would have erupted in anger had he known that his schoolboy son was a 'would be' volunteer. Both of them could often be seen running across the open space behind Anderson Crescent. My sister Doreen and Paul were still good friends; like a lot of young girls, she had joined Cumann na mBan (the IRA's female armed section) and she helped Paul Fleming and other volunteers when she could. Paul would often drop into my mother's in Anderson Crescent to see her. On the face of it, he appeared to be a nice young man who I remember being well mannered. He had a lot of time for my mother and father, as they had for him, though I noticed on more than one occasion that he would no sooner sit down in their house than a foot patrol would pass by. He'd obviously spot them on his way somewhere and didn't want to be stopped so he would just drop in to my mother's so as not to be seen. He would stay awhile and then leave when the coast was clear.

I was at my mother's one morning when the RUC and the army arrived to raid the house. It was that day that I saw first-hand what it was like to be raided by the British Army. Two young soldiers wrecked my mother's living room, smashing her little china cabinet as they searched for weapons or explosives. Upstairs they threw my brother's CB radio against the wall, smashing it as they went through his room. In my parent's room, one soldier pulled out all the drawers in my mother's dressing table and, finding my father's Second World War medals, threw them out of the window into the garden below. To me that was tantamount to a blasphemous act.

They took Doreen's room to pieces, ripping up her jeans and holding up her underwear and laughing at one another. They violently overturned her little dressing table, smashing the glass plate that sat on top of it. They had a sniffer dog with them, which peed on the landing before they left. After finding nothing in the two hours they were there, they issued my father with a 'Confirmation of Damage' certificate so that he could claim compensation from the State. It took us hours to calm my father down as he cursed the English pigs for the chaos in his home.

Later that afternoon, as I helped Doreen put her room back together, she laughed as she sat on the floor lifting the bits and pieces that had earlier been neatly laid out on her dressing table. 'What are you laughing at?' I asked.

'Bloody stupid cunts. They wouldn't know a safe house if it jumped out in front of them!' Asking her what she meant, she lifted a container of Avon talcum powder and tipped it out on the floor. I nearly died when I saw several rounds of 9 mm ammunition lying amidst the fragrant white powder.

'Jesus Christ, Doreen. Are you mad?' I exclaimed. 'You could have been caught. Do you not realise that if the army had found these you and everyone in this house would have been arrested and you would probably have gone to jail for years?'

'Listen Willie, those fuckers would need to get up early in the morning to catch me and they would need a better sniffer dog than that thing they had with them.'

I didn't know whether to laugh at her daring and cunning or be angry over her recklessness. Later that night, Paul Fleming called in to see my father and hear all about the raid. Of course, he nipped up to Doreen's room to see her and presumably took his little 'arsenal' with him when he left.

On this particular day in May 1974, Paul and Liam spent most of the afternoon in Paul's garden. I saw them once or twice as I looked out of the kitchen window and they were obviously up to something, because they would stop talking when anyone walked past the garden, which was next to the park. I never saw either of them again, but a few days later as I was passing Strabane Old Road there was an almighty bang and everyone ran out into the street. Smoke could be seen rising above Dolly Shotter's bungalow. People began to run towards the scene of the explosion and I could hear someone in the distance calling for help. Within minutes it was emerging that Dolly and her father-in-law had been blown up and it was being said that Mr Shotter was dead. This was clearly a bomb that had gone wrong, it couldn't be anything else. Someone ran past me and shouted, 'It was that wee fucker Fleming!'

By the next afternoon, even the dogs in the street seemed to be barking Paul Fleming's name. Apparently, Dolly had spotted Paul and Liam out of her kitchen window putting something into her dustbin. She never said anything but became anxious after they hopped over her fence and left. Dolly guessed there might be something 'stashed' there and assumed that they would come back later and lift whatever it was. Like most people, she knew that the IRA moved weapons and explosive devices around when foot patrols were in the area. Alfie Shotter, a frail man in his fifties, had no time for republicans, especially Paul and Liam, whom he'd often chased from his yard. Unlike Dolly, he was not afraid of them and had often rebuked her for putting up with them. Dolly made her way out of the kitchen, only to be met by Alfie, who walked past her, opened the back door and stepped out into the yard. Dolly froze, hoping he wouldn't go near the bin. As he approached the bin she ran out and shouted at him, 'Alfie! Don't go near that bin!' As he started to lift the lid she grabbed him by the arm, struggling with him as she did so, but it was too late. The bomb exploded as soon as he lifted the lid. Alfie Shotter was killed outright and Dolly was flung across the yard, losing a leg in the blast and sustaining horrific facial injuries. The Army and the RUC, who regularly patrolled Gobnascale on foot, had a habit of checking back yards, hedges, outhouses and sometimes even dustbins, something that hadn't gone unnoticed by Paul and Liam.

I was due to meet Alan a week or so later and I thought he would want to know about the bomb – not to act on my information but more out of establishing the facts. But such was the talk round the estate that there was no need. Within seventy-two hours, Paul Fleming and Liam Duffy were arrested and held at the RUC's interrogation centre at Castlereagh for seven days. Both of them were eventually charged with Alfie Shotter's murder. At just eighteen years of age, Paul Fleming was sent to jail for twenty years. Liam Duffy, sixteen years old, couldn't be dealt with by the courts and was instead detained in prison at 'the Pleasure of the Secretary of State'.

* * *

In the summer of 1975, Mary discovered that she was pregnant. We were delighted, even more so when she came back from the hospital one day with the news that she was expecting twins. It had been confirmed by a scan and she even had a little black and white photograph showing them in her womb. I spent the next two months showing anyone who would look the little photo and felt really proud of myself. Father Duffy, our local priest, told us that 'this is God's way of rewarding you for past pain and suffering'. Then, a few weeks before Christmas and a month before the babies were due, Mary was admitted to hospital in severe pain. Dr Martin was in charge of her treatment and he organised some kind of injection so that the babies would stay in her womb and not be born prematurely, at which point she went into renal failure and a helicopter was placed on standby to take her to a hospital in Belfast. During the night the babies were born and immediately placed in incubators because they were very weak and gravely ill. The two little boys were christened in the morning by the visiting priest. Little William and Thomas Carlin were fighters, and Mary sat by their incubators and prayed that God would not take them from us. Sadly, they died that afternoon and left us all devastated. It was a horrific replay of how we had lost little Sharon back in England years earlier. I could not believe or comprehend that it was happening to us all over again.

In the mourning period after the boys were buried it struck me that I had been back in Derry since 1974 with little to show in terms of my new job gathering intelligence. Over the first twelve months of my new undercover career I only met with Alan three times, and I still wasn't sure what I was supposed to be doing. This feeling reached frustration point by early 1977, when things appeared to quieten down in Derry. But it was only a brief hiatus of inaction for me. Alan and MI5 knew that we had a telephone in our hall and I had mentioned that the Fleming family would often ask to use it to speak to family and friends at home and abroad. My handler provided a mini tape recorder, which was slotted into the phone, and it would record the Flemings and another republican family as they talked about IRA bombs in England and how the Provisional's economic warfare would 'make the Brits sit up and notice us a thousand times more than any bombs exploding in the centre of Derry'.

Another handler, 'Andy', eventually took over Alan's role and let it be known that the strategy of bombing economic and strategic targets – particularly in London – was the brainchild of Martin McGuinness. However, the IRA's strategy was not solely confined to planting bombs in large English cities. By 1977, the organisation was moving into a 'leftist/anti-capitalist' phase when it also targeted rich industrialists and multinationals on the island of Ireland. Some were to be kidnapped, especially in

the Republic, while others in the North would be assassinated.
Even more than McGuinness, his partner in the axis dominating
Northern Command, Gerry Adams, had fallen under the
influence of ultra-leftist Trotskyite thinkers, who goaded the IRA
into committing 'anti-capitalist acts' of terrorism. The net result
was a number of squalid murders of businessmen, including the
shooting dead of Jeffrey Agate, the managing director of the
American multinational Du Pont, in Derry in February 1977.
Du Pont wasn't just a factory, it was a massive plant just outside
Derry, spread over several acres overlooking Lough Foyle. They
employed hundreds of workers, mostly Catholics, and brought
in millions of pounds to the local economy. There had been a
number of attacks on businessmen in the past, but the IRA's
justification for these was that they were either members of the
UDR or worked with the RUC or British Army. Jeffrey Agate
didn't appear to fit any of these categories. This looked like
another cock-up and I could just imagine the outcry that would
follow, let alone the reaction of the RUC and the army in our
area.

On the night of Jeffrey Agate's murder I was at home when
my neighbour, Colm Dorrity, appeared in my hallway with a
young boy dressed only in a white shirt, black trousers and black
shoes. He had no jacket and was visibly shaken, not to mention
the fact that he was bitterly cold. He looked about seventeen
years old. 'Wullie,' said Colm, 'this wee man here is looking for
your Doreen. He called at your father's first and your father sent
him over to you except he knocked on my door by mistake.'

Colm was anxious to leave so I said, 'Okay, leave him
with me.' I showed the boy into our living room and Mary
immediately rose to get him a blanket and some coffee. It soon
became clear to me that this young boy must have been up to no

good somewhere because he was from the Derry side and was totally lost. 'I'm Willie and that's Mary. What do you want me to call you?'

'Everybody calls me Shorty.'

'Shorty, you need to calm down and relax, you're in safe hands now and I think you should stay here the night. We'll get you sorted in the morning.' Later, I got into bed and realised, 'That wee man must have been involved in the explosion at Agate's home and lost the team he was with.' By the next morning, the news of Agate's murder had reached London and across the world to the White House, given that Du Pont was American owned. On every TV and radio station north and south of the border, politicians and ordinary everyday people were demanding revenge for his murder. Ian Paisley added more fuel to the fire, threatening to bring Ulster to its knees by organising an impromptu loyalist workers' strike.

The Peace Movement, which had marched with thousands of women in Belfast the previous year demanding an end to the war, was now talking openly of marching in Derry. The Bishop of Derry, Edward Daly, called Agate's killers 'cold blooded murderers with no sense of shame.' Jimmy Carter, then President of the United States, speaking from the White House said, 'Mr Agate's murder was a senseless act on a businessman who represented an American Company and whose only crime was to bring employment to the city'. He added, 'the manner of his death will only further divide communities in Northern Ireland and bring unwarranted shame on all good, decent Irish Americans.' Trade Union representatives at the plant were planning to hold a protest strike. The only people who were silent were the IRA.

I decided to leave the house for a while and called London to let them know about my lodger. They viewed the matter with great concern and Andy agreed to fly over the next day and meet up with me in Portrush on the northern coast.

'Well, well,' said Andy, after I had explained everything to him, 'this is going to be tricky. Look, Willie, you and I both know that it's 99 per cent certain that this little shit was implicated in some way in the murder of Mr Agate. However, knowing it and proving it are two different things. Furthermore, how would you explain your house getting raided when it's never been raided before?'

'That's easy,' I replied. 'All you need to do is arrange for every house in my block to be hit, starting with next door to me, and it will be thought that he was found by accident.'

'Okay, and what do we do after the RUC charge you with harbouring a terrorist and implicate you in the murder? Sorry Willie, but you're not thinking straight, so this guy gets off. While he's under your stewardship and being monitored by the IRA, you'd better pray that the RUC don't stumble over him or that some informer doesn't give you away.'

After several hours discussing the matter it was decided that the information would be logged but not passed on because it could incriminate me and, worst of all, blow my cover, which London did not want. I was to get rid of Shorty as soon as possible, but only when it was safe in the eyes of the IRA. After that, Shorty could be picked up at some other time well away from me.

A week went by and we did our best for Shorty, but he was becoming a nuisance and a real pain in the arse. Deep inside he was a cocky wee shit who spent most of the time admiring himself in the mirror. He also had his fair share of drink every night and would often get very cheeky in our conversations. A few nights before he left us, he and I were having a beer and the conversation led to God and the church. He was slightly tipsy because he couldn't really drink that much. Mary felt sorry for him no matter what he'd done, because as far as she was concerned he was some mother's son. As a keep safe, she had bought him a St Joseph's prayer on the way back from the chapel. He laughed at her and asked her, 'What good is this going to do me?' Mary explained that it would keep him safe and read the inscription on the back, which said that saying the prayer regularly would keep the person safe. She read out that it had often been carried into battle and the holder would never fall into the hands of an enemy nor would poison ever have an effect on them. Shorty got up, weaved his way past us and went into the kitchen, bringing back with him a bottle of bleach. He thumped it down heavily on the coffee table and challenged Mary, 'Go on then, drink that, missus, and show me how powerful your prayer is!'

Mary was embarrassed and left the room, taking the bleach with her, while I stood there shaking with anger. I could have planted one on him right there and then. He seemed to lose control because he got up, went to the bottom of the stairs and put on the jacket that had been sent over to him. 'What are you doing?' I said.

'I'm goin' down to Annie's Bar to get a fuckin' drink,' he replied, belligerently. Part of me wanted to open the door and kick him the fuck out into the street, but the sane part of me said I should stop him. I grabbed him around the shoulders and tried to persuade him that it was foolish to go to the pub; besides, the word hadn't come from the Derry side that he could leave the house. He became aggressive and lashed out at me. I was about to grab him again but decided to hit him instead, then I hit him once more just for Mary and St Joseph. He was now trying to kick out at me so I threw him onto the stairs and grabbed him by the throat.

'Listen to me ya wee cunt, you don't seem to realise the trouble you're in. Just about every policeman, every soldier and every informer in Derry is looking for you and if they don't get yee, half the population of Derry will string you up by the balls for the fuck-up you and your friends made out at Altnagelvin last week. On top of that the word amongst the boys is that you and your friends weren't supposed to do what you did.'

He tried to speak but I was choking him. As I eased my grip he wheezed, 'That's a load of shite. The job was given the go-ahead.'

I told him I couldn't care less but he was going nowhere. I let him up and ordered him back into the living room.

'I'll get you fucking shot for this,' he said, looking into the mirror at the blood on his lips and nose.

'Finish your drink and get to sleep.' I wasn't sure of the importance of what I'd just heard or the ramifications of beating up an IRA volunteer. As I went to sleep I decided this guy had to go. Doreen and the boys had all steered well clear of my house because of the danger of being seen coming and going, which was good security but didn't help me when I needed to speak to them.

The next day I walked down to Fleming's to see if Lynn Fleming was around. She and Doreen were good pals and I felt sure that she was bound to know that I was keeping someone from over the town. Luckily, Lynn was coming around the corner and I stopped her. 'Lynn, I'm having problems with the young guy I'm looking after,' I said. It was Lynn who suggested that to get Shorty sorted out I should go over the town and see Martin McGuinness.

* * *

When I knocked on the door of his Brandywell home, Martin McGuinness was sitting on the sofa with a pink safety pin in his mouth, changing his baby's nappy. The famous Derry IRA commander spoke through his teeth as he enquired how he could help, and I wondered how many times in these typical domestic situations McGuinness had to deal with callers making some kind of complaint, seeking advice or looking for help from the IRA. I had been lucky to catch him, so to speak, as the legend went that he was more often than not on the run across the border from the Brits and the cops. To get an audience with him was fortunate.

I briefly explained the problem with Shorty, who was still billeted in my house even though he was currently Derry's most wanted man after the Agate murder, and outlined our problems, including my scuffle with him the night before.

McGuinness immediately understood the gravity of the situation and put the baby down on the sofa, keeping a close eye on it. He turned to me and said with a smile, 'So, you want rid of him, do you?'

I thought for a second and then replied, 'No! Not until it's safe for him. But he needs to be told that he can't go to the pub or be seen in the area.' I also explained how Shorty had threatened to have me shot for restraining him.

Martin stood up and ushered me to the door. 'What's your name again?' he enquired.

'Willie Carlin,' I replied.

'Anything to John Carlin?'

'No, but I have heard of him.'

'So, you're not in Sinn Féin?'

'No.'

'Right, Willie, leave that with me and I'll see somebody after and get it sorted out for yee, okay? In the meantime, you tell him that if he attempts to leave your house again, he'll be in deep trouble.'

I realised immediately that McGuinness meant what he said; one word from him and for us the Shorty problem would quickly be over.

At half past ten that night, a man came to our door and asked to speak to Shorty alone. Mary and I sat in the kitchen with Mark, who had become friendly with Shorty because when he was sober and not being cocky, he was quite likeable. After a short while, Shorty and the man came into the kitchen.

Shorty put out his hand and shook Mark's hand. Then he turned to Mary and said, 'Mary, I'm sorry about the other night, it was only the drink talkin'.' He then produced the St Joseph's prayer from his jacket and asked her if he could keep it. Mary smiled and nodded. He came around to my side of the table and put his arms out to give me a hug. I stood up and put my arms around him. I patted him on the back. 'You take it easy.'

For a brief moment I thought he was going to cry. The man who had come to collect him thanked Mary, winked at Mark and within minutes they left by the back door. At last we were over our ordeal.

Over the following days, the protests and marches subsided. Jeffrey Agate's funeral was a very sad affair. The sight of his poor wife standing by his graveside will be ever fixed in my memory. She was just an ordinary working-class girl from Newcastle in the north east of England, thrust into this extraordinary situation and consumed by grief. As I watched, I just couldn't get my head around the reason for his murder. For a murder it was, and even ordinary nationalists, who whilst not agreeing with the IRA could sometimes understand their rationale, did not agree with this killing. After all, the IRA claimed to be protecting the people of Derry from the British Army and the RUC. However, the reality for Derry people was that far from protecting them from these occasional thugs, anyone in Derry, even unarmed businessmen, were fair game to be murdered so long as it suited whatever screwed-up strategy the IRA thought they had. The IRA never admitted its involvement in Agate's murder, but later in the year they made a veiled attempt to explain the thinking behind it. The killing only strengthened my resolve to keep working in my undercover role, which was still tentative at this stage.

On 14 March 1977, another business manager, James Nicholson, was murdered as he visited the Strathearn Audio factory, in west Belfast. Like Agate he was English and, like Du Pont, the factory employed mainly Catholics. The outcry that followed led the IRA's Northern Command to issue a notice in Dublin through *The Irish Times*, stating, 'In all cases, those executed by the IRA played a prominent role in the effort to stabilise the British-oriented Six County Economy.' The notice added, 'Those involved in the management of the economy served British interests.' However, there is no denying this was yet another squalid murder in the IRA's leftist phase, when they behaved like the ultra-left gangs causing mayhem in Europe such as Germany's Baader–Meinhof group. They imagined that by killing the odd businessman here and there they were somehow striking a blow against the entire capitalist system. It was pathetic, stupid, cruel and insane.

* * *

In the spring of 1977, the Reverend Ian Paisley – one of the men I personally blame for the eruption of the Troubles – was threatening a replay of the 1974 Ulster Workers' Strike. Three years earlier, an alliance of unionist politicians, loyalist paramilitaries and pro-British trade unionists overthrew the first ever power-sharing executive at Stormont. Paisley was now leading from the front, whipping up the likes of the Ulster Defence Association for a second general strike. This time it was in response to what he claimed was a deteriorating security situation, though many saw it as an attempt by Paisley for a putsch. Although I had nothing but contempt for Paisley and his sectarian form of politics, his strike would provide the inroad for me into Sinn Féin activism and unintentionally beat a path towards Martin McGuinness.

The strike began on 3 May 1977. The next day Mickey Roddy, who lived beside us on Rose Court, called in to see me, 'We're trying to organise cars to go over the border to Buncrana and bring back necessities for the people in the area.'

'I'm up for that, Mickey,' I said. Mickey originally came from Bishop Street, on the Derry side. He was an ex-Official IRA member and was now a member of Sinn Féin. He was a decent bloke and I had a lot of time for him. We called on Colm Dorrity, who had also expressed an interest in doing something to help 'stock up'. Colm had collected money from various families and pensioners who were worried that the power would go off, and a lot of them were scared because of their experiences of the 1974 strike. We visited bakeries and grocery shops across the border in Donegal, buying up reserves of staple foods in case supplies were cut in the North due to blockades by the loyalists. The IRA even saw to it that I was paid for the petrol I used going back to Donegal for torches, batteries, paraffin heaters and candles. I was becoming known in the district as a community activist.

The power workers on the east coast of Northern Ireland pulled the plug on the regional electricity supply. With no power and no television, the residents in Gobnascale became used to sitting around the fire at home trying to find things to talk about. Tommy McGlinchey, the local coal merchant, saw to it that Gobnascale was well supplied with coal and told people they could pay when they could afford it. Out on the streets the residents were already used to having no streetlights and walking around at night in the dark. Even the local bar was open, so you could go there at night and have a drink by candlelight; needless to say that never really caught on. There were intermittent power cuts, but it wasn't as bad as anticipated and this time the strike didn't succeed. Roy Mason, the hard-headed Labour MP and Northern Ireland secretary, refused to give in to Paisley's many demands – as was widely predicted at the time – and the strike collapsed after just thirteen days.

By the summer of 1977, our family life hit an all-time high. Mary and I had decided to try one more time for another baby, though after our experience with the twins I was very apprehensive. Still, I shouldn't have been because on 3 July at Altnagelvin Hospital, Mary gave birth to a little girl, who we named Maria. Mary and I were over the moon and I remember being so delighted that as I drove back home to tell Mary's parents, I went around the roundabout at the hospital four times, whooping and yelling out of the window. For the next eight or nine months I was totally dedicated to Maria, and it seemed everybody was really pleased for us given what had happened to Sharon and the twins. Maria was the apple of my eye.

* * *

By the following summer I was back to my old routine again, and it was in late September 1978 that I was invited to a republican meeting in Gobnascale to discuss the forthcoming march celebrating the tenth anniversary of the Derry riots. The 'boys' from the IRA were the main representatives, but it was here that I met Eddy McGowan, a painter and decorator by trade and a committed Sinn Féin activist who lived with his wife Maeve and family on the estate. Also present were John Carlin (no relation), Mickey Roddy and Tommy McGlinchey. Tommy had been the victim of a UVF car bomb attack at his home on Fountain Hill. He had lost both legs, but that didn't stop him from leading a full life and driving a specially modified car. He was an active member of Sinn Féin, was well respected by the people at the Top of the Hill, and held a lot of sway in the Waterside. The meeting was a fairly quiet affair as we planned a strategy for the march from the Waterside railway station up Duke Street and over the Craigavon Bridge. Ian Paisley and the loyalists of Derry were adamant that the Waterside was a Protestant area and that the march was an aggressive action designed to upset the unionist population. They made it quite clear that they were going to hold a counter demonstration and prevent the Sinn Féin march from taking place. (At this stage I was still a 'civilian', not a member of Sinn Féin but someone who sympathised with them.)

As we left the station on 8 October 1977, we were about to become involved in one of the bloodiest riots the Waterside had ever seen. The rally was attacked by loyalists from Bonds Hill and from behind Nixon's garage on Spencer Road. In fairness to the RUC commander in charge, he did his best to organise protection for our march. However, a lot of the young RUC men sympathetic to the unionists weren't so protective as they joined in 'baton charging' the march, leading to running battles with them as well as attempts to defend ourselves from the loyalist crowds. It took over an hour to march 150 yards to the bridge and a further hour to cross it. Even as we reached the Derry side, we were attacked by gangs from the Protestant Fountain Estate. All in all, over one hundred marchers were injured and seventy RUC men were left maimed, with most of their injuries being sustained as a result of being bottled and stoned by loyalists. Ironically, later that evening at the casualty department of Altnagelvin Hospital, RUC constables sat united with republicans as they all waited to be treated for their injuries.

* * *

Over the previous four years I had met quite a few men from MI5, all of whom didn't really have a clue as to the grit and determination of the republican movement in Derry. But they were beginning to understand – partly, I hoped, through my political reports – that whilst not giving total support to the IRA, ordinary decent nationalists had no time for the British government, the British Army, and least of all the RUC. One critical fact I relayed to MI5 was that, contrary to their belief, not all IRA volunteers were 'unemployed, mindless thugs'. Indeed, a lot of them were either employed or attending some form of further education, and some of them were quite astute in their thinking. I had also reported that one of the 'boys' in the Waterside was talking about a new structure which would see them form into small 4–5 person groups known as cells that would make it harder for informers to penetrate (or so they thought). My handler Andy assured me that he would pass on the information about these new cell structures to the army. Yet with no clear role for me as a 'spy', and feeling no sense of achievement, I drifted into the public domain in an entirely different manner.

I was singing in pubs and clubs and making a few extra pounds to help supplement our income. I was quite popular out of town in what were known as 'singing pubs'. Most of the lounges would have a group who would play from 9 to 11.30pm. I would be announced as the guest artist and would sing and play guitar from about 10 to 10.30pm. Singing was my hobby and it wasn't long before I became 'Billy Carlin' the country singer and found myself in some demand. Within two years I was fronting my own group, Billy Carlin and the Envoys, which toured around Donegal as well as Derry. I loved country music and I felt happy on the road, away from the political maelstrom; it was a welcome hiatus in my secret life as an agent.

The covert world, however, was never far away and my meetings with MI5 contacts were becoming more frequent, especially since I had a new handler who called himself 'Ben'. The location of our conversations had also changed. Before they were held in car parks and picnic areas, but now we had a house at our disposal in a spot outside Limavady on the road to Castlerock. I would enter the house through the back door, which led straight into the kitchen, where I would usually find Ben waiting for me, notebook at the ready and coffee brewing. At first it was interesting working with him. He appeared different from the others, more open and down to earth. He had a very low opinion of the army and said of the RUC, 'I wouldn't trust them as far as I could spit.' He was a Catholic and an only child, and his parents, whom he would visit quite often, lived in England. At only 5 ft 5 in, he wore a tweed jacket, corduroy trousers, glasses and smoked a pipe. He wasn't the usual MI5 'type' I'd been used to dealing with. The other thing he did was drink, and whiskey was his favourite tipple.

We wouldn't meet at the house very often, instead Ben would arrange for us to go to a hotel or somewhere on the coast. His favourite was the Londonderry Arms in Carnlough on the Antrim coast. He preferred lunchtime meetings, which was good for me even though it meant that I had to sit and watch him consume large quantities of Bushmills whiskey. I wondered why, with a house at our disposal, Ben preferred to meet at other venues, and I was soon to discover the reason. I was on my way to meet him on the Antrim coast one lunchtime and as usual turned right to head up the coast road out of Limavady, which went straight past the house. As I drove up the road, a red Peugeot came out of the gates of the house and headed back into Limavady, coming straight towards me. I had the shock of my life, for there in the passenger seat was Martin McGuinness, bent forward as if he was reading or looking at something on his knee. I quickly looked the other way in the hope that the driver (whom I couldn't place) didn't recognise me. As I drove towards Carnlough I could feel my right foot shaking on the accelerator and sweat running down the back of my shirt. A little further on, I stopped at a layby and got out to catch my breath. What the hell was Martin McGuinness doing coming out of an MI5 house? I was late for my meeting with Ben, who by now had consumed a considerable amount of Bushmills, and I didn't share with him what I had just witnessed. However, a few weeks later I had an even bigger shock.

One afternoon after seeing Ben I was heading back to Derry to attend a meeting on Cable Street when I spotted Ben sitting in his car outside Martin McGuinness's house. Ben had often told me that if he could meet McGuinness he 'could put him wise' and let him know what was really going on 'behind his back'. I thought it was just the drink talking but here he was outside Martin's house with no telling what he would do or say if challenged. He stood out like a sore thumb, and I knew that if Ben was caught it would only be a matter of time before he told his interrogators about his work, and of course about me. I drove past him, turned around and parked a few yards behind his car. I ran to the driver's door and beckoned him to wind down the window. Immediately, I could see that Ben was very drunk!

'Listen, Ben,' I said with some urgency, 'you're sticking out here like a sore thumb and it won't be long before someone arrives and will challenge you. So, for fuck sake get out of here before you get us both killed.' That seemed to sober him up a bit because he started his engine and left.

Later, I phoned Alan Rees-Morgan in London and explained my situation. I told him that Ben was dangerous and he was going to get himself and me killed and that I wanted to leave MI5. Alan insisted that he thought I was being a bit hasty and said that he would come and see me. Two weeks later, Ben informed me that his boss was coming over for a visit and wanted to see me. He obviously didn't know that I had asked for the meeting. The three of us met at the Killyhevlin Hotel near Enniskillen, and Alan suggested that he and I go for a walk alongside the lake adjacent to the hotel, leaving Ben on his own. I put it to him that I thought Ben was dangerous and getting out of control. 'I'm sure he's an alcoholic, Alan.'

'Look,' he replied. 'You live here and in a way you've become immune to the danger. Ben views Northern Ireland as a very scary place and he has had a few bad moments elsewhere in the province.'

'But Alan,' I said, 'if it's so scary what the hell is he thinking about going to McGuinness's house?'

'Willie, you're on a very, very long road and there will be many upsets along the way. Your information about Sinn Féin's activities in Derry is vital to my office in London, and as for Ben's drinking and turning up at the McGuinness household, I'll look into that. But I have to tell you that most of our lot have a tipple at lunchtime and in the evening, it goes with the territory. Leave it for a few weeks and see how you get on.'

By the time Alan and I got back to the hotel, Ben had ordered lunch and some lagers. Alan left after lunch. Ben obviously didn't have a clue what we had talked about because he was keen to know what we'd discussed and if he'd been mentioned.

Due to deteriorating conditions amongst the republican prisoners in the Maze prison, and the increasingly volatile security situation across the country generally, I started to distrust Ben and often missed meetings. After a further meeting with Alan Rees-Morgan at the Ballygally Castle Hotel on the Antrim coast a few weeks later, it was agreed that I should go to London for a little break. I stayed at the Penta Hotel in London and had at least five meetings over the weekend with Alan and a woman he introduced as 'Paula', his secretary. She was an odd woman. Although Alan often chatted about life in the North and the trials and tribulations of working there, Paula was more interested in Martin McGuinness and his views on things.

'She's no secretary,' I remember thinking as we dined on the thirteenth floor of the Hilton Hotel on Park Lane. They lived in a different world and thought that visiting St Paul's Cathedral and the Tower of London would help me unwind. The truth was I was bored, as well as being out of my depth and not used to such luxuries. By Sunday night I was on a flight back to Belfast and I promised Alan that I would give it another go and try and stick with Ben. I never saw Alan Rees-Morgan again, though years later I would recognise his secretary Paula when she was on television being announced as Stella Rimington, the new head of MI5.

Despite telling Alan in London that I would try to make the relationship work, I still couldn't get rid of my mistrust of Ben and I decided that I would definitely terminate my arrangement with MI5. On 10 December 1980, my final meeting with Ben was a pretty frosty affair. I knew by his manner that he didn't know why I was leaving and I never told him. Before we parted he handed me a plastic bag with £2,500 in it. Presumably this was the salary I had accrued with MI5 during my time in service, though it did not seem an awful lot for the potential danger to which I had exposed Mary and the children.

CHAPTER 3

FRU FOR YOU

The first hunger strike at Long Kesh had begun on 27 October 1980. Seven republican volunteers went on hunger strike demanding the right not to wear the prison uniform or do prison work, to be allowed free association with other prisoners, and to organise educational and recreational pursuits. After more republicans joined the strike, including three women at Armagh prison and several loyalist prisoners, on 18 December, about one week after I had stopped working for MI5, the strike came to an end after it appeared some kind of deal had been struck. However, on 1 March the following year, a young IRA volunteer who was little known in republican circles began the second hunger strike. His name was Bobby Sands, and his strike was the culmination of a five-year protest that had begun in 1976 when the British government withdrew Special Category status for convicted paramilitary prisoners. As Sands continued his fast, further prisoners joined in the hunger strike and those engaged in the 'dirty protest', though not participating in the hunger strike, called off their actions so as to highlight Sands's protest. Within days, Sinn Féin was organising meetings and rallies to which Eddy McGowan, Mickey's friend, had invited me.

On 5 March 1981, Frank Maguire, MP for Fermanagh and South Tyrone, died and there was to be a by-election. Initially, it was to be a non-event with Maguire's brother Noel tipped to win the seat, but Bernadette McAliskey (née Devlin), formerly an independent republican MP for Mid Ulster, insisted that she would contest the seat and would 'only stand aside in favour of an H-Block prisoner's candidate'. The IRA leadership, though appearing to be very reluctant, gave their approval to her stance, though the word in Derry was that Martin McGuinness was against it.

By 22 March, Francis Hughes, Raymond McCreesh and Patsy O'Hara from Derry had joined Sands on hunger strike. O'Hara was not an IRA volunteer but the leader of the INLA prisoners in the blocks. After many meetings and private discussions, Sinn Féin decided to nominate Bobby Sands to contest the by-election. By 29 March, Noel Maguire along with Austin Currie of the SDLP had withdrawn their nominations, leaving a straight fight between Sands and Harry West, the unionist candidate who held the seat in the 1970s. With a week to go before voting I was travelling the length and breadth of Fermanagh and Tyrone, putting up posters, distributing leaflets and campaigning on the doorstep on Sands's behalf. When we came across SDLP supporters we told them that though they had no candidate they should still vote because a vote for anyone other than Sands was a vote for 'Maggie'. We tried to persuade potential voters that this was a fight between a dedicated Irishman and Mrs Thatcher.

The Fermanagh and South Tyrone by-election and the hunger strike increased my profile around Sinn Féin, but one incident during this period only bolstered my determination to work against the organisation and continue my perilous undercover existence. It was 7 April 1981 and a peaceful afternoon in Gobnascale when I wandered over to my mother's house on Anderson Crescent. Inside the house we were chatting about the hunger strike when my mother stood up and pointed out of the window saying, 'There's a girl coming down our steps and she seems to be crying.'

I paid little attention as my mother went to open the door and just carried on talking to my father. I heard her say, 'Come on in dear and sit down' and seconds later, my mother re-entered the living room with a girl in her late twenties saying, 'Willie, this wee girl is in a dreadful state. Go and get her a drink of water.' I went to the kitchen as the girl entered and sat on the sofa. She was well dressed with fair hair and she had a clipboard gripped tightly in one hand. As I handed her the glass I could see that she was still very upset; her hand shook as she took the water from me. She sipped it and said timidly, 'Thank you for your kindness.'

'What's wrong, love?' asked my mother, bending down beside her. The girl sighed and explained, 'I called at a house at the end of the street and the man said he would have me shot if I didn't leave the area. As I was coming down the steps a man from another house shouted at me to get out of the street.' I stood up, moved my mother out of the way and bent down beside the young woman. My God! I thought. She's a 'census collector'!

The much-talked-about 1981 census was underway in Northern Ireland. Sinn Féin had asked people not to participate, saying the information would be passed to the security forces and it would lead to republicans being harassed and arrested. Graffiti appeared on walls across nationalist areas of the North urging people to 'Burn the census.' The IRA had warned the Census Office in Derry that its representatives should stay out of republican areas, calling them 'agents of the Crown'. I realised this young woman in our house was in grave danger. 'What's your name?' I asked.

'Joanne Mathers,' she replied.

'Don't you know what you're doing is dangerous?' I asked. She handed me her clipboard and explained that she had been briefed to stay out of Gobnascale but Anderson Crescent would be okay. Sure enough, her map had Anderson Crescent listed alongside Irish Street, which technically it is. It's mainly a nationalist street with only a few republicans in it and this girl just happened to call on two of them. She didn't know the area, explaining that she came down from Strabane. My mother and Joanne began talking as she relaxed and calmed down. She was a pretty young girl and explained that she had left her job as a town planner to assist her husband in running his farm at Tamnabrine, near Strabane in County Tyrone, and she was fascinated by my mother's stories of life on her farm in Convoy in Donegal. Indeed, she had only taken the job collecting census forms for a few days to earn a little extra money for her and her husband. She had a little boy, whom she called 'Shane', and told us that he was the same age as Maria, our little girl whose photograph she admired.

As it was now getting late in the day, I suggested that perhaps she should move out of the street and head for the safety of Irish Street. 'If you go from here, down the street you'll see Irish Street Estate in front of you and you will be safe enough then. However, you might like to call into Nelly Shongo's house three doors from the end of the street, or across from her you could try Betty Kearns.'

Joanne stood up to leave and thanked my mother. She pressed her hand into mine and said, 'God bless you.' As she was halfway up the steps she turned towards me. 'Will you watch and make sure I'm okay?'

I smiled, 'Of course.' I watched her as she went into Shongo's and came up the steps again. As she crossed the road she smiled back and gave me a confident wave. She was a lot happier now than she was an hour ago. Then she went up the steps to Betty's house and knocked. I could see her with her back to me waiting for a response. Just as the door opened a masked man ran from the side of the house and tried to take the clipboard from her. As she struggled to keep hold of it, I heard a shot and saw Joanne fall forward into the hallway. Horrified, I started to run down the street towards her, but then turned and shouted for my mother to phone an ambulance. As I turned back towards the house, a second shot rang out and I could hear screams in the distance. I caught sight of the masked gunman as he fled across the waste ground at the back of Anderson Crescent.

By the time I got to Betty's house the gunman had obviously gone. A few people had started to gather and I pushed my way into the house. There was glass and blood everywhere; the gunman had pushed his way past the man of the house and crashed straight through the glass vestibule door. As poor Joanne lay bleeding to death on the floor, he tried to wrestle the clipboard away from her. But with her dying grip she held on and in a final moment of anger and frustration he shot her again in the back of the head, causing blood and matter to spray all over the wallpaper and down the side of the leather armchair that sat a few feet inside the door. Joanne Mathers was shot twice and had still managed to cling to her clipboard, which she had been given in the Guildhall in order to earn £5 for the day's work.

As I turned to let the ambulance men pass me, a neighbour looked at me and snarled, 'Willie Carlin, you're nothing but a pack of murdering bastards.' I didn't know what to say. Surely the IRA wouldn't have authorised such a shooting. The boys at the Top of the Hill had committed some terrible acts, most of them 'fuck-ups', but this was cold-blooded murder and I knew it.

Within twenty-four hours the IRA in Derry moved to distance themselves from the murder and issued a statement saying, 'This killing was probably carried out by those intent on discrediting the election campaign of Hunger Striker Bobby Sands.' It was a pathetic attempt to justify cold-blooded murder and all of Derry knew it. Ironically, twenty years later Sinn Féin's Mitchel McLaughlin would call on all republicans to complete their 2001 census forms.

Fuelled by anger over what they had done to poor Joanne Mathers, I made up my mind that after the election was over I would phone Alan Rees-Morgan and try one more time with MI5. The following day Eddy called for me and we were off to Fermanagh, which meant having to put Joanne's murder temporarily out of my head while I joined the campaign trail to get Bobby Sands elected to parliament. On election day this meant 'personating' or stealing votes.

Personating was where you collected voting cards from electors who couldn't or wouldn't vote. The card was passed to a worker who would go to the polling station, hand it to the clerk, receive a voting slip and then vote for whoever they'd been instructed. Different cards at different polling stations, together with a collection of coats, hats, wigs and glasses, could gain a candidate a lot of votes. Stealing a vote took a bit more nerve. Here a worker was sent to a polling station without a card and claimed to be someone they weren't and all they needed was the correct name and address of the voter. The electoral officer would check the list and, provided the name and address given was correct and on the electoral register, the worker was able to steal that person's vote. This was always done early in the day by targeting doctors, nurses, solicitors and business people who normally left their voting until the evening. Pink slips were issued to those particular voters who arrived at the polling station in the evening. They used the slip to cast their vote and went home happy, but what they didn't know was that the pink slip was only used on the day of the count to calculate how many votes had been stolen or personated. They were not given to the candidate and the vote that was personated or stolen was the one that counted.

All in all there were just over a hundred activists from across the North working the entire area in mini-buses and cars. We were organised into small groups of five or six and ferried around the polling stations. I voted in nine different polling stations with cards that had been given to me in each area. Others claimed to have voted fifteen or sixteen times further up the country. Looking back, we could have done more because while there was no want of polling cards there was a problem with transport, but I was reliably informed that we had personated and stolen well over a thousand votes. Bobby Sands beat Harry West by 1,446 votes, and I was never sure if Sands would have won had we not stolen and personated on his behalf. However, I was jubilant, as were most nationalists – never mind republicans. Victory cavalcades went around Derry that night as it was clear there was a republican vote here in the North just for the taking. In the weeks that followed, the attention of the world focused on the H-Blocks and the hunger strikers, particularly Bobby Sands MP for Fermanagh and South Tyrone, and many people came to the prison to see him.

Bobby Sands was never advised to go on hunger strike by Sinn Féin but they never encouraged him to come off it either. However, all sorts of dignitaries did try. The European

Commission for Human Rights tried, the Pope's envoy tried, and the whole Catholic population prayed for him. Night after night on the streets of the North there were vigils at which people marched with a covered coffin, lighted candles and concluded by saying the rosary. It showed just how much of a bond there was between the Catholic people and Sands, something that unionist politicians couldn't understand. They couldn't see that Sands was a Catholic first, a republican second, and he wasn't going to be abandoned. All over Derry black flags hung from houses and lamp posts as we waited for news. In the final days before his passing, Sands lost his sight and drifted in and out of consciousness. Finally, on 5 May 1981, Bobby Sands left us, and so began weeks of funerals, marches and riots.

The British government came under attack in the House of Commons over their handling of the Sands affair. Mrs Thatcher, the Prime Minister, said 'Mr Sands was a convicted criminal. He chose to take his own life. It was a choice that his organisation did not allow to many of its victims.' This was seen at the time as a clear reference to the murder of Joanne Mathers.

On 14 May there was a rally in Gobnascale which ended beside the Spar shop on Strabane Old Road. Over 400 people attended and Eddy McGowan asked me to address the crowd and perhaps read something suitable for the occasion. I gave a speech full of rhetoric and anti-British sentiment and also read out a poem that I had written about Bobby Sands and Francis Hughes, who had died two days earlier on 12 May. The poem began:

> In the month of May in the year '81
> Irish history was made but not with a gun
> Two young Irishmen who'd never really met
> Died peacefully and the world was upset ...

The final verse was:

> But when this war is over and Irish freedom is daily news
> They'll build great big monuments to volunteers like Bobby
> Sand and Francis Hughes.

As I stepped off the platform and the applause rang out I was approached by a man in a light-brown duffle coat. 'That was a great speech, Willie. You did well.' Then he said, 'Sinn Féin are holding a rally at The Diamond on Sunday and I was wondering if you'd like to read out your poem on behalf of republicans here in the Waterside?'

I was gobsmacked. Me! Take part in a big Sinn Féin event? And all because of a poem I had just penned. I wondered if my handlers back in MI5 would think of it as some sort of cosmic joke. 'Of course,' I replied.

'Great. Just ask for me at the platform. The speeches are due to start at about three o'clock, okay?'

'It'll be a pleasure to address the rally,' I said. 'By the way, what's your name?'

'Mitchel McLaughlin,' the man replied, as he walked off with two other men.

So that was the Mitchel McLaughlin, I thought. I had often read what he had to say in the local papers and also heard Eddy talk about him, but I never dreamed that he would approach me to do anything on behalf of the movement. Mitchel was in his thirties then and was a very active member of Sinn Féin, which he had joined in 1966, long before the current troubles. He was christened John Mitchel and went to the same school as me in the Bogside. He was only one of a handful of Sinn Féin activists who thought politically, and he had single-handedly brought Sinn Féin to where it was at that stage. He was very intelligent and articulate, but he was not a great public speaker and preferred to work behind the scenes. It was clear this was a man who was going places in the movement and it was good from my viewpoint to get to know him.

* * *

The next day I phoned Alan Rees-Morgan in London, but to my surprise the line was dead. I tried several times without success, and back in the house in Rose Court I tried to figure out what to do next. Perhaps getting in touch again was the wrong thing to do; maybe I should just carry on as I was and not have anything more to do with them? In the end I decided to give it one last try, so I went to a phone box out of town and phoned the army at Ebrington Barracks.

I knew that the officer on duty would take my call and record it in his 'Night Duty Report Log'. As the phone was lifted at the other end, I took a breath. 'My name is Sean [my code name for messages in MI5] and I would like to speak to the Company Intelligence Officer.'

'I won't be able to contact him until tomorrow, is there anything I can do?' came the reply.

'No, that's fine,' I said. 'Just pass the message on and say that I'll ring tomorrow at 3pm.'

Promptly at 3pm the next day I called again and sure enough I was put through to the CIO, who had been given my message. I explained as much as I could and asked if he could get in touch with Alan, back in London. At this point he suggested that he and I meet up and establish my identity (for security reasons) and then he might be able to help. I agreed.

Two days later I waited in the car park at Altnagelvin Hospital as instructed. Shortly after 2pm a blue Hiace van stopped beside me and the driver motioned me into the back. I was quite nervous and was beginning to regret that I'd ever phoned. I soon found myself sitting in an enclosed area in Ebrington Barracks, home to the Army's 8 Infantry Brigade, chatting with two English soldiers about my background, my army number (24056669), my regiment and my work with MI5. They wanted to know why I wanted to return and seemed to understand when I told them of Joanne Mathers's murder. An hour later, after giving me a number to contact them on, 'Eddie' and 'John' (as they called themselves) drove me out of the barracks and dropped me off in the car park of the local health centre. I was back at Ebrington Barracks, where my father had taken me all those years ago, and this time under the cover of a new extremely secretive intelligence force.

As I crossed at the junction of Spencer and Dungiven Road, I watched the blue Hiace van disappear into Ebrington Barracks. I'd had what I thought was a very successful meeting, but something bothered me. Who were these people? They certainly weren't MI5, and if they were from the British Army Intelligence Corps, they didn't look or behave like it. Back at Ebrington Barracks, Eddie and John were wondering about me too. Who was I and what were my motives? All that they knew was they'd just met someone who claimed to be a former soldier working undercover for MI5 until the previous year, with a contact name of Alan Rees-Morgan in London. I thought they were two ordinary soldiers who lived in a different world from me, an MI5 agent sent into conflict to work undercover and take down a secret criminal organisation. In actual fact, they were soldiers from a very special unit of the British Army.

Although I didn't know it at the time, I had just contacted the Force Research Unit (FRU).

The FRU was a secret unit of British soldiers exclusive to Northern Ireland. Most of them were hand-picked from various regiments throughout the British Army and trained by elite SAS teams in England. They had been set up in 1980, and when I contacted them had around 170 personnel, eighty of them officers. There was also a backroom staff of over forty soldiers whose job was to collate the intelligence brought in by handlers. The FRU didn't appear anywhere on MOD directories and the entire operation was run behind the backs of most politicians. They had their own budget and the soldiers were officially posted (on paper) to the 14th Intelligence Unit at Headquarters NI, often referred to as 14 Det. They were represented by a colonel in the Tasking and Co-ordinating Group (TCG), which included MI5, the SAS, the RUC Special Branch and the army. This group met weekly at Gough Barracks to pull together all security and intelligence information throughout the province.

The small Ebrington Barracks unit was relatively new and was still in the process of being 'kitted out'. Eddie and John sat in the reinforced Portakabin that was their office and discussed my claims of being sent to Derry by MI5, my reasons for leaving the previous year, and why I wanted to work for them once again. The FRU were trained in intelligence gathering and 'tout recruitment', and they followed strict procedures in both recruiting and handling 'informers'. Mostly this was by turning someone who had been arrested to work for them, but sometimes bribery or threats were involved. In my case Eddie and John found themselves in a bit of a dilemma. Not only had they just met someone *offering* to 'work' for them, but someone who claimed to be a British soldier already working undercover for MI5. More incredible still was that the man they had just met was friendly with known IRA volunteers and seemed to know a hell of a lot about the political intentions of Sinn Féin. They spoke to their boss (an army captain) in charge of the 15-strong team based at the camp. In turn he contacted his boss at Lisburn and told him of the bizarre meeting that two members of his team had just had, and the officer in Lisburn immediately filled out and sent a Military Intelligence Source Report (MISR) to the Irish Joint Section (IJS, a joint MI5–MI6 operation) based in Belfast. Details of the meeting were then passed to the Joint Intelligence Committee (JIC) in London, often in those days chaired by the Prime Minister, Margaret Thatcher. Subsequently, my former handler from MI5, Ben, was contacted and asked for a brief.

Because of my complaints about Ben's continued alcoholism, he had been posted back to MI5 headquarters in London, where he now worked. Needless to say, although he confirmed everything to the army officer, Ben wasn't too complimentary about me. Within a week, Eddie and John were given the news that I was real and a sergeant from the unit was assigned to work with me. He was warned that I had shown republican sympathies in my previous role as an agent and they should tread carefully, not least because I told them I would work for nothing – something they had never encountered before. After all, their main recruiting method was bribery and money. They even considered the idea that I might be a 'plant', intending to set them up.

As I climbed into the same blue Hiace van a few days later, I had no idea of the world I was about to enter. Within half an hour I was at Ebrington Barracks, sitting in a room with a sofa, a chair and a coffee table, the style of which I recognised as army issue (officers' use). There was a huge map of Derry on the wall with various coloured pins scattered across it. To my left was a window that overlooked a small fortified complex and a corrugated canopy under which was parked the blue van, as well as a white Ford Transit. An armed guard stood at the locked gates ensuring that no one entered the complex. Off to the right about fifty yards away I could see a roundabout and a huge flower bed. Also visible was the edge of a building that I recognised. Now painted green, it was the very same guardroom that I saw as a boy when my father brought me here after his football match with the Sea Eagle Rovers.

The door opened and a young man in his late twenties wearing Levi jeans and Nike trainers entered the room. He asked if I wanted tea or coffee. 'Tea please.'

'How do you take it?'

'NATO standard,' I answered.

'What does that mean?' he asked, with a puzzled look.

As we sat there and chatted about my background, he gave away little about himself. I had to assume that as he wasn't taking notes the conversation was being recorded or monitored from another room. As he motioned me to sit on the chair opposite him, he asked me to call him Steve and then began his little speech. Steve was very polite and tried to engage me in friendly talk. He had an obvious Geordie accent, which he tried unsuccessfully to hide, and the only time he seemed uneasy was when I asked him if he supported Newcastle or Sunderland. He quickly changed the subject. It soon became clear that Steve was very interested in the IRA families I knew quite well. He wasn't in the least bit interested in republican politics, the hunger strike or Sinn Féin in the Waterside.

* * *

A few days later at the hunger strike rally in The Diamond I ended up on the platform beside Mitchel McLaughlin, Martin McGuinness, Seán Keenan (an IRA leader from the fifties) and Barney McFadden, a seasoned volunteer from the same era. When it came to my turn I delivered my poem again, this time to over 2,000 republicans. I knew how to deliver a monologue and when I started there was a deathly silence. As I finished there was a huge eruption of applause from the crowd, which rang all the way down Carlisle Road and onto the roundabout at the end of the bridge. Then the shouts of 'IR, IRA! IR, IRA!' Afterwards, Mitchel congratulated me as he introduced me to Martin McGuinness. 'Martin, this is Willie Carlin from the Waterside.'

Martin shook my hand, 'How are yee doin', Willie, it's nice to see yee again.'

'Do you know Willie?' asked Mitchel.

'Aye surely, Willie had a wee bit a bother one time and he came to see me to get it sorted out, isn't that right Willie?'

'You surely did, Martin,' I replied.

As we stood there talking, fighting broke out at the Carlisle Road end of the rally and we quickly made our exit down through Butcher Gate and into the Bogside. By nightfall we were back in the Waterside.

The next day I decided that I was fed up messing about with the very inactive Sinn Féin branch in the Waterside and drove over to the Bogside to see if I could get any advice about what to do about it. I arrived at Cable Street just after 10am as a young girl was opening the door of what I assumed was the Sinn Féin centre. Her name was Bernie Coyle and she worked in the office. I followed her into a very badly lit room – it was a bit of a dump if you ask me – and as she put the keys on the desk she said, 'I saw you yesterday and you spoke very well. That was a lovely poem, could you write me out a copy?'

Of course, I replied, and sat down there and then and wrote it out for her. She was delighted. 'Now, what can I do for you?'

'Well, I have a bit of a problem.'

'Okay,' she said, and pulled out a neat writing pad.

'Oh, it's not a complaint!' Just at that moment the door opened and in walked Seamus Keenan, whom I'd briefly met at the rally the day before.

'What about yee kid? That was some turnout yesterday? You played a blinder by the way. So, what brings you over here?'

'I was hoping for a chat and to have a wee look around to see what it is you all do over here?'

'Why would you want to do that?' he asked, curiously.

'I want to spy on yees,' I said.

He just laughed, 'Well you better come on upstairs with me because Bernie knows fuck all.'

Bernie gave out a snicker of laughter and threw her pen at Seamus as we headed upstairs. As we sat, I couldn't believe what I'd just said. I remember thinking that I wished I could be a fly on the wall in this room. I explained my frustration over Sinn Féin in the Waterside, how inactive I thought they were, and of my attempts to get to one of their Monday meetings, but they never seemed to turn up. Seamus thought a while. 'Look Willie, it's the middle of the hunger strike and everybody's very edgy around here. I suppose it's worse in the Waterside. I'll have a word with Mitchel and I'm sure either Eddy McGowan or John Carlin will get back to you.'

By this time Bernie had brought us up some tea and sat listening to Seamus. 'Don't hold your breath waitin' on John Carlin!' she said. Soon, people started to arrive downstairs asking for Bernie, and Seamus needed to crack on with a statement he was preparing for the *Derry Journal*. I said my goodbyes and left, not knowing what to think of that damp dump of a place, which was so famous in our city. Mind you, I was now where I wanted to be and it was all down to me getting noticed and standing out in the crowd. So much for keeping a low profile.

Within days of that meeting all hell broke loose in Derry when two IRA volunteers were shot dead by the British Army. The volunteers in question, George Mc Brearty and Charles 'Pop' Maguire, had been tracking an undercover soldier in their car. As he drove past Aranmore and Cromore Avenue he spotted them, and since his backup car was only a few hundred yards away on Southway, he drove towards it. George, 'Pop', Hugh Brady and another volunteer prepared to shoot at him, but the soldier turned and fired at them at the same time. One of the volunteers was hit in the crossfire whilst George and 'Pop' both fell dead onto the road. Hugh Brady tried to lift one of them into their car but he couldn't manage it. It was a disaster for their families and the republicans in Derry, and there was another funeral to organise on Cable Street.

That night Eddy McGowan came to see me and I was invited to go with him to the funerals of George Mc Brearty and 'Pop' Maguire. He also wanted to chat with me about joining Sinn Féin; I was being officially invited to join the party. I would no longer be an outsider looking in on the republican movement and reporting what I had seen; I could now offer my new handlers first-hand insight into Derry Sinn Féin, and possibly get closer to Martin McGuinness. That chance increased in less than a year as Sinn Féin began the inexorable push towards full-blown politics.

Mitchel McLaughlin paid a back-handed tribute to the new post-hunger strike Northern Ireland secretary, James Prior. Banished to Belfast because Margaret Thatcher saw him as a 'wet' and a One Nation Tory who didn't like aspects of her new right revolution, Prior embarked on another attempt to bring about devolution into Northern Ireland. This would first entail elections for a new assembly in the autumn of 1982, a decision Mitchel described as having 'given us a penalty kick'. It would open up the potential of a big electoral test for Sinn Féin.

He uttered these words at our Sinn Féin meeting on Cable Street. Once the minutes had been read, Mitchel announced that the nominations for the election were now open. Then he said, 'And I nominate Martin.' Without any further comment he sat down and passed round a packet of Polo Mints. Everyone there who thought they might be able to nominate someone from their cumann just sat there and said nothing. Mitchel will tell you that he nominated Martin first in case he might have been nominated himself, but nothing could be further from the truth.

I relayed back to my new handlers how Martin had been reluctant to stand, but Mitchel was working behind the scenes with Gerry Adams, Tom Hartley and others to bring McGuinness around and convince him. The problem was that when Martin discussed it with the IRA Army Council it became clear that he might have to resign his post along with Adams, who was very keen to do so anyway. He and Martin had alternated as chief of staff and officer commanding Northern Command since 1977, and giving up the control he had on the IRA was something Martin didn't want to do. In the end, Gerry Adams persuaded Martin that both of them should remove themselves from their posts 'officially' in order to head off any 'IRA men' claims in the media. They would let it be known to some friendly journalists that they had stood down in order to contest the elections.

As the election drew near, Sinn Féin pulled out all the stops to get Martin elected, and it was this campaign that changed the way the republicans did things in Derry. Breakfast meetings were introduced, think tanks were set up, a publicity department (me and Seamus Keenan) was brought into use and volunteers came out of the shadows to work alongside Sinn Féin members and knock on doors (this time without masks). We went out campaigning, encouraging voters to get out and vote for Martin McGuinness No. 1 and Cathal Crumley No. 2, under the proportional representation rules. Within days, Martin's poster was all over the city and out in the countryside of the constituency. Those people who didn't want to go to a polling station gave us their polling cards in order that we could try and repeat what I'd seen in the Sands election. It must have been the sight of the electoral activity that lifted McGuinness's spirits and gave him hope, because up until then he hadn't been all that fussed and was a bit depressed, but I understood that because he was suffering from 'Gilmour-itis'. IRA volunteer Raymond Gilmour had become a 'supergrass', working secretly for the RUC from 1977 to 1982, and was now in protective custody. Up to thirty of Martin's volunteers from Derry had been arrested solely on his testimony and were being held on remand in Belfast awaiting trial. Essentially, the bulk of the Derry Brigade was behind bars. I suspected McGuinness was also a bit apprehensive about not getting elected to an assembly seat, which, like all Sinn Féin candidates, he had promised not to take in Stormont.

Just when everything was going well in Derry, the 'fuck-up squad' in Gobnascale struck again. Colm Carey, from a very dysfunctional family, had served time for being a terrorist and was now a local drunk. One night Colm, who had been drinking over in the Derry side, stole a bottle of whiskey from a shop on his way home. He was reported for anti-social behaviour to the local volunteers, who had for months been receiving complaints about him, and it was decided that he should be punished by kneecapping him – shooting him in the back of both legs. The brave volunteers went to his home, where they found Colm in a drunken stupor and dragged him out into the garden for his punishment. They couldn't get hold of 'a short' (a revolver), so instead they lifted a rifle from an arms dump behind Bards Hill. They raised his right leg and shot him from close range. The high velocity rifle bullet ripped right through his arteries and nearly severed his leg at the knee. Then they turned him over and shot him in the other knee, blowing his leg to smithereens. The volunteers ran off leaving Colm alone, and within minutes he bled to death in the garden of his own home. Neighbours just peered through their windows, as it wasn't wise to come out of your house after hearing loud shots like that. Colm Carey was the first person to die in the North as a result of being kneecapped. The brave volunteers who murdered him even marched behind his coffin on the day of his funeral. One of them was the same IRA volunteer who had earlier murdered Joanne Mathers. She had paid with her life for £5 and now Colm paid with his for the price of a bottle of whiskey.

A few days before the election I had a routine meeting at Ebrington Barracks with my contact John. During the meeting he introduced me to a man named Alec from London (who was not military). He was very interested in how I thought Sinn Féin would do at the election and was absolutely over the moon when I told him of our plan to get Martin elected. Alec made it clear to me that it was imperative that 'Martin McGuinness gets elected

to the Northern Ireland Assembly'. This was intriguing, and
Alec stressed that there was a school of thought in London who
differed from the main body of government. They believed that
if Sinn Féin had elected representatives it might be possible to
make some headway with the parties' socio-economic demands.
Alec said they knew that Gerry Adams would undoubtedly get
elected, but for me – Willie Carlin – it was vital that 'You do all
you can to get Martin elected. It's only the first step down a very
long rocky road but it's important that by next week Martin
McGuinness is an elected representative of Sinn Féin. Do you
understand the importance of what I'm saying, Willie?'

'Even if it means breaking the law through vote stealing to
achieve it?' I asked.

Alec just smiled. 'Whatever it takes, Willie, whatever it takes.'

It proved to me that this new army unit was not 100 per cent
tasked by the military machinations of the IRA's Derry Brigade;
it had a politico-strategic mission as well: to encourage, cajole,
persuade and aid those forces in the republican movement
towards political action rather than armed struggle.

The school of thought personified by Alec got its way on 20
October 1982 when we started stealing votes at the Clondermot
School Polling Station on Irish Street in the Waterside. After
thieving the polling cards of doctors, nurses and other medical
staff from the local hospital we were voting early and often to
put our '1' and '2' beside the Sinn Féin candidates on ballot
papers. We even stole the votes of the nuns from the Good
Shepherd Convent.

Sinn Féin took over 10 per cent of the valid poll in the North
and won five of the seventy-eight seats. The SDLP took just
8 per cent more than us, but in Derry Martin McGuinness was
elected on the first count. He got 8,207 first preference votes

whereas the DUP's Gregory Campbell only got 5,305. Indeed, Campbell was only elected on the twelfth count as the 'last man standing' and never achieved the required quota of 8,058. We had stolen and personated over 800 votes throughout the city, but it was clear just looking at the count that McGuinness might have made it without our voting scam. Martin was ecstatic and revelled in his victory. There would be no going back now, Martin McGuinness had entered the dirty world of politics and Gerry Adams would teach him how to ride his military horse along that road. As celebrations went on through the night I wondered if Alec and his colleagues back in London were also toasting McGuinness's entry into politics.

* * *

The euphoria that followed Martin McGuinness's election victory had gone and we were soon back into our everyday routine. In November 1982, what was left of the IRA on the Derry side decided in their wisdom to take 'supergrass' Raymond Gilmour's father from his home on the Creggan Estate as a hostage, threatening to kill him if his son didn't retract his evidence against thirty-five of his former comrades, which included three boys from Gobnascale, Gary, Harry and Brian. It turned out that Patrick Gilmour wasn't actually kidnapped, more advised to go with the volunteers in order to put pressure on his son.

Through the country and western scene I got to know Dolly Shotter quite well; she was still in recovery after incurring horrific injuries in the 'dustbin bomb' explosion at the rear of her home in 1974. My band always arranged transport for Dolly if she said she needed it because she was confined to a wheelchair and getting to the local country and western club wasn't easy. Often Dolly would invite some of us back to her bungalow for a drink, lasting into the wee small hours. Dolly was married, but technically separated from her husband, Patrick (known locally as Derek), whose father had been killed in the explosion. Derek was tall with long, well-groomed dark hair. He was a bit of a playboy and always dressed well, and he could often be seen around town in an expensive leather jacket, Wrangler jeans and cowboy boots. Even though Dolly and her husband lived apart, they still had an on/off relationship. With his good looks, his car and plenty of Dolly's money, it was easy for Derek to attract young girls whilst keeping it a secret from Dolly, who often hoped that he'd change his ways and they might get back together again.

However, girls weren't the only secret Derek kept. He was an active member of the Irish National Liberation Army (INLA) and ran a small team who were often seen in the district. They were regarded as 'wasters' by the IRA, with no weapons and no nerve, and were the butt of jokes amongst the boys in Annie's Bar, who would laugh at their antics, their failure to successfully carry out any jobs, and their lack of credibility in the area.

Although the INLA cell that Derek Shotter led might not have carried out any attacks, at least they didn't make any balls ups either. However, Derek Shotter was about to strike at the very heart of the British Army in Derry, and would become infamous as the most wanted man in the North. On the evening of 6 December 1982, Derek Shotter drove into the countryside and met up with Dominic McGlinchey, the leader of the INLA, and several other senior INLA members. They loaded a bomb into Derek's car and drove separately back into the city, where Shotter picked up his girlfriend and then headed out of the

Waterside along the A2 towards Ballykelly, some twenty minutes away from Derry, which was home to an entire British Army garrison. Arriving in the village, Shotter drove into the quiet car park of the Drummond Hotel and sat there in the car, waiting for the rest of the team to arrive. He reached down into the well behind him and lifted out a bag containing a box. Inside the 6x4x3-inch box was the bomb. It wasn't a very big bomb compared to the hundred-pounders used by the IRA, but the INLA didn't have the same kind of finances or contacts as the IRA, and tended to steal most of their explosives. In this case was 5 lbs of commercial explosive of the type used in industrial quarrying. Shotter reached into the box, turned on the switch to activate the bomb, and set the timer as he had been instructed. Once the other members of the team arrived they all drove the short distance to the Droppin' Well public house, parked and walked inside, taking the bag and the bomb with them. The place was packed with off-duty soldiers who were enjoying a disco and generally having fun on a night off with their mates, girlfriends or wives. The fact there was a disco on this evening was a bonus, thought Derek, as he, his girlfriend and the other members of the team made their way into the function room and sat down at a table.

The DJ stood a few feet away, the music was loud, and the multicoloured lights flashed to the beat of 'Come on Eileen' by Dexys Midnight Runners. The air was thick with cigarette smoke, and the sound of English accents cut through the noise as Derek Shotter nervously looked around in case he was spotted by any of the soldiers who regularly patrolled Gobnascale. He stood up and slowly worked his way around the edge of the room to the bar and ordered a pint for himself and a drink for his accomplices. My young cousin, Priscilla White, was serving

behind the bar as part of her weekend duties at the Droppin'
Well and had no idea who Shotter was as she admired his good
looks and gave him his change. Priscilla, daughter of my uncle
Robert, lived just a few hundred yards from the bar and was
well known in the village. She had been asked by the owner's
wife to help out that day and was enjoying her evening's work.
After sitting for over fifteen minutes with the bomb ticking by
his right foot, Derek slid the box with his outstretched leg along
the polished wooden floor until it disappeared behind a large
ornate pillar, one of four that helped hold the roof in place. He
and his girlfriend moved through the couples, now dancing to
the music of Slade in the centre of the function room, and made
their way towards the doors that led to the hallway.

As they got into the car, Shotter took one final look back to
make sure that no one had spotted them. After a few seconds
he started the engine and drove nervously out of the car park,
followed by the other car. Within minutes both cars were speeding
towards Derry. Inside the Droppin' Well, the normally vigilant
soldiers didn't notice the box behind the pillar and carried on
drinking and dancing. At 11.15pm the bomb exploded with such
force that the sound of it was heard miles away across the River
Foyle in Donegal. The explosion was devastating, the people
sitting at the tables nearest the bomb were blown completely
to smithereens and the pillar collapsed and brought the entire
ceiling down on top of the dancers on the dance floor. The roof
was blown off, with parts of it landing hundreds of yards away,
and the building crumpled and came crashing down onto the
revellers inside. Within minutes, local people rushed to the pub,
which now lay in ruins, and tried to pull men and women from
the rubble. Holding handkerchiefs to fend off the smoke and
fumes, they pulled at bricks and wooden beams in an attempt to

get at the survivors, who could be heard screaming, 'Please help us', 'Oh my God', and one man calling out to his wife.

One of the rescuers uncovered a hand in the rubble and pulled at it, only to be left holding an arm severed at the elbow. The stench of death and charred bodies filled the air, choking the rescuers, who could be seen bent over, vomiting and unable to take part any further. The sound of sirens would carry on into the early hours of the next day and rescue teams worked on into the night. As light dawned on 7 December, the normally sleepy village of Ballykelly was overrun by the RUC, Special Branch, forensic teams, and the Special Investigation Branch of the British Army. By midday, just about every journalist and television crew who had arrived was camped out around the little village, beaming their news to the world. As people laid flowers near what was left of the building, it was emerging just how successful Derek Shotter and his bomb had been. Eleven off-duty British soldiers (average age twenty-one years) from the Cheshire Regiment were killed together with six other people, four of them women. Sixty-five casualties lay in critical condition at various hospitals.

My young cousin, Priscilla White, was one of those on the critical list. The blast from the bomb had blown her a good thirty feet to the other end of the room and her legs were blown completely off. She had horrific injuries and lay in intensive care, clinging on to life as my uncle, aunt and cousins kept vigil around the clock at her bedside. Ironically, Pricilla sustained exactly the same injuries as Shotter's wife, Dolly, sustained after the IRA's 'dustbin bomb'. The disgust, shame and anger I felt over this attack removed any doubt I ever had about my undercover work. I also knew that Sinn Féin would regret this night, and I wasn't the only one. The fear and the thought of reprisals forced the IRA to take the unusual step of denying any involvement in the bombing.

Back in Gobnascale, Derek Shotter had decided to go on the run over to Donegal. In doing so he drew attention to himself and thus started the rumour among those in the know that he must have been involved. Soon afterwards, fired-up soldiers came into Gobnascale and began to extract their revenge on the residents, particularly any known republicans. They smashed their way into houses, kicked down doors and beat up anyone or anything that got in their way. They wrecked bedrooms, kitchens and living rooms and dragged into Land Rovers anyone they could justifiably get their hands on. They even managed to recover a weapon and some bomb-making equipment belonging to the IRA.

A few days later I had a pre-planned meeting with Frank. As we sat in Ebrington Barracks, I passed on the rumour amongst republicans about Derek Shotter being responsible for the INLA bomb. They were already aware of it and were so badly affected that they asked me to try to discover his whereabouts if he returned to the area. I told him about Priscilla White and how angry I was and that I would see what I could do. We weren't the only ones looking for Derek. Shortly after arriving home I took a call from a man wanting to speak to one of my neighbours, Piercy, a well-known volunteer. After listening to him, it was clear that the IRA was trying to find Derek as well. The race began to see who could find him first, but it would be some time before Derek Shotter was seen again.

CHAPTER 4

SINN FÉIN ON THE RISE

Out of the blue one afternoon I was summoned by Seamus Keenan to Cable Street. As I entered the now-familiar office, Bernie greeted me with, 'He's upstairs,' and I found Seamus sitting at his desk with all the Derry party leadership reports laid out in front of him. Anything of importance happening in Derry Sinn Féin was there in black and white for me to see, including various financial reports that showed the debt of each of the branches. After about an hour or so, Seamus took me into Mitchel's office and said, 'I've a wee job for you.' He opened the cupboard next to Mitchel's desk, the contents of which were like an Aladdin's Cave. 'I'd like you to help me go through all this stuff, categorise it and lift out anything you think we should be doing something about. Have a wee look and see what you think.'

I was looking at hundreds of documents, instructions and leaflets from the Northern Ireland Assembly office; minutes and papers on housing, education, agriculture, health and, to some extent, security. There were also letters requesting assembly members to attend various meetings at different venues. Whilst Martin and Gerry Adams had not taken their seats in the assembly, they were still entitled by law to receive all the information from Stormont on a daily basis. It was obvious that

Martin and Mitchel were reading these, making notes, and in some cases jotting down personal thoughts on yellow Post-it Notes. It was no surprise that all of the documents were well-read and had lots of comments. On the shelf at the bottom of the cupboard lay twenty or thirty unopened brown envelopes, each stamped 'On Her Majesty's Service'. It seemed that for some reason they had lost interest in reading anything more to do with the assembly, and upon checking the envelopes it looked like this had happened just after Christmas. Seamus produced four folded cardboard boxes, saying, 'You can file the stuff you think we should keep in these and we'll sling the rest.'

'I can't read all these over here, given all that I'm doing for my other job on the site and now as the spokesperson for the cumann [party branch].'

'Well you can take some away and read them when you get a chance; but make sure you bring them back because we've got our own views on what we should keep.'

As I scanned through everything, I came across all the voting registers from the assembly election here in Derry. Registers from the Creggan, Rosemount, Shantallow, Carnhill and of course the Waterside. Clearly marked were the names and addresses of all those who had voted for Sinn Féin and those who hadn't. I don't know why but I decided that I wanted to have these and go through them and see if I could find some kind of pattern that might help us later.

As I stood there, astounded at what was in front of me, I thought of Eddie, my handler back at Ebrington. Surely, military intelligence would be interested in Martin's views on these subjects, not to mention all the voting registers. Various departments at Stormont were sending details to Martin McGuinness, of meetings and discussions on all sorts of subjects including the opinions of senior civil servants with regard to the security situation. I felt like it was my birthday.

'Seamus,' I asked, thoughtfully, 'Why do you want me to do this?'

'Because it's very important to us and I trust you to do it properly and he [nodding towards Mitchel's desk] also thinks so.'

After some general chit-chat, I returned to the Waterside to see Mickey Pick (brother of our chairman, John Carlin), who was at his mother's house in Anderson Crescent. 'What about yee?' he said, as he showed me into the living room. I had to be careful what I said to Mickey, not really knowing how he felt about me right now, or what his relationship with John was like. Pick gave me the minute book together with £17.50 that was the cumann's total financial resources. I went back home and sat down to go through the minutes. As to the £17.50, having seen the state of the other cumann's finances, at least *we* weren't in the kind of debt they were all in. That afternoon I decided to invest in some stationery and went to Lane's on Spencer Road. I purchased two A4 ledgers, a ream of paper, a selection of pens, envelopes and a book of stamps, then went home again and copied the cumann's 'Procedures for Meetings' from the one in Cable Street.

A few days later, I walked into Ebrington Barracks with all my paperwork and the registers from the election in a carrier bag from Kelly's Supermarket. The FRU and its political masters now had a valuable insight into the running of Sinn Féin in Derry. I took Eddie through the goings-on in Cable Street and my new Sinn Féin position. He was delighted, but he was more interested in IRA activity in the city. I asked him to have a look at the registers to see how the people of Derry had voted for the IRA and Martin McGuinness. He was clearly not interested in what I was showing him. 'Look Eddie, can you not see that the people of Derry voted for Martin and the IRA?'

'Yes,' he said. 'I heard it on the radio.'

'But Eddie, if this vote was replicated across the North the IRA would be able to get èlected under a Sinn Féin banner. Can you not see that? Jesus, Eddie, Gerry Adams was the first candidate elected in the North with 10 per cent of the vote! His team hammered every candidate.'

'Willie, I'm a soldier. I'm not really into this voting stuff.' Eddie was confused and was not really getting what I was hinting at.

'Eddie. Look, as you know I used to work for Alan Rees-Morgan and MI5. It was you that checked me out. Now here I am with the very stuff he and MI5 wanted and you don't seem interested. Can you not get this to him or at least pass it to someone. Can you not show these registers to someone who knows about politics?'

'Okay, Willie, leave them with me and I'll speak to someone.' I gave him the Kelly's bag containing the registers and he put it down next to him against the wall. Looking back now I have to admit that I was a little presumptuous in my thinking, but it goes to show how I felt at the time. I felt a sense of achievement that I had finally obtained the kind of information that MI5 thought might be possible. I was no visionary but I knew we had done something unbelievable.

* * *

By early May 1983 I was running a team in the campaign to elect the first Sinn Féin local government councillor in nearly fifty years – Seamus Kerr from Omagh. Sinn Féin was rapidly becoming a stronger movement than it had ever been and Derry was the only city in Northern Ireland where there was massive potential for the party's electoral success. At the same time, things in Derry were in full swing and meetings with Mitchel McLaughlin and Seamus Keenan were beginning to give me an insight into how their minds worked.

For a long time, Martin McGuinness had been an active member of the IRA and had gone on to become the chief of staff. Recently, however, he had been persuaded by Gerry Adams that politics was worth looking at as another means of hitting at the British government. Even though it was said he had formally resigned as chief of staff, McGuinness was still seen by the IRA as their leader and often found himself divided between the war and the political path. Mitchel McLaughlin mirrored the opinions of Gerry Adams, and his sidekick Tom Hartley, and advised Martin on the rights and wrongs and the dos and don'ts of politics. Mitchel was cleverer than Martin on this front. Not only did he have the ability to guide people into elections, he also had the skill of being able to choose people to make sure of the results. He was a very deep thinker, again not unlike Gerry Adams. He was well read in history and, to him, a ten-year plan in Ireland was merely a moment in time. Looking back, he was probably (maybe still is) the best political strategist that Sinn Féin ever had.

With the general election declared for 9 June 1983, politics was now the order of the day. Even though some IRA volunteers regarded Sinn Féin members as people who hadn't the guts to commit to the war, Sinn Féin was no longer a front for the IRA or, as used to be said, an organisation that just sold papers. The previous year's assembly elections had begun to change that view and the following month's general election would result in that myth being blown away completely.

On the home front, my activism in Gobnascale was also developing rapidly. The Action on Community Employment (ACE) scheme was going well and the park was beginning to take shape. We were doing what we could for the residents' housing problems; back gates and windows were being fixed or replaced and vandalising flats was now a definite no-no. At Ebrington, my relationship with Desi, my new handler, was also growing. We didn't always talk about work and sometimes we would meet outdoors and talk about our families, my time in the army and how he ended up in the Intelligence Corps. He often spoke about his wife, who he said was German, and he confided in me that he lived in married quarters just outside Belfast. His hobby was bird watching and sometimes he would be more interested in telling me about the different species of birds that visited Northern Ireland from colder climates than the information I had for him. This used to annoy me at first but I got used to it in the end – it was just Desi and how he was. If anything, it told me that he trusted me and was comfortable in my company. We would often sit and wonder what people would say if they found us together with binoculars not far from Magilligan prison. There were even times when the RUC would show an interest in us as they drove past, but they always stopped short of enquiring who we were. I liked him, and within a short space of time he was asking for more political information from Cable Street.

It got to the point where not only was I meeting Desi, there would occasionally be a well-dressed Stephen or Mark, who would turn up seeking more detailed information about my views on Martin's or Mitchel's opinions and politics in general. They were also interested in the Northern Ireland Assembly papers that were being sent to Martin. It was Desi and the visitors who helped me focus on what I was trying to achieve. I held the view that if Sinn Féin could be successful in politics and win ground in the North, this would lead to concessions from the British government who would be forced to recognise the political aspirations of nationalists and republicans in Northern Ireland. I often found myself taking unopened envelopes to these meetings for Mark to read the contents. The thought occurred to me that given that he was a civil servant from Stormont, it would have been much easier for his dispatch department at Stormont to give the papers straight to him and save on the postage, photocopying and me endangering my life to deliver them to him. But obviously it was the hand-written comments by McGuinness and McLaughlin that they were really interested in.

The IRA in Derry seemed to be 'muzzled' at this time, with most of the attacks on the security forces happening in Belfast, Armagh, Fermanagh and Tyrone. This was mainly because Martin's brigade had been torn apart by the informer Raymond Gilmour, and active IRA men in Derry found themselves involved in a holding operation. Some of the attacks that did take place in the city during this period were carried out by volunteers on the run and living over the border. It was risky but necessary in order to demonstrate to the Security Forces that the IRA in Derry was alive and well despite Raymond Gilmour. We were in the age of the supergrass, and no IRA member felt safe.

* * *

On the evening of 10 May 1983, just a few weeks before the general election, I was in my car on my way out of the estate, destined for Sinn Féin's office on Cable Street, when I saw two masked men run up the waste ground from Robert Street towards the back of the houses on Strabane Old Road. I turned around and parked outside the VG convenience store and chatted to Mickey Gallagher, the owner. Within minutes we both heard a shot and saw the two men run off over the waste ground. I jumped out of the car and together with Mickey we ran towards the rear of the houses.

I climbed the few steps to where two other men and an elderly woman had already gathered. The woman was screaming, 'My God that poor woman has been shot!' We followed the two men into the house through the kitchen and into the living room. The smell of gunfire still hung in the air. One of the men knelt beside a young woman lying on her back on the floor, eyes wide open as if she was staring at the ceiling. A pool of blood lay all around her, seeping into the carpet. 'Jesus!' I thought, 'surely not again, not another fuck-up.'

The man kneeling over the body stood up and sighed, 'I think she's dead.' The woman was Alice Purvis, daughter of the elderly lady who sat dazed on the chair in the corner. Alice was married to a British soldier and she had decided to visit her mother, who lived there alone in the house. Although soldiers were prohibited from entering the city – never mind entering a republican area when off-duty – her husband had come with her for some reason, so he was clearly there without informing his superiors, who would have stopped him. As they sat in the living room drinking tea, two masked men burst through the door and shouted, 'Irish Republican Army! Stay where you are.' There then followed a struggle as one of the gunmen attempted to shoot the soldier. Alice shouted at her husband to get out as she struggled with the gunman. 'You'll have to get past me first!' were the last words she ever spoke. The gunman, who was struggling to get away from her grip, lifted his handgun and shot her in the head at point blank range before running out of the house in pursuit of the soldier, who had by now escaped.

I couldn't believe it. Here we were preparing for an election and the 'fuck-up squad' had struck again. Needless to say, I left before the RUC arrived and a few minutes later met up with Mickey Roddy and Eddy McGowan. They didn't have to say anything but I knew what they were thinking. They felt as bad as I did. We agreed that this job must have been a 'quickie'. Someone had obviously spotted Alice and her husband arriving at her mother's and passed on the word. The gun would have been drawn within minutes and there would have been no time to seek permission, not that a cell needed permission. But this was no ordinary IRA unit, this lot came with a track record for carrying out operations that led to civilian deaths and caused communal outrage. By 10pm that evening, every road in and out of the estate was blocked. Houses were being systematically taken apart by what seemed to be hundreds of British soldiers and RUC men.

There was a scary eeriness about the area. People were standing around in groups, talking about the poor old woman and the murder of her daughter. I even heard one woman say with reference to the site where I was project manager, 'They should close that site down because it's just a meeting place for the IRA.' Shortly after meeting Eddy and Mickey, we walked towards the building site. We didn't say much about the shooting, we didn't have to; Eddy and Mickey were nothing if realistic. The lights were on in the office and there were soldiers everywhere. As we attempted to enter the site, an RUC man informed us to stay right where we were. I demanded my right, as the project manager, to have access to the building during the search. Two of his colleagues grabbed me by the neck and threw me into the hallway. As I went to get up and moved towards my office, one of them kicked me in the back and sent me sprawling through the door. He then grabbed me, drew his revolver and said, 'I'll give you fuckin' access you wee bastard.' I thought he was going to shoot me. His colleagues continued to wreck my office, throwing papers and files into the fireplace. One of them even smashed the phone with his submachine gun (SMG). It was then that I recognised him, it was 'Big Ian'. I had served with Ian in the army and my memory of him in the Queen's Royal Irish Hussars was as a drunk and a troublemaker; he was often up on CO's orders for one charge or another. So useless was he as a soldier that he was sent off to the cookhouse for most of his career. He was never allowed to be active in the regiment, never mind allowed near a gun. Now here he was, a full-blown member of the RUC, armed to the teeth and backed up by the might of four of his colleagues. 'Ian, what are you doing here?' I said in an attempt to strike up some calming conversation.

He lunged towards me and pinned me against the wall. 'Trying to find out which one of your friends murdered that poor wee woman. But then you wouldn't know anything about that, you wee Fenian bastard.' His breath stank of alcohol. These guys were on a mission. Later, as I walked in a daze through Gobnascale, I saw four flats on fire; only days earlier they had been refurbished by the Housing Executive at my request. As the fire brigade arrived, women and children could be seen screaming out of windows in the flats above the fires; then the rioting began. Petrol bombs and stones rained down on the fire officers and the RUC accompanying them. I ran down the steps towards the Spar shop on Strabane Old Road and shouted at Mickey Roddy's son and Mousie Concannon to stop their rioting. Just then two masked men emerged from behind the shop. 'Right lads, that's enough,' said one of them, 'if you want to help, get yourselves down the bottom of the Trench Road and keep the Brits busy.' I soon realised that they were two of my workers.

'What's up, boys?' I asked, feeling nervous.

'We're going to try and draw these bastards up towards Sandville Terrace and see if we can take a couple of them out,' said one of the masked men.

Feeling brave or angry (I'm not sure which) I said, 'You need to do something to make up for what happened earlier on.'

'Look Willie, we've just arrived. Why don't you dry your eyes, go home and leave this to us?'

One of the women who'd been watching shouted at me, 'I hope you've got something to say about this and your workers in Friday's *Derry Journal*, because by God we will. You're either being used or you're conning us, and we're sick of it.'

I was so ashamed. Not only had the IRA bungled the entire operation, they had managed to kill an innocent Derry woman in the process. As I lay in bed, I couldn't imagine the repercussions or what could be done to salvage the situation. I also knew that as a spokesperson for Sinn Féin I would be asked for a statement. Drifting off to sleep, I dreaded the next day although, as with the Joanne Mathers murder, this callous killing of another innocent only made me more determined to keep up my secret war against the armed campaign.

Over the next few weeks I postponed two meetings with my handler Desi, knowing all he'd be interested in was the Alice Purvis shooting. Whilst I trusted Desi, any information on this killing was being sought high and low by all the agencies and Desi might be tempted to pass what little I knew onto the RUC.

This would only have led to more raids and more riots, just when the estate was settling down again. Instead, I spent most of my time travelling between breakfast meetings on Cable Street, Gobnascale, and electioneering with Martin McGuinness and his team as we headed towards the general election. Cable Street had now become the focal point of most Sinn Féin activity in Derry, and the majority of people who came and went from the office were from one branch or another. The office downstairs had files on most of the areas and reports and statistics from advice centres; examination of these files clearly showed how far Sinn Féin had come in activity on the ground and in the political field. It was also the case that the offices upstairs were once used for various private meetings between individuals from the IRA, when plans were discussed between them and actions approved. These days, however, the IRA stayed well clear of Cable Street. Besides the fact that it was well known to the security forces, they were beginning to understand that discussing an action with senior Sinn Féin officials like Mitchel usually ended in political advice that resulted in the plan having to be rethought.

As the election approached, the meetings on Cable Street, which were at times hectic, were endless. Starting at 7.30am, there were days when it seemed like every chairman, PRO or secretary was in the building. Seamus and I were churning out statements by the hour, most of which had the desired effect. There were a few times when people were too busy to come to Cable Street or had to leave to go elsewhere, and Seamus and I found ourselves alone with a very subdued Martin McGuinness, discussing how one statement or another should be worded. Martin found it difficult (in those days anyway) to relate to the problems of ordinary people, and left to his own vocabulary

Martin's articles tended to be very warlike and technical. He was particularly fond of the phrases 'the armed struggle' and the 'occupational forces of the British Crown'. He didn't understand that the vast majority of the people of Derry weren't in the least bit interested in a united Ireland but were more concerned with their quality of life and bigger issues like heating for their housing, social security, jobs, health, education and the everyday issues, which to them didn't involve the British Army or the RUC.

Back then he didn't seem to realise that the advice centres in Derry were making their mark: winning over nationalists who for over sixty years had been educated in the practice of abstentionism and who now saw it as their opportunity to vote against a unionist, as opposed to voting for a nationalist. He also had difficulty in understanding the proportional representation system, which involved first and second preference voting. Second preference votes to Martin were sympathy votes from the SDLP electorate but they were vital to us, a lesson we had learned during the 1982 elections. Sinn Féin had taken over 64,000 first preference votes (10.1 per cent of the poll) and won five seats. The Alliance party only took 58,851 votes (9.3 per cent of the poll), but they still managed to win ten seats as a direct result of second preference votes.

Though Martin always listened, he didn't enjoy these discussions and I understood where he was coming from. He was used to aiming his words at the British Establishment or hard-line republicans. Strangely enough, both sides read his words very carefully, looking for signs of 'softness'. During one of these discussions, I managed to persuade him that the reader of these articles was not as articulate, or as knowledgeable, as he was and that he should remember this was merely an exercise in electioneering and not an exercise in promoting republican theories. It was at one of these meetings that I took a chance and said to him, 'Look, Martin, we understand your point of view but you have to understand that the wee woman from Creggan isn't interested in the war. She wants to know when she's going to get central heating in her house. She wants to know when the glass in the park is going to be cleared up so that her children can play there. She will vote for you if you show her that you care about these issues just as much as you care about the war.' It was at this meeting that the phrase 'remember the wee woman from Creggan' was born. I remember Seamus looking at me and saying, 'Fuck me, you've got some balls Carlin!'

'Just telling the truth Seamus,' I said.

Unlike the rest of Derry, I made sure we sent literature and details about Martin McGuinness to every unionist and loyalist home in the Waterside, to let them see that we were engaging in real politics. It also helped that this material landing on their doormats in the morning would get right up their noses, which was something that Martin loved. Late afternoons were spent back at Cable Street, where we organised Martin's evening, known as 'pressing the flesh'. On one occasion we persuaded him that he should visit the Waterside and also campaign in the more rural areas of the ward, like Ardmore and Lettershandoney. This was difficult to organise and very risky, because our team had loyalists, assisted by the RUC, on our backs nearly every night. Putting up posters or tricolours on the Derry side was easy because no one dared touch them, whereas in our area, no sooner had we put them up – sometimes amidst stone throwing – than the loyalists would rip them down again.

After one final meeting on Cable Street, some of the pressure I'd been under in the 1982 assembly election went away. Each cumann in Derry was to run their own personating teams, leaving me and the boys to run our own operation in the Waterside, and what an operation it was. The night before the election we had 300 voting cards that we'd collected around the houses from people we couldn't persuade to vote. However, we had a different problem in the Waterside because although our people were republicans who would vote, the polling station was on the loyalist Irish Street. They would have to run the gauntlet of loyalist stone throwers, who aimed at anything or anybody coming out of Strabane Old Road and heading up Irish Street to the Protestant school. Then there was the RUC, who deliberately P-checked everyone coming out of Gobnascale on the pretence of seeking IRA men. A P-check (personal check) was the security forces' way of back-checking your identity: your name, address, date of birth, whether you had a criminal record or not, etc. The information on a subject was so detailed that it also gave the officer a grading of suspicion as to involvement in terrorist activity, which was anything from being an outspoken republican to a known IRA volunteer. The crazy thing about this war was that the RUC knew most of the volunteers by sight and the volunteers knew most of them too.

Election day was different to the previous year; this time I was more detached from the operation in the Waterside because our people knew what to do and just got on with it. Instead, I spent the day driving around the different polling stations in the city, tallying the personating as well as the general turnout. Just after 7pm it was clear that personating was up and Martin was holding his own. John Hume of the SDLP was polling heavily in every area in the constituency, and in Rosemount very few people were voting for Martin. It was clear that in Rosemount and Creggan the SDLP were pulling out all the stops and their voters were turning out in droves. In contrast, we had exhausted our real votes and the personating teams had finished, so something had to be done if the election was to be turned around.

I turned to two volunteers, Pat Coyle and Danny McLaughlin. 'Pat, take a team to Rosemount, and Danny, you take a team up to Creggan. Get up there and start fights with the RUC and close down those two fuckin' stations.' Teams headed to Rosemount and Creggan and as trouble started the fights spilled over into the street, causing the polling stations to close and preventing SDLP supporters from voting. They reopened again with only minutes before the close of polling, losing John Hume hundreds of votes. That's the third way of reducing votes for your opposition. By 1am we were all back at Cable Street surrounded by telephones and two televisions. We watched through the night as various members of the Dimbleby family and other political correspondents brought us the results and predictions from various constituencies around the mainland. As dawn broke, it was clear that Margaret Thatcher had been re-elected as Prime Minister and the Conservatives were back in government. McGuinness was devastated, and he pondered the future saying, 'That's all we needed, four more years of bans, legislation and harassment.'

Mitchel replied, 'Well I did think that Labour would give her a run for her money, but I should've known.'

It was a remarkable piece of political naiveté on McGuinness's part. He had totally misread the political situation in Britain and ignored all the commentators who had predicted a Thatcher victory over a disastrously split Labour Party. Nothing could console McGuinness over the Tory hat-trick. 'I think she'll take this as a mandate from the British people to come after us now that she's been re-elected,' said Martin, visibly upset.

Two local political facts were becoming obvious: Gerry Adams and Dr Joe Hendron (SDLP) were head-to-head for the seat in West Belfast, brought about mainly by Gerry Fitt, the sitting MP, who refused to go away and stood as an independent. Meanwhile, John Hume was doing his usual political 'walking on water' and was drowning Martin in his spray, something we all knew would happen anyway but didn't talk about. By the time all the results were declared there were a number of factors worth examining: Gerry Adams had won West Belfast with 16,379 votes, a majority of 5,445 over Hendron, who polled 10,934, followed by Fitt with 10,326. Combining Hendron and Fitt's vote, it could be seen that over 21,000 people in West Belfast voted against Adams. Fitt's intransigence handed Gerry Adams the seat on a plate. As I looked at the result I wondered, given the size of the West Belfast constituency, how many of Adams's votes were personated or stolen. It was well known amongst republicans and nationalists that Adams's election machine was the best in the country.

There was another notable split in the province amongst nationalists in Mid Ulster. Unlike West Belfast, this split went against us. William McCrea (DUP) beat Danny Morrison by only seventy-eight votes, a seat we thought Danny could win. Because Mid Ulster is a mainly rural constituency it must have been difficult for Danny's team to personate. Later in the year Danny was heard to say, 'If I had had the Derry team, I would've won. It was wasted on McGuinness – who couldn't win.' We also suffered defeat in the notorious Fermanagh and South Tyrone seat. Originally held by Bobby Sands and retained by Owen Carron, the difference this time was the entry of the SDLP, who had previously abstained. This caused another split, allowing Ken Maginnis (UUP) to win. To my surprise, although

John Hume romped home, Martin didn't do as badly as I thought he would. By the end of the day we were turning defeats into victories, as we tended to do, and were celebrating that the Sinn Féin vote of 102,701 had gone up from the previous year (10.1 to 13.4 per cent). The total SDLP vote of 137,012 had fallen from 18 per cent to 17.9 per cent. McGuinness was still disappointed, because his vote in Derry (as predicted) had fallen to 10,607. But Gerry Adams would bring him round again by congratulating him on his achievement and keep him on track.

* * *

After the general election, life in Sinn Féin became less hectic. The very same day that Margaret Thatcher lifted the exclusion order on Gerry Adams, preventing his movement within the United Kingdom, the IRA in his constituency paid her back by killing a 20-year-old British soldier in a remote-controlled explosion in Ballymurphy. One month later, on 13 July 1983, when many Orangemen were hung-over from the annual 12 July celebrations, four members of the UDR were killed in a land mine attack near Ballygawley. The bombing was intended to be a baptism of fire to the world of politics for Ken Maginnis, him being an ex-major in the UDR. Ghoulish as it sounds, the whole of Cable Street celebrated at the news. Now that the election was over, the IRA was off the leash again – except in Derry.

I was able to concentrate on the ACE (Action for Community Employment) scheme, and made fewer appearances at the impromptu meetings on Cable Street. When I did visit, it was to go through documents and files which I would take away for my handler Desi, who for the most part was interested in what I was producing; as were others from the Northern Ireland

Office whose visits now became more regular. All the while I was passing political information to my handlers, the RUC had begun to harass me on a regular basis. On one such occasion I was stopped on Fountain Hill by an RUC patrol. Confronted by a police inspector who was renowned for his ruthlessness – a man full of hatred who instilled fear into the IRA in the Waterside – he emerged from the safety of his Land Rover and approached my car. Assisted by four armed RUC men, the inspector reached into the car, grabbed me by the neck and pulled me out onto the road. As he twisted my tie and was choking me, he said, 'I have it on good authority that you're a bit more than a community worker, you wee bastard. If you appear in court one more time to help your murdering friends, I'll arrange for you to be put away in a box.' With that he hit me smack on the chin and I dropped to my knees. One of his accomplices lifted my right arm above my head and smashed it against the wheel of the car, at which point I must have passed out.

When I came around, a young couple who were witnesses to what had happened sat me up and made sure I was okay. They took me to the hospital, where it was diagnosed that I had a dislocated shoulder. In the meantime, one of the boys came down from Annie's Bar and drove the car to my house. My shoulder still pops out sometimes to this very day, thanks to an RUC inspector who punched an undercover agent. What the inspector was referring to were my by now regular appearances in court providing character references or witness statements for various IRA men who were being charged with minor offences. It's well known in Sinn Féin that during my time in Northern Ireland, I appeared over a dozen times in various courts throughout the province, ensuring the release or dismissal of charges against members of the IRA and the INLA. Being an ex-British soldier of exemplary character and a dedicated community worker, my word was always taken over that of some members of the RUC.

I began to see less of Martin McGuinness, who was now heavily involved with Adams in planning for the removal of Ruairí Ó Brádaigh and Dáithí Ó Conaill of Sinn Féin, who had become known as the men with long rifles. Ó Brádaigh and Ó Conaill spent all of their time in Dublin and rarely ventured into the North, yet they controlled a lot of Sinn Féin's thinking about the future. An ardent abstentionist, Ó Brádaigh was becoming a liability and would have to be removed before Sinn Féin could tackle the thorny issue of becoming involved in day-to-day politics, both in the North and in the south. As the war was in the North, and the politics of the future was in the North, it was clear that Sinn Féin should be led from the North. Martin's travels and discussions with other Sinn Féin activists were preparing the way for Gerry Adams to become the next president of Sinn Féin.

A bigger problem for Martin was persuading the IRA leaders that he wasn't going soft on them but that there were battles to be won in the North on the political front, which would give them more power to negotiate when the time came. Although this wasn't easy for him, it wasn't as difficult as it would have been just a year earlier. Sinn Féin now had hundreds of members and thousands of supporters, whereas the IRA was becoming depleted. In Derry alone membership had fallen from over a hundred to less than forty, and the same was true in other areas in the North. There were new IRA volunteers, and others who had been promoted. Some of them were recruited after the hunger strike, and were used in our involvement with elections, and others, now leaders, were aware of Martin's views but still saw him as their leader; and if it was good enough for him it was good enough for them.

I now had on my books ten hard-line republicans, eight of whom either had been or were still active IRA men. I say this because, unlike the IRA on the Derry side who stuck rigidly to the rules, our guys drifted in and out depending on the job, so you never really knew who was active and who wasn't. As our relationship developed, they would bring me their problems. Whether it was a letter from the DSS, a pending court action, or the need to be off the site for a few hours, I was gradually able to gain their trust. There was an assumption in their minds that I was a bit more than just a community worker or an ordinary member of Sinn Féin. So far as they were concerned, if I was coming and going out of Cable Street on a regular basis I must have the ear of senior republicans on the Derry side. Though I wasn't in the IRA, they trusted me with their information and their weapons; on several occasions they made me aware that guns, ammunition or explosives were being stored overnight on the building site so that I could keep watch over the site if they had to be away for any reason. It was also now the most secure area on the estate, with a twelve-foot high fence, large padlocks on every door and shutters on all the windows.

Early one Friday in July 1983, I was locking up the three flats, one of which was Dee O'Donnell's and Mark McChrystel's joinery workshop, and there in the corner of one of the rooms for anyone to see were three Armalite rifles, together with a clip of 7.62 mm rounds. 'Jesus,' I thought, 'these fuckers are starting to rip the arse out of this.' I looked around in case there was anything else but as the windows were boarded up, it was difficult to see through the gloom even with the light on. I wandered over to the fireplace where I could see a shopping bag, crumpled up but not tied closed. In my naiveté, I reached with both hands to lift it out of the hearth whilst attempting to look inside at the same time. Suddenly, I heard the unmistakable sound of a clock ticking and at the same time noticed some wires protruding from the bottom right-hand corner of the bag and disappearing down beneath the grate in the fireplace. 'Fuck me', I thought. 'I've just activated a booby trap that was probably meant for the Brits.' I started to shake and lowered the bag gently down again. I didn't know what to do, but I knew I had to get out of there before the whole building was brought down on top of me. I ran out of the flats and straight through the gate, slamming it behind me, and made my way quickly down the Trench Road, leaving my car in the car park. Once home I sat in silence until about 3pm, smoking about ten cigarettes and going continually back and forth to the toilet; I couldn't stop shaking. I was in a terrible state and couldn't think straight. One minute I was lifting the phone to call Desi, then I changed my mind to call Eddy McGowan. Changing my mind again, I decided to phone Paddy McNaught, then again maybe I should phone Martin? My brain was scrambled, but as the hours passed, I managed to calm down and convinced myself that if it had been a booby trap it would've gone off by now. Maybe it was fear, it certainly wasn't bravery, but I decided to go back to the site and see what was in the bag, taking my briefcase with me.

Within ten minutes, I was pacing up and down in front of the bag, glancing occasionally at the Armalites. There were no wires leading from the fireplace, all I had to deal with was the bag. I lifted it gently, taking care not to take the pressure off the grate. I peered into the bag, the clock's ticking almost as loud as the sound of my heart pounding in my ears. Inside the bag there were half a dozen or more bullets of varying sizes, two Ever Ready batteries with wires running between them, two metal objects about six by four inches, and a small white block wrapped in cellophane – which looked like a firelighter. Then there were the wires that went down beneath the grate. Gently releasing the pressure on the bag, I took a pen from my jacket and tried to probe at the items, but my hand was shaking too much. I grabbed my right wrist with my left hand and steadied myself to have another go. I pushed the pen at an angle under the clock and attempted to lift it from its position. I could feel the sweat running down my back and sides from underneath my arms, and I was convinced the whole of Gobnascale could hear my heart thumping. The clock fell over and it was suddenly clear that it wasn't attached to anything. Using the pen, I gently lifted the wire up from under the grate; that went nowhere either.

I don't know how long I was there, but I was now afraid that the owners of the guns and the bomb – either the IRA or the INLA – would come back at any minute. Or worse still, the Brits would arrive. Either way, I had to get out of there. I stood up, grabbed the bag, closed my eyes and yanked it from the grate. The silence was the nicest sound I'd ever heard. Stupidly, I shook the bag again – just in case – then I opened my briefcase and stuffed the bag inside. I could only manage to close one clip, which meant I had to carry the briefcase under my arm, as I set off back to the house.

Back home I phoned Desi to arrange a meeting, but he was away for the weekend and the person on the other end was reluctant to transfer me to anyone else. Eventually, I managed to convince him I was in trouble and needed to see someone right away. He told me to drive to location 'E' (the Ness Woods just outside Derry), where I would be picked up. I left the house, taking with me more Sinn Féin documents which I had intended to give to Desi anyway. Within half an hour I was sitting in Ebrington Barracks, having a cup of coffee with an operative called Frank, who looked like a homeless person. With his long, unkempt red hair and glasses, complete with ill-fitting combat jacket, he reminded me of someone making his way to Glastonbury Festival. By this time, I had calmed down completely and I started to talk Frank through the documents and reports. He just sat and listened, looking bored, as if I was speaking a foreign language, but towards the end of our meeting suddenly I woke him up.

Opening the briefcase, I handed him the bag. He looked inside, paled and dropped it onto the floor. He turned and ran out of the room, and after what seemed like ages a member of the bomb-disposal squad arrived dressed in the heavy suit of body armour designed to withstand a bomb blast and any fragments of shrapnel it might produce. Before he could examine the bag, I picked it up and handed it to him. The Perspex on his visor was all steamed up and I could feel his hand shaking as I placed the bag in his fire-proof gloved hands. I could hear the muffled sound of him talking into the microphone inside his visor as he turned and left the room. I was now the opposite of afraid and was suddenly consumed with laughter. The tail of his bomb-proof body wrap – which was supposed to be clipped between his legs – was trailing behind him and he reminded me of a kangaroo.

Frank came back some time later and whispered in a very nervous manner, 'Well if that's all, I think we'd better get you out of here.'

'That's not quite all. You better sit down again.' As I reached into my jacket to take out my wallet he sat back in apprehension, wondering what surprise I might produce this time. I took out a quick sketch I had made of Dee's workshop, clearly marked with the location of the three Armalites and ammunition. Frank left the room again, and on his return said, 'I can't seem to get hold of anyone to deal with this right now. If you phone in the morning and ask for John, we might be able to do something about it.' With that, we left.

The next morning (Saturday) I visited the site to do some paperwork as usual. Eddy McGowan called to see me, as did Gerard 'Bogey' Logue, and young Willie Fleming. No one asked for the keys to Dee's workshop and I never offered. At lunchtime, I called Ebrington from home and spoke to John. I walked him through the events of the previous day and confirmed to him that the rifles were still there. On asking, I advised him that in my opinion the best time to break into the site to recover the weapons would be between 3am and 4am the following Sunday, when everyone would be asleep. I put the phone down and tried to forget about it.

At 11.45 that night my sister Doreen rang in a panic and told me that someone was breaking into the site and Eddy had asked her to contact me. I got dressed, jumped into the car and headed to the site. As I pulled up, my headlights caught a fair-haired man in his late twenties wearing a bomber jacket, jeans and trainers, climbing over the fence and trying to escape. Another man, similarly dressed, quickly followed behind him. The smaller of the two ran past the passenger side of my car, heading out of the car park. The other crouched down as if to hide. Word had spread before I had arrived and the boys were already there. People began opening their doors, looking towards the park. Dee O'Donnell, one of my employees and a volunteer, arrived almost at the same time, as well as Paddy 'Lambsie' McNaught and 'Bogey' Logue, two seasoned volunteers. The second man was still motionless beside the gate, hiding behind the bushes. Dee hadn't spotted him and came towards me with Bogey shouting,

'Go and draw a fuckin' weapon'. Dee ran off. By this time, a crowd had assembled at the gable wall of Fleming's house and began stoning the intruder running through the car park. I ran towards the man hiding behind the hedge, and as I did so he got up and started to run towards the site gate. I grabbed him by the leg and whispered, 'You'd better get to fuck out of here.' Then someone shouted, 'Watch out! He's got a gun!' and I could hear people screaming and shouting.

The man in the car park, who was being stoned and now believed his partner was trapped, pulled out a 9 mm Browning and was waving it in the air. He pointed it towards me and I fell to the ground just in the nick of time; the sound of the bullet whizzed past my head and lodged in the ground behind me. He was now backing out of the park, gun in the air, as his friend caught up with him. Only when they were clear of the green on the edge of the car park did they both turn and make a run for it. As I got up, someone shouted, 'Quick, Willie, get in your fuckin' car.' A masked and armed man jumped into the passenger seat of my car. I had no choice but to speed after the two men, who were now making their way up the Trench Road, past the Rushy field. As my car swung into the Trench Road we briefly lost them, then we spotted them again as they entered Woodburn. Seeing they were going in the wrong direction my passenger couldn't believe his luck, and he wound the window down to shoot the one nearest to us. Before he could do so they turned right, leaped over a fence and were gone into the night. We cruised around the area for about ten minutes and then returned to the site. The whole estate now seemed to be awake, standing around in anticipation of our return. Several people stood around while Eddy and Mickey told people that the show was over and they should all go home. Later, as I was talking to Doc and Colm Dorrity, Bogey came over and asked me for a word. He wanted the keys to the site to see if the Brits had got anything. As we walked he looked at me and said, 'Fuck me, Carlin, you're one brave wee man.'

'Why?' I asked.

'Tackling an armed SAS man? Jesus, Willie, he could have stiffed you.' He had seen me grab hold of the guy as he tried to get over the fence and thought I was trying to catch him. As I got into my car, I told him to keep the keys but to get them back to me by the next night so I could open up on Monday morning. They also wanted to lay in wait, just in case others came back.

The next morning it was all over the local news that shots had been fired at a crowd in Gobnascale, with no IRA involvement. The army issued a very unusual statement saying that it was two undercover soldiers. That was a first. Later that day, like good citizens Eddy and I went to the RUC station on Spencer Road and reported the incident. Asked how I knew it was a 9 mm Browning, I produced the casing that had been given to me by one of the local youths. An understanding officer on the desk informed me it was an offence to keep such a case and made me promise to hand it in later that day. Returning to Gobnascale, Eddy told me that he and the boys suspected something was up because for the first time that he could remember, the RUC never turned up to harass the people leaving Annie's Bar; the usual Saturday night stand-off between them and the youth of Gobnascale never happened.

Arriving at the site on Monday morning, I opened up and headed straight to my office. Lambsie and Bogey arrived soon after and we sat round the fire. Eddy came in and took a seat in my chair. The word 'panic' came into my head once again.

'Well, that was some night,' said Lambsie.

'Did they get anything?' I asked.

'No, the site was clean. They must have just been nosing around.'

Later that morning I had reason to go next door to see Dee. The rifles were gone, and after some discussion about Friday night and the reinforcements he was making for the site, I returned to my office. While I was dictating a letter, I heard a row outside. Looking out the window I could see some INLA members scrapping with one another man, throwing punches. Apparently, the fight started because the bag with the bomb-making equipment had been put there earlier in the week by one of them. It went unnoticed by the IRA, who had turned up on Friday morning to store the rifles, and not only were they now blaming one another for Friday night's incident, the INLA men were accusing the Provisionals of stealing their explosives. Unknown to me, I was also being blamed by the two members of military intelligence for setting them up and starting a riot.

When I had time to think, it was clear the IRA now trusted me with their lives and their weapons. It was also evident that the opposite was true of military intelligence. Their decision to enter the site at 11.30pm, despite my suggestion to go in the early hours, was proof of this. It was also obvious they had stood down the RUC's regular patrols that night, which gave rise to Eddy and the boys knowing 'something was up'. This action had potentially endangered my life.

That Thursday, I sat in my car in a car park in the centre of Limavady watching them, watching me. Earlier that day, Desi had called me at home, which was a first because in all my time working with military intelligence no one had ever phoned me, so tight was the security. Desi simply rang and asked if I could come and meet some people who were only available that day.

He said it was important, so I agreed. As I waited, my emotions began to get the better of me. I was convinced that the people who had requested to see me were probably SAS and would give me a hard time over the weekend's fiasco.

I tried to calm down and stay positive in the knowledge that Desi would be pleased with the amount of internal Sinn Féin communiqués I had with me, together with a number of policy discussion documents. The van arrived on time and I climbed in. This red Toyota van had no gap in the wooden partition so I wasn't able to speak to the driver. As I visualised the turns in my head, I realised we were heading for Derry and Ebrington Barracks.

On our arrival I was shown into a room that I'd never been in before and was immediately confronted by a tall red man with an equally tall colleague. They spent over two hours accusing me of 'setting up' the soldiers who had attempted to break into the site. Their interrogation was relentless and it got to the point where I became very angry with both of them. I don't know what possessed me but I just stood up and walked around the coffee table to the man opposite me and shouted. 'Listen you, if your men had come onto the site when I suggested, you would now be in possession of a number of Armalites and hundreds of rounds of ammunition. Instead, either you or someone in your team didn't heed my advice and you sent those two young soldiers to what could have been an early grave. You, or someone, ordered the whole fuck-up. You are no better than the "fuck-up squad" on my estate.' On and on I went until he motioned me to calm down and sit. But I just went around both of them and walked out the door where I was met by Desi, who'd clearly been listening. No one came after me and Desi went into the room for a chat. A short time later he came out and motioned me downstairs and into the van. That was the only time I ever saw that man or his colleague. Over the next few weeks, the FRU team were a little more guarded during our debriefs, except for Desi who thought the whole thing was very funny, especially the way I had verbally attacked the 'SAS boss', as he called him.

Leaving Desi, I began to drive back to Derry, and just as I was driving through Greysteel I passed a cream coloured Ford Cortina, the same as mine, parked at the side of the road. Sat in it were Martin McGuinness and the man I had seen a few years earlier coming out of the house on the Castlerock Road. This time I just looked the other way and drove on. I wasn't as nervous, though I still couldn't figure out what he was doing there or who the man was. As I drove I remembered Ben and the time I'd caught him outside Martin's house in the Brandywell, and him saying, 'If I could meet McGuinness I would tell him what's really going on behind his back' and that 'I would put him wise'. Still, I told myself, it was none of my business and McGuinness must know what he's doing.

CHAPTER 5

A RISING STAR IN THE MOVEMENT

After the incident in Gobnascale I was so trusted at Cable Street that I could go to any door or cabinet in the building and read whatever I wanted. My discussions with Martin McGuinness, Seamus Keenan and Mitchel McLaughlin continued and I now completely understood Martin's dilemma. He was trying to persuade the more radical members of the IRA that holding a seat on the Northern Ireland Assembly while at the same time being one of their leaders was merely a tactical move – as was his involvement in the general election. He was now coming under an almost daily barrage for making comments like 'Sinn Féin could take over from the SDLP'. Gerry Adams and others were able to get away with remarks like this because, unlike Martin, the IRA didn't see them as out and out military men. Sinn Féin organiser Danny Morrison's call to fight the Brits 'with an Armalite in one hand and a ballot box in the other' was now a reality; something the IRA in Derry had believed would just go away. Though it was rumoured he wasn't the chief of staff anymore, the Derry Brigade often turned to Martin for advice and he found himself anguishing over what to say. There were times when I felt sorry for him.

That summer I had to organise accommodation for forty members of NORAID, who were visiting Northern Ireland to supposedly investigate discrimination against Catholics. This was of course nonsense; NORAID had been coming to the province every summer for years, to tour republican areas and see for themselves how the war was going; and for republicans to show them how much we needed and appreciated their fundraising in the US on our behalf. They were led to believe their money was vital to our campaign, and while it took up a lot of my time, I did it to stay in the limelight and in the good books of those senior republicans in Derry who had organised the visit. After they had disappeared back to the US, we started preparing for November's annual Ardfheis, another committee and more meetings.

We spent evening after evening writing submissions to the Ard Chomhairle/Central Committee, who would decide the agenda for the two-day summit. Top of the agenda was to have Gerry Adams elected president of Sinn Féin. Hundreds of motions, ranging from setting up Sinn Féin advice centres to scrapping the Éire Nua, or 'New Ireland', idea forever, together with other motions ensuring Sinn Féin would in future be controlled by us in the North, were being drafted and put forward for consideration. It was considered a privilege – indeed an honour – for a cumann's motion to be adopted, placed on the agenda, debated and carried in Dublin. This was the movement's way of demonstrating that the hierarchy acknowledged and took note of its grassroot members. The reality of the situation was the opposite, the Ard Chomhairle was made up of Gerry Adams and other senior IRA members from the North, who simply passed their requests for certain motions down the line to the grassroots. It was a top-heavy, leadership-led relationship in the party.

Meanwhile, the IRA in Derry was having its own discussions. Apart from a few incidents, they'd been kept relatively quiet during the year and were becoming increasingly apprehensive about Sinn Féin's position within the republican movement. The IRA in Derry was historically the poor cousin of their counterparts in Belfast and Armagh, with plenty of bungled operations behind them. Outside Derry the IRA had been led by men who were ruthless and who cared little about public opinion, whereas in Derry the IRA had beliefs of their own, nurtured by devout Catholics like Martin McGuinness. His attitude, methods, outlook and beliefs were sunk into the minds of volunteers and young leaders. The Derry Brigade, now seriously affected by Raymond Gilmour's accusations and the impending trial, the constant suspicion of informants in their midst, and the frustration at the change the movement was undergoing, left younger volunteers frustrated and edgy. The main players on the brigade staff had no difficulty with this quiet period. They had been hand-picked or approved by McGuinness and were, to some extent, his disciples. Some of them were also members of Sinn Féin, and they were aware of the forthcoming Ardfheis and the move to have Gerry Adams and Mitchel McLaughlin promoted to positions of real power. They were also aware of Sinn Féin's overall, albeit patchy, strategy to contest future elections and extract concessions from the British government.

On 26 September 1983, a few weeks before the Ardfheis, Martin McGuinness authorised the release of old Paddy Gilmour (Raymond Gilmour's father), whom the IRA had held for ten months. Gilmour had not retracted his evidence and all the volunteers that he'd named were still under arrest. The IRA had achieved nothing and Martin knew it. One of the reasons Paddy was released that weekend was to relieve pressure on the IRA volunteers in the south who were looking after him, and other volunteers who were engaged in non-military activities. These volunteers were needed for a separate, very important operation. The previous day, a long-planned escape from Long Kesh resulted in thirty-eight members of the IRA seizing a lorry in the compound and shooting their way out of the prison, killing one prison warden and wounding another. Gerry Kelly, one of the prisoners, was now needed to assist McGuinness on the outside. One other prisoner to escape was Ciarán Fleming, Lynn and Paul Fleming's cousin from the Waterside. Paddy Gilmour's minders, together with other volunteers throughout the province, were needed in vehicles at various pick-up points along the border over the next two days. Technically, Gilmour had been released on the Saturday, but he was held just over the border in Donegal until Sunday night. Donal McDermott from the *Derry Journal*, who had been alerted by Mitchel about Gilmour's imminent release, was seen emerging from the dark with Mr Gilmour and was filmed by the BBC and ITN, 'who just happened to be standing about at the border that night'.

Attending the historic Sinn Féin Ardfheis in Dublin on the Sunday, the press was asked to leave and voting began to oust Ruairí Ó Brádaigh as president of Sinn Féin. Needless to say, Gerry Adams was elected president by the power of northern votes, and others, like Mitchel, would be moved to higher positions. Earlier, as Ruairí Ó Brádaigh rose to speak against the motion, Gerry rose and reached out to shake his hand, which Ruairí took but not without passing a snide remark. As I watched, I was reminded of those British politicians who hated one another, shaking hands for the cameras. Every member in the hall stood and applauded; they all had their own reasons. On the whole they were congratulating Gerry Adams on his election, but they were also glad to be rid of Ruairí Ó Brádaigh.

There was an air of expectancy as Gerry Adams began his speech in Irish, then in English. He had two things to achieve, the message to the IRA had to be clear: Sinn Féin was no longer a paper-seller or money collector for the PDF (Prisoners Dependants Fund), and he had to placate the IRA and let them know these things were not to be achieved at their expense. If anything, he had to get them back on board to catch up with Sinn Féin. After a short time, he addressed that issue, 'I would like to elaborate on Sinn Féin's attitude to armed struggle. Armed struggle is a necessary and morally correct form of resistance in the Six Counties against a government whose presence is rejected by the vast majority of the Irish people ... There are those who tell us that the British government will not be moved by armed struggle. As has been said before, the history of Ireland and of British colonial involvement throughout the world tells us that they will not be moved by anything else. I am glad therefore to pay tribute to the freedom fighters – the men and women Volunteers of the IRA.'

As Gerry Adams sat down, the hall erupted. People whistled, cheered and stomped their feet as if calling for more. Gerry rose, passed Danny Morrison to where Martin McGuinness was sitting, grabbed his right hand with his left and pulled Martin up. Both men now stood together, arms raised in the air. The delegates in the hall went wild and began to chant, 'SINN FÉIN IRA, SINN FÉIN IRA, SINN FÉIN IRA!' Both men took applause from their respective supporters and the Northern republican family of Sinn Féin and the IRA were now united in a common objective. As I sat there I knew that this marriage of convenience – arranged for Gerry's benefit more than Martin's – would be hard to divorce. It must have been a strange feeling for McGuinness, who at one time was the blue-eyed boy of Ó

Brádaigh and Dáithí Ó Conaill. These two men would have done anything for Martin as they had admired him so much. Now here he was just a few years later turning his back on them whilst Sinn Féin removed them from high office. However, as Adams and McGuinness stood there that Sunday, I couldn't help wondering about these two men now standing together on the platform in Dublin and the image of Martin coming out of what was an MI5 safe house (or at least it used to be) still haunted me. At the time I just couldn't figure it, and it would be a few years yet before I would one day find out the truth. Ruairí Ó Brádaigh was, of course, proved right in his prediction that this seminal moment would mark the start of a long retreat from armed struggle. The following Tuesday I was back in Ebrington Barracks, where I spent over three hours going over all that had happened at the conference.

* * *

A few months later at a gig in our country and western club I sat beside Dolly Shotter. After the show, she invited a few of us back to her place for a drink and a bit of craic. Dolly disliked the IRA intensely, and had similar views about some of the people in Sinn Féin, but she didn't see me as one of them. She often said that I was more like a community worker who had to side with Sinn Féin in order to get things done in the area. No one at Dolly's that January night was aware of the rumours about Derek, and as we sat there drinking and talking, the phone rang. Dolly decided it was private and started wheeling herself into the hall to take the call. As I was sitting near the living room door, I got up and opened it to allow her through. I held the door slightly ajar, making sure not to close it, and listened to as much of her conversation as I could, whilst at the same time pretending to be interested in what was going on in the room. I realised it was Derek Shotter on the line and he was trying to come and see her to borrow some money. 'You can't fuckin' come here,' hissed Dolly. After some further exchanges I heard her say, 'Okay, look. I'll be here after six, so if you come about seven, I'll be in. Now don't come any earlier because the Brits are everywhere during the day. Right, then, I'll see you tomorrow night.'

I stood up and walked away from the door towards the fireplace as we waited for her to come back to the living room. She took some time, which was better for me in case any of her other guests had noticed I wasn't quite focussed on their conversation. After her return, we all sat chatting for a few more hours before I said my goodnights and left.

The next night I sat near her house and waited for Derek to arrive. Shortly after 7.15pm he walked up to Dolly's house and went in, but before I could do anything he came out again and began walking down the hill towards the Derry side. I was caught on the hop. My car was well known so it would have been foolish to crawl along behind him, but I had to do something – and fast! I didn't want to let him get away now that I had him in my sights so I decided to ditch the car and follow him on foot and hope that no one would pick him up. After crossing the bridge he entered a private club in Foyle Street. The club was well known for music and drink on a Sunday night and was owned by a local market trader and businessman. I got a car from nearby Foyle Taxis and went back to the Waterside to see if I could find a local IRA volunteer whom I knew. That's when I found Bogey Logue, so I told him that I knew everyone was keeping an eye out for Derek Shotter (still on the run for the Droppin' Well massacre) and that I'd just seen him going into the club on Foyle Street. Bogey never questioned how I knew about the hunt for Derek, I suppose he just assumed that I had been asked as well. 'Are you sure?' he said.

'Honestly, I was walking back over from the Bog when I saw him. He was on his own,' I added.

'Right,' was all he replied.

I waited for about ten minutes before deciding to drive back to Foyle Street myself and see if anything was happening. Once there, I parked in between two buses and waited out of sight. Couples came and entered the club but other than that there was nothing unusual. Suddenly, out of nowhere a car appeared from the direction of the Foyle Road and stopped right outside the club. The doors opened and out got Martin McGuinness and big Mickey McNaught from Bishop Street. Mickey didn't appear in public with any other republicans that often but was rumoured to be well connected to the OC in Derry. Soon after they went inside, another car arrived and four men ran into the club. I decided that I was in the right place at the wrong time. Whatever was going to happen, I didn't want to be anywhere near, so I drove back to the house and phoned my handler in Ebrington Barracks. He wasn't too pleased about having to get out of bed at that time of night, but said he would pass it on. I went to bed hoping that Shotter would be caught for his terrible deed. Now, I don't know who told who what, or who followed who from the club, but Shotter wasn't lifted. I called Frank at Ebrington again to see why not and he told me that 'it wasn't easy and to lift Shotter there and then would have meant having to lift McGuinness as well.'

'For fuck sake,' I protested. 'This man murdered fourteen British soldiers and left my cousin maimed for life and all you can say is it's not that easy!' Thinking about it, though, I knew he was right. The politics of war and my cover had ruled on this occasion. Four days later Derek Shotter was arrested along with his girlfriend and both of them were charged with planting the Droppin' Well bomb and the murders. Along with other charges he would eventually stand trial and go to jail for life. However, at my next meeting Frank told me something extraordinary. It was actually two members of the IRA in Derry that had followed Shotter after he left the club. He had stayed the night, first at a safe house in Shantallow before moving to another one the next day. Those IRA volunteers passed the information to the Provisional's OC in the Bogside, and within an hour another volunteer was given 'permission' to tip off the RUC as to Shotter's whereabouts. It was this call that led to his arrest.

You need to think about that for a second. For the IRA in Derry to give permission for a volunteer to tip off the RUC as to the whereabouts of another 'senior republican' was a first. You could describe it as 'treachery' from within the 'republican family', and so radical and dangerous was it for the IRA in Derry to sanction such an action it could only have come from McGuinness himself. His reasoning, however, was understandable. Because Shotter and his team in Derry were causing havoc, attempting the most impossible attacks, this was endangering civilian life and giving the security forces the excuse to step up their raids on all republicans. When the IRA planned and executed an attack on the security forces they were able to pre-empt the authorities' reactions, move volunteers and arms around, and generally try to be one step ahead of the Brits and the RUC. When Shotter and the INLA did anything in the city, the IRA was in the dark and the subsequent raids often caught them and the entire movement on the hop. The INLA in Derry had always been a thorn in McGuinness's side for that very reason.

Though he used the excuse that they were indiscriminate and endangered civilian life, the real reason was that he didn't know what they were planning. Whatever Shotter was asked that night in the club, he refused to co-operate. Within the INLA Shotter had become a bit of a hero, but in Derry he was a liability which they couldn't deal with for fear of causing open warfare between the IRA and the INLA.

McGuinness detested the INLA for their arrogance and their disregard for his 'republican principles'. He viewed most of them as no more than thugs who used the INLA to line their own pockets and cause trouble amongst republicans, but he did admire their leader Dominic McGlinchey and some of their more senior members. He had no time for their antics in Derry, however; indeed he would later attack their behaviour in a speech delivered to the Ardfheis at the Mansion House in Dublin when replying to a motion that 'Sinn Féin should desist from condemning other "Freedom Fighters"' – a clear reference to Martin's continued disapproval of the INLA in Derry. Such a motion would never have got onto the agenda or been approved by the leadership, but it was 'deliberately proposed' specifically so that Martin could stand up at the Ardfheis and make a public condemnation of the INLA. He referred to an incident outside a pub in Derry which led to a major fallout between the INLA and himself. That led to a big standoff one night between McGuinness, two IRA volunteers and three members of the INLA. The house belonged to a well-known INLA man in Derry, and trivial as that sounds (what's new about a fight in a pub in Derry?), it involved a very senior IRA man and his wife. Needless to say, the so-called motion was defeated.

Derek Shotter was released under the Good Friday Agreement and still resides in the Waterside, where he is known as the

'Quiet Man'. I often wonder if Shotter, in his years of silence, ever wonders how he was set up by the IRA in Derry for arrest; that if he had not been followed that evening by IRA volunteers from safe house to safe house the security forces might never have caught up with him. The 'Quiet Man' would certainly have the right to cry out loud about betrayal.

* * *

Every scam and move we made to winkle money out of the ACE schemes, and also the Northern Ireland Housing Executive, was known to military intelligence. Not only did they know what was happening, they also knew what was going to happen. By now, on alternate weeks, I was meeting another contact with Desi. His name was Kevin; a really good guy who was interested in what I was doing and anything to do with Sinn Féin and their intentions. Kevin, or 'Ginger', as he liked to be called, was unlike any other contact I'd ever dealt with. He was well dressed, well spoken, and not in the least bit interested in guns or explosives – at least not with me anyway. I was secretary of my local Sinn Féin branch by this time and had just been elected as the Derry delegate to the then Comhairle an Limistéir, which liaised between Sinn Féin in Derry, Omagh and Dungannon, and was chaired by Francie Molloy. My appointment was reported in the local paper in Omagh, something I didn't know until my FRU handler showed me a copy of it. Everything discussed at this co-ordinating committee for Sinn Féin branches in the west of the province was being passed to military intelligence. Though he would occasionally ask how the boys were doing, Ginger was delighted at my new appointment.

I had also opened up a local Sinn Féin advice centre and we began to deal with the public on a day-to-day basis. Our office was so well equipped and laid out that it even became the envy of Cable Street, who for years had prided themselves in the fact that they owned their own building. The Sinn Féin centre in Creggan, while well used and staffed, was a bit of a joke, and Pat Coyle in Shantallow was still working out of a caravan. The Northern Ireland Housing Executive had adopted a policy of recognising Sinn Féin as acting legitimately on behalf of the tenants in the area. We had the contacts and could get results. Mitchel even asked me to help one of his relatives, who lived on Bishop Street, with a housing problem that he couldn't solve, which I managed to fix for him. Then, out of the blue one night, I was asked to go to Shantallow House and meet Joe McColgan for a chat. McColgan was married to Martin McGuinness's sister and could easily have fitted into the IRA in Armagh or Belfast. His job with British Telecom and his knowledge of electronics had earned him the reputation of being a wizard when it came to electronic timing devices. He was also 'alleged' to be ruthless with a gun. Indeed, it was well known that Joe was one of McGuinness's inner circle. I asked Martin if he had any idea what it was about: 'No idea, Willie.' This was another one of those moments where I became concerned and afraid. I didn't like meeting senior members of the Derry Brigade without knowing why. If I was ever discovered by the IRA, this type of meeting with someone like Joe McColgan would be used to lull me into a trap. I was very, very scared.

I arrived at the Shantallow House pub at 6.30pm as instructed. The bar was virtually empty except for Pat Coyle. He bought me a drink and, as we talked, a yellow British Telecom van pulled up and parked outside. A man in his early thirties, dark-haired, moustached but clean-shaven, blue shirt and jeans, with black boots and carrying a clipboard, came into the bar. This was Joe McColgan, the trusted lieutenant of Martin McGuinness. After buying him a pint, Pat Coyle left the two of us alone. I could only guess that he was there to make sure I met safely with Joe. Taking a sip of his beer, Joe began by asking me about the Waterside, the ACE scheme and how it worked. He asked how it was funded, how come I managed to employ volunteers, and how we were able to get the whole thing off the ground. After I had explained the process at length, he suddenly changed the subject and asked me what I knew about ASU (IRA Active Service Unit) activity in the Waterside. I hesitated, not knowing what to say, and decided honesty was the best policy, so I walked him through each operation that I knew of.

'I'm surprised you know that much,' he said.

'Well it was my job to cover for them,' I replied, 'and to tell you the truth, sometimes they are their own worst enemies.'

He looked at me, screwed up his face and nodded. 'Don't tell me: Alice Purvis, right?'

'And others, Joe. But to be fair to them, they've all got hearts of gold and believe passionately in our armed struggle.' I couldn't believe these words had come out of my mouth. I was now using the very words that we'd been persuading Martin McGuinness not to use during elections. I suppose it was the adrenaline, and who I was sitting with, that made my mind switch automatically to his level.

Joe changed the subject again. 'Now, you really do have to tell me about Sandville Terrace.' I walked him through how it came about and how we'd managed to refurbish the building with materials I'd ordered for the site. He smiled and said, 'You'll be fine.'

'What for?' I asked.

'Pat over there is the treasurer of Sinn Féin but he's stepping down soon, so I think given your know-how, you should put your name forward when the vacancy comes up.' Before I could ask him what the hell he was talking about, he polished off his lager, patted me on the back and left the bar.

I drove back to the Waterside trying to figure out what was going on. The next day, I was discussing the problems we had on Cable Street with Briege Curran and Mitchel. The typewriter they were using was antiquated and just couldn't do the job or cope with the workload anymore. Mitchel said to Briege, 'If you ask Willie nicely, I'm sure he might be able to get you a new one, after all he could be the next treasurer.'

Joe McColgan came in, sat down and started chatting to me. He spoke about how elections cost hundreds of thousands of pounds. Not only was it becoming a pain getting the money, it was also becoming more and more difficult to account for it, as a lot of it needed to go through Sinn Féin's books. He went on, 'Sinn Féin needs someone who can do more than just fill in "money in, money out", backed up with receipts and balanced up at the end of every month. That's known as a treasurer. The movement needs someone with a business mind who can invest and raise money, take risks and at the same time be trusted by the whole family. Your name just happened to come up. Yours isn't the only name by the way, but you will be asked to put yourself forward for the post. If you do, you'll know that you have our approval.' He got up and pushed the Sinn Féin minute book, which lay on my desk, onto the floor. 'Put it this way,' he said. 'I'm not in Sinn Féin.' He smiled. 'Keep in touch,' and with that left the office.

At the next Waterside Sinn Féin meeting, I allowed my name to go forward on the understanding that in the unlikely event of me becoming treasurer, I'd have to relinquish some work in the Waterside, namely secretary of the local branch. Then I discovered the Bogside cumann had nominated Barney McFadden as treasurer. On hearing this I was confused; the cumann in the Bog was practically controlled by the IRA. As Mitchel called the meeting to vote between Barney and me, I raised my hand, 'Mr Chairman, whilst I was willing to consider the role, I'll concede to the Bog's candidate, Barney McFadden, who probably has more time and is better located.'

Martin McGuinness, who had just sat down, turned to me. 'Your cumann's nominated you, Willie. They obviously feel that you have what it takes to undertake this role.'

'I agree with Martin,' said Mitchel, 'it would be better for all concerned here, and in the interest of democracy, that you allow your cumann's nomination to stand.'

I reluctantly agreed, though I was still puzzled. Why would Martin want me elected to this post, one that was normally held by a trusted IRA member? By 10.30 that night I was the new treasurer of Sinn Féin in Derry, defeating Barney nine votes to two.

As the Derry treasurer I was in a new position of responsibility and influence; my handlers would be pleased with that outcome. There were two sets of accounts books: one for all to see, which showed a steady income from the cumanns through various fundraising, and outgoings that left the books reasonably balanced with little or no money in the bank. The only time there appeared to be large amounts of money passing through those books was at election times. The other set of books told a totally different story. As I gazed at them, I couldn't believe what I was looking at. There were no receipts and no debts, just details of money coming in regularly. Even without studying them it was clear that I was now in charge of four bank accounts, all of which contained a considerable amount of money. They were in ordinary people's names, none of whom I knew. A quick check at the four balances informed me that I was now the custodian of hundreds of thousands of pounds, all legal and above board.

As the weeks and months passed I was to meet several businessmen from the city who made regular contributions to Sinn Féin. Of course, there was also corruption and collusion. The owners of at least six businesses allowed their failing operations to be bombed in order to get compensation. They would re-open bigger and better businesses which were of course free of debt thanks to British state compensation, and Sinn Féin would receive a valuable contribution towards the cause. Sometimes volunteers took advantage of that strategy and would bomb a business at the request of the owner, get the compensation and then split it with the volunteers, who would keep it for themselves. This was known as a 'homer', an inside job designed to earn money for the cell. I started to meet complete strangers from the Derry side and over the border who would contact me either requesting money or giving funds.

Shortly after my appointment, Martin asked me to meet a man in a car park in the Waterside (just by the bridge). He gave me the car registration and asked me to call the man 'Andy'. Jesus, I was scared; Andy isn't exactly an Irish name. But Martin reassured me he was a very successful businessman from across the border and it was necessary for me, as the 'treasurer of the movement', to meet with him. Treasurer of the movement? This was a new term to me. If anything, I had very little Sinn Féin money in the two relevant accounts. Martin told me that Andy had several businesses over the border, so I agreed to meet him and discovered that Andy was a willing participant in carrying and laundering money for the movement – for a 'cut'. One of his businesses in Buncrana was cash-orientated, and as he lived and banked in Derry, the RUC and the Brits were used to him crossing the border with money on a regular basis, usually in the form of Irish punts (the pre-Euro Irish currency), and with all the relevant cross-border paperwork. It was not unusual for Andy to bring over two or three thousand pounds in punts. What the RUC didn't know was that his business, while very successful, generated only a few hundred punts at the weekends – the rest was ours.

I could tell when the money was brought over the border because it would turn up in my Sinn Féin account after Andy had obviously banked it in Derry. He spent the next four weeks ferrying reasonable amounts across the border, though never too much that he drew any attention from the authorities. Having brought the money to Derry he would deposit smaller amounts into his own bank, where it would be transferred later to my Sinn Féin account. It would often take weeks for the total amount to arrive, as the money was drip fed into the account. After that first meeting, the only time I met Andy was to give him receipts, which were made out in his businesses's names and were passed to me from various wholesalers around Derry and the North so as to try to match the money he brought up and put in his bank. His own accountant would have been suspicious and would have noticed the money missing from his business.

Notwithstanding this method of raising funds, I was soon to suspect that a lot of the money came from robberies. One afternoon, for example, two IRA units in four vehicles parked in the main street in Carndonagh, Donegal, just before 2pm. Twenty minutes later they had robbed the only two banks in the town with slick military precision and drove to Letterkenny, where they changed cars and split up. One of them headed for Buncrana and gave the proceeds to their contact, who locked the money away in a safe. There were many robberies like this, but this one stands out in my mind for two reasons in particular. Firstly, at the time of the robbery it was reported the robbers had netted far more money than was being stored. This gave rise to some suspicion within the movement as to who took the rest. It couldn't have been the IRA men because I don't imagine the boys waited for the money to be counted, or that they knew how much they had taken. Suspicion then fell on my businessman, but it was eventually decided that whilst he could've taken the money, it was unlikely. Besides, even if he had he was too valuable an asset to lose. The IRA held their own inquiry over the border and concluded the problem wasn't at their end at all but that the bank's managers were probably lying for insurance purposes. (You can work that one out for yourself!) The second reason was that the IRA claimed responsibility for it and went on to state in the *Republican News*, 'The successful operation was due to the daring of the volunteers and the excellent intelligence gathering that allowed them to return safely to base.' I heard more later about this so-called 'excellent intelligence'. Apparently, the local garda sergeant in Carndonagh used the only police car to take his wife shopping on a Wednesday afternoon to Letterkenny, leaving only a young Garda and a bicycle for any emergency or 'rapid response'. Of course, it has to be said that there was the other little matter of him being alone and unarmed.

I also involved the movement in more imaginative fundraising. For example, to help raise funds for one of our so-called community groups, all Sinn Féin supporters, of course.

One time we helped set up a committee and assisted them to raise funds for a 'camera workshop' in the Bogside and then make a film about how the Troubles affected the youth of the area. After drawing up a constitution and electing a committee, chaired by an English leftist sympathiser who I didn't trust, we were up and running. We even managed to scam money out of Channel 4, who at the time were running a late-night community action programme. Grants were available for the right 'youth group projects', so I applied and we were granted one of the minor grants, which helped them set up their project and later make their film, which showed the daily life of youth in the Bogside.

As the group of six now stood on their own feet I was able to create two full-time positions for a manager and an administrative assistant in the room at the house that was their workshop. It was approved under the government's ACE scheme, which gave them both £90 a week each instead of unemployment benefit of just £30 a week. I was also able to buy them office furniture and other essentials. They were a great team and even provided Cable Street with the added value of being able to take photos of anything Seamus Keenan wanted for the local press. So, we doubled our money and gave local people a grounding in photography while using the Channel 4 and ACE support money to create a picture library for Sinn Féin.

***

Given my experience in electoral fraud, as well as leeching money from British government schemes, I was asked by my FRU handler if I could talk to some people from across the water in England. They said they were from some committee or other to do with reviewing the electoral process in Northern Ireland. They had with them some of the very voting cards that I had handed in as evidence of personating. We talked mostly about the system of personating and then stealing votes and the difference between the two. The woman on the committee was interested in my view on how it could be combatted. The answer was obvious, I said. 'Once a resident had successfully applied to be included on the electoral roll, they should have to apply for some sort of photo identity card to prove that they were who they claimed to be.' As for stealing votes, 'It shouldn't happen as long as ID was needed, with or without a voting card.' She was in favour of voting cards being necessary in order to vote but I pointed out to her that in certain areas in Northern Ireland there were those employed by the Post Office on both sides of the fence that would go to great lengths to see to it that voting cards did not arrive. 'If you go down that road, you'll have an outcry from here to London from all parties,' I said.

She looked at one of the men present. 'That's something that hasn't come up in the past.'

One of the men asked me, 'Do you really believe that workers would interfere with Her Majesty's mail? After all, it's a criminal offence.'

He clearly underestimated the real situation and, I thought, was rather naive. 'Look,' I said, 'if you introduce legislation that makes it necessary for voters to have ID plus their voting cards, I can assure you, you'll be making a rod for your own back. In fact, I can foresee a situation where an election day will turn into a circus. You might even have to rerun elections due to the number of requests you'll receive from *all* parties who'll claim that members of their constituencies were disenfranchised by not receiving their voting cards in the post.'

He seemed to get the picture. The woman, who was obviously the head of the delegation, thanked me, 'You've certainly given us food for thought.' And that, as they say, was that.

Meanwhile, back out in the real world, the political situation was getting hectic. I was attending meetings on Monday, Tuesday and Wednesday nights, and travelling to Dungannon every other week. I was almost full-time working on Cable Street, as well as trying to manage the ACE scheme. On top of all this, we had a delegation of English miners visiting the city and I was roped into organising fundraising for them. When the delegation first arrived, a lot of the younger republicans could only identify with their accents and wanted to know why we were 'hosting Englishmen' in Derry. They didn't know that the British government had already closed twenty-odd pits and paid off thousands of miners the year before. Entire families had lost their livelihood; some of them were even about to lose their homes. We raised a few hundred pounds at functions in Shantallow House and the Bogside Inn, and another few hundred in The Rocking Chair, but it was hardly enough to even pay for their trip. In fact, they probably spent more than that on drink while they were in Derry! I also organised white buckets for them to collect money in the city centre. All they managed after two whole days outside Wellworth's department store and down the Strand Road was around £480. Unfortunately for the miners, Derry was the wrong city to try to raise money from a general public who didn't really have any to give. It must be said though that the people of Derry were very sympathetic to their cause and those who couldn't give promised to light candles for them and their families, such is the belief in the power of prayer in Derry.

Over in Waterside on the Friday night, some of the nutters from the local IRA 'fuck-up squad' told them to approach Martin

McGuinness for weapons to 'sort out the fuckin' English Cops' who were being used by Margaret Thatcher to try to defeat them. One IRA volunteer, known locally as 'Curney', said, 'Listen to me; you've got to hit them in the balls. Stiff a couple of cops and you'll tip the tables on them.' Another of the IRA unit turned to the miners. 'He's right, but if you get the weapons, don't be shooting any cops on the picket line. What you have to do is send out "scouts" and find out where the fuckers live. Find out where their wives go and what school their wains go to, then turn up some morning and stiff two or three of the cops in their driveways. I promise you, Thatcher will shite herself and have a rethink.'

There then followed a conversation about weapons and how McGuinness was the man to authorise their issue. It was typical of these 'know-it-alls' in the Waterside who thought just shooting everyone who got in your way was the answer to every problem. The miners did speak to McGuinness, but he told them that 'industrial disputes' were not the place for weapons, though he did promise future financial assistance as well as a donation. Before they left I was despatched to the bank in the city and withdrew £2,000 in total. I presented it to the miners as a donation from the republican movement in Derry. Had the British press got hold of that, they would have made as much controversy over it as the allegations that the NUM were receiving secret donations from the Soviet Union and Colonel Gaddafi. It was a lot of money in those days, but Martin approved it so that was fine by me.

* * *

The European elections were coming up in June 1984 and Sinn Féin didn't have a candidate. Gerry Adams was recovering after being shot by the UDA in March on his way back from a court appearance and was considering the pros and cons of standing against John Hume. An Adams victory against Hume would be a major shock for the British government and would give the organisation an international voice which Margaret Thatcher would not be able to silence. Defeat, however, would be a disaster and give Thatcher ammunition to use against us. The other problem for Adams was that some elements of the IRA in Belfast didn't like the speed at which he was pushing the movement down the electoral road and taking McGuinness with him. Defeat for Adams would give the ultras the opportunity to re-open the whole discussion of the 'ballot box theory', yet a victory would put them back into their corner. The word on the ground was that this was a golden opportunity to garner sympathy votes from SDLP voters following the attempt on Gerry's life. Given the right sympathy vote and a good campaign, and with enough personating and vote-stealing across the North, we believed he could win. However, no decision was taken initially as the hard-liners in Belfast made a decision of their own which would ensure that Adams lost any sympathy he had with ordinary nationalists.

On 8 April 1984, two IRA gunmen shot dead 22-year-old Mary Travers as she walked home from mass with her parents. She was the daughter of the magistrate Tom Travers, who had been trying a case against Adams the day that Adams was shot by the UDA. Travers, who was the real target, was shot six times in the attack but survived. Nationalists always had mixed feelings about IRA actions. To them, some were understandable and some were not. But to shoot dead a woman on her way home from mass was seen as a sacrilege and unforgivable. Given the fact that the attack was seen to be linked to Adams, any hope of sympathy from nationalists, who might normally not vote Sinn Féin or support the IRA, was now completely out of the question.

With Adams off the list, McGuinness was left with a dilemma. Martin hated losing anything, from an argument to a Gaelic football game. After all, he hadn't initially agreed with the hunger strike 'in case it failed', and he vetoed any volunteer from Derry attempting to join it. He made it known he hadn't been too keen on the election campaign of Bobby Sands 'in case Sands lost', nor had he been convinced at first on the necessity to stand in the assembly elections of 1982 'in case he lost.' And he didn't want to stand in the general election of 1983, even though that was all about building a Sinn Féin vote and not about him winning.

Now here we all were, sitting round a table talking with him about another election. The fact was he and Adams suffered from the same illness, 'fear of failure', and he didn't fancy another defeat from the Blessed John Hume. But he had learned something from British politicians. Turning to Mitchel McLaughlin, who was chairing the meeting, he said, 'Mr Chairman, I'll have to decline the nomination in order to spend more time with my family.' You could have heard the laughter down the street, though to be fair to Martin, his wife Bernie was by now seven or eight months pregnant. In many ways, Martin had more to lose than Adams did, if he had stood. McGuinness knew he couldn't beat John Hume, no matter what Sinn Féin did for him. In that respect Martin was right not to stand.

As June approached, Danny Morrison was seen as a suitable candidate. He was well liked by both republicans and nationalists because of his manner, charm, twinkling smile and the fact he liked being in the public eye. For him to lose against Hume would not be viewed by the media in the same way as a defeat for Adams or McGuinness.

It was around this time that I nearly blew the whole army intelligence operation at Ebrington Barracks and caused a panic that went all the way to Belfast. In the run-up to the election I was on Cable Street nearly every afternoon. One day I was upstairs in Seamus Keenan's office and running late for a meeting with one of my handlers, someone senior from London, and I just knew that I wasn't going to make it. The spy craft rule was that if you had a meeting on the hour and were going to be delayed there was no need to contact anyone. You simply turned up an hour later at the same spot where you would have been picked up. This was known as the second hour. It was long past the first hour and was now heading for the second hour. As the meeting was with someone from London, I determined that I had to make that meeting. Not really thinking, I decided to use the phone downstairs in the Sinn Féin office. I knew that the phones on Cable Street weren't bugged, thanks mainly to Joe McColgan's BT engineering skills, but I needed the call to look routine and I didn't want Mitchel, who was sat in the next room, to interrupt me. Once downstairs I simply picked up the phone, dialled the number at the barracks and asked for Eddie. Anyone listening would think I was phoning Sinn Féin activist Eddy McGowan, which I often did. The office was very busy and no one took any notice of me as I said 'Hello Eddie. Look, I'm just not going to make it. Is there any chance of meeting up at six o'clock?'

'Okay,' replied Eddie, 'six o'clock, same place.' Then I went back upstairs and got back to what I was doing. I attended my secret meeting with the handler later that day and thought no more of it.

Two weeks later, Seamus Keenan sent me into a deep shock. I was writing a press statement about Gobnascale at his desk when he came in with a bundle of his own. As usual I asked him if he had anything interesting. 'You better believe it, kid,' he said, handing me one of the statements. Reading it, I went weak at the knees and nearly passed out. It was a statement about the British Army trying to recruit someone to spy for them, and there in the middle was my contact phone number, the one at Ebrington Barracks I had called a fortnight earlier.

'Was this for real?' I asked Seamus, almost certain my cover was blown.

'Fuckin' right, and it's going on the front page of the *Derry Journal.*'

A few days later at a meeting in Ebrington Barracks, Eddie wanted to know if I knew how the IRA had got hold of the number. What I didn't know was that it wasn't just my number; others in Derry (unknown to me) had the same number. Eddie made light of it and gave me a new number. As it turned out, it was my fault, though I believe army intelligence blamed someone else.

It transpired that the phone bill on Cable Street was regularly monitored and someone became curious about this strange number. They were familiar with the regular ones but checked all of the numbers not seen before. This one was completely new so the person concerned simply dialled it – and quickly hung up when a young English Corporal answered. It was then passed to Joe McColgan, who checked it out at BT and discovered the number was allocated to Ebrington Barracks. On discovering what it was, the IRA decided to use it to their advantage and claimed that the British Army had tried to recruit a local man and had given him that number. Though the date and time of the call was logged on the bill, Joe McColgan was not able to narrow it down to me. For a long time afterwards, the phones were monitored in an effort to try and catch whoever had dialled the number. Needless to say, I never made such a stupid, dangerous mistake like that again.

After an ordinary polling day of 'stealing and personating' around Derry's schools during the European election on 14 June 1984, we all knew that things hadn't gone as well as our previous outings, but we expected that. We stole and personated more than usual because we knew that our vote would be down. Firstly, there was really only one seat available, and Morrison was never in with a chance against John Hume. Secondly, our supporters also knew that and some of them just didn't see the point in making the effort. Lastly, our election effort had scared a lot of Hume supporters into believing Sinn Féin publicity that Morrison could win, an error on our part. Consequently, they turned out in force and Hume polled over 150,000 votes. Our target had been 100,000 votes, which we missed by about 9,000. That wasn't bad I suppose, given the circumstances. The only person who wasn't happy was Danny Morrison. Nobody had told Danny, who wandered Tyrone, cigar in hand like General Patton, that he couldn't win. He was gutted when our vote fell by 11,000 on the previous year of the general election. He didn't appreciate that at this point, as political horse-trainers, we were basically a two-horse stable. Though we sold it as an increase of 50,000 votes compared to the previous European election experience, which wasn't hard to do given that it was as far back as 1979, the fact was the vote went down, not up. We were only kidding ourselves by talking such nonsense because Sinn Féin didn't contest the 1979 election anyway, as it was Bernadette McAliskey who stood as an independent.

With the European elections behind us and our political machine well oiled, it was now time to consider what to do about next year's local council elections, which was the next obvious political race to run in. But we still had to persuade the IRA members, who had been very quiet in Derry after the murder of Alice Purvis and were afraid as they waited for the outcome of Raymond Gilmour's trial, which involved the arrest of the most experienced volunteers in Derry. The ones that were still at large were either down across the border just sitting around the 'White House' (an IRA safe house in Buncrana) or in Derry waiting to see what would happen next. Gilmour had crippled the IRA in Derry by turning police informer, and Martin, who was in a permanent daze, steered well clear of the few volunteers that were left in the city.

* * *

At the end of July 1984, Seamus Keenan advised me that Martin Galvin, the NORAID spokesperson, had been banned from entering Northern Ireland by the secretary of state. Whilst Galvin's contribution towards the armed struggle was good PR for the movement, he wasn't vital to any plans at the time. However, Adams wanted him to address a rally in Belfast in a few weeks' time. This was meant as a token of recognition for the part he played in fundraising in America. Shortly after his and NORAID's arrival in Derry, I was asked to bring him to our centre and show him how his money was being spent. I took an instant dislike to him as he bragged about how his fundraising was vital to our cause, as if we owed him something. After an hour or so the sound of the twang in his voice annoyed me intensely. My father had no time for Americans and their ways;

I couldn't understand his attitude at the time. Now here was Galvin doing the same to me. He was waiting in my office for a lift to the Derry side where he was due to meet Martin. The car never came and I reluctantly offered to take him myself. By the time we got to Cable Street there was very little time left to meet Martin McGuinness, so he was quickly taken away and then sent to a safe house somewhere in the city. At the time I didn't think it important enough to phone and tell my contact, because I was sure that there wasn't much they could do and that Galvin wasn't that important to them. However, the next time I was to see Galvin would be on the nine o'clock news, taking part in an incident that would play on my mind for many years.

On 12 August 1984, Martin Galvin climbed up onto the rostrum to make a speech at the anti-internment rally commemoration at Andersonstown in West Belfast. His appearance was like a red rag to a bull to the RUC, who had surrounded the rally having got wind of Galvin's attendance. Suddenly, all hell broke loose as at least twenty RUC men charged the platform trying to get hold of Galvin, who was quickly removed by a crowd who surrounded the microphone and disappeared with him into the back streets of Belfast. Another group of armed RUC men emerged and so incensed and embarrassed were they that they began to fire plastic bullets directly at the crowd. Gerry Adams asked everybody to stay calm and sit down on the road and the pavements. As they did so a number of people fell to the ground, badly injured. One of the injured was 22-year-old Sean Downes, who never recovered and died a short time later. That night there were riots all over West Belfast.

I was overcome with regret. Had I not been so cavalier and had contacted my handler, Galvin might have been arrested and

Sean Downes might still be alive. Later, at a meeting with Desi he helped me square the circle of guilt by saying, 'Willie, Gerry Adams was the one that was cavalier. He used innocent Catholics as a barrier between Galvin and the RUC. And you can't tell me that Adams didn't know the trouble Galvin's appearance would cause.'

CHAPTER 6

MARTIN OPENS UP

One afternoon in the summer of 1984, I was at Cable Street when Mitchel McLaughlin asked if I fancied taking part in a debate. 'What's the issue?' I asked.

'We want to hold a debate between both sides of the movement in Derry about the wisdom of taking our seats on the City Council.'

I was taken aback. 'What, us and the IRA?'

'Both sides of the movement,' he repeated, not wishing to use my words.

'Okay,' I said, 'when and where?'

He told me he hadn't yet reached agreement but was hoping for two teams of four speakers on each side. The venue would have to be somewhere away from public view. Over the next week the debate was organised in the safety of the upstairs lounge of The Bogside Inn and would be closed to the public. I was to lead and propose the motion: 'Sinn Féin believes that we should contest and take our seats at the next city council elections.' I had three other Sinn Féin members in my team and we were opposed by the 'other side of the family' who were represented by two hard-liners from Creggan and two volunteers from Shantallow.

The lounge was packed, with over eighty people gathered from all sides of the movement to witness what Mitchel had called 'a relaxed discussion with a serious side to it'. He was using the absence of most of the hard-line IRA men to generate the discussion and the debate, which 'if carried' could be claimed as the wish of the rank and file of the movement in Derry. If the motion was to be lost, he could claim it to have been a useful exercise in the art of 'healthy discussion amongst republicans'. Martin McGuinness was conspicuous by his absence. I suppose it wouldn't have been wise for him to be seen to be taking part. True to form, Mitchel didn't take part either, instead opting to act as chairman and 'bell-ringer', should anyone overrun or get carried away. He, like Martin, was now riding two horses and didn't want to fall off either of them.

We did have a very special, surprising guest, however. The hereditary peer and senior barrister Lord Gifford was in Derry, visiting and advising the families of volunteers who had been arrested on Raymond Gilmour's evidence, and he had been invited along as an observer. He sat out of sight in the corner, with few people even knowing he was there. I was called on to open the debate, which I did to cheers of the Sinn Féin cumann from the Waterside and boos from the IRA volunteers in Shantallow. One by one each of the speakers gave their five-minute contribution. The atmosphere was mostly light-hearted, as boos and cheers rang out around the lounge. Each speaker spoke with authority and passion, defending their views robustly. All in all it was a very good debate, which I felt needed to end with a rousing plea.

I was called upon to sum up for the motion. I spoke passionately about the need to change the way we did things on behalf of our electorate in republican areas of the city. I told

them that 'blowing up the Guildhall now and again was futile!'
That got them going so I drove on hard, despite boos and cheers,
'We need to take our seats in the council and on the committees
and represent our people who are being misrepresented by the
SDLP. We can change the politics of our city but we can only
do this from inside the chambers of the Guildhall. We can put
the OUP and the DUP into the dustbins of that building, instead
of the bombs we put there in the past.' More cheers and boos
rang out as some of the guys from the Waterside urged me on.
'They thrive on the fact that we don't take part and they elect
themselves into council positions in our absence. We must take
our seats and take on the responsibility which will be given to us
by the republican families in this city next May.'

Just as I was getting into my stride, Mitchel rang the bell. I
had overrun my summing up. By now I was being cheered on
by the majority of Sinn Féin members in the lounge and decided
to ignore Mitchel and carry on. I moved from behind the table
and out onto the floor and carried on despite Mitchel's protests.
Soon people were chanting, cheering and stamping their feet,
both in response to what I was shouting and to the fact that I
had told Mitchel to be quiet and not interrupt me.

As I was about to sit down, someone shouted, 'Military
victory over the Brits is the only way!' I turned towards the
voice and said, 'Okay, let's assume that we beat the Brits and
kick them out. What are you going to do then, eh? You'll have
no experience of the mechanisms of politics at a local level, never
mind nationally, and we in Sinn Féin will be eaten for breakfast
by the unionists, not to mention Fine Gael in the south. You'll
be led like lambs to the slaughter!'

The chanting in the lounge urging me on was like adrenaline,
but I realised that I had better sit down and be quiet. After

everything had settled down and before Mitchel called for the motion to be voted on, he introduced Lord Gifford and asked if he would address the gathering and comment on the debate. He was a very eloquent speaker, though a bit nervous, which I suppose, given the area he was in and the company he sat in, was understandable. He told the gathering, who sat in silence, 'I am very impressed by your understanding of the issues involved and have learned a lot from just witnessing the discussion.' Then he said something that brought a cheer and gave me a lot of personal satisfaction, 'You may not be aware of it but the rules and procedures governing debating are handed down by the House of Lords, which as you all know is the upper chamber of the British parliament. So it was noticeable that all you republicans abided by those very British rules, except, that is, Mr Carlin. He was the only one of you who broke the rules of the House of Lords by refusing to obey the chairman and continue with his summation.'

The roars of laughter could be heard far away as they emanated from the open windows of the lounge of the Bogside Inn. It's a night I shall never forget and it was the beginning of the end for the movement's pro-abstentionists in Derry. When Mitchel eventually gained control and asked for a vote on the motion, it was carried unanimously. I felt very proud, at long last the people of Derry would be able to vote for Sinn Féin knowing that we would be taking our seats and truly representing them. Though it was already policy, it needed to be debated and understood so that there could be no internal disputes later. It was also a personal victory for me, for which Mitchel congratulated me by telling me that I had been brilliant. I thanked him and asked, 'What would you have said if we had lost?'

He smiled. 'Aha! I would just have told everyone that it was your idea and that well intentioned as you were, it really wasn't the right time to have such a debate.' I just smiled at the thought of his cheek and craft. I also thought about my handlers, knowing that they too would be as pleased as I was over this major political shift in the movement.

Mitchel McLaughlin had used the absence of the 'hard-line' members of the IRA, now locked up in jail, to have a 'friendly debate' while already knowing the outcome. This was yet another demonstration of his shrewdness in gently nudging the movement in Derry in the direction he wanted it to go. This man will go a long way, I thought. Gerry Adams might have Tom Hartley as a guide in Belfast, but Martin McGuinness had Mitchel McLaughlin. It was a strange team compared to Belfast, but a winning combination all the same.

***

By 1984, Sinn Féin were well established in Derry, with three advice centres on the city side and a new one in Gobnascale. 'Skilled and competent' activists manned the centres, dealing with everything from housing, benefits, pensions, wife-battering, child abuse, to the usual RUC and army harassment, house raids and the general enquiries that we always received. Because of the strong showing on the ground and our 'always available' policy, as a political force Sinn Féin was becoming more than a match for the SDLP.

I remember, for example, when BBC Two's *Newsnight* brought a TV crew to Derry to make a programme about Sinn Féin. This was the second time the BBC had been to Derry within a few months, though this time Mitchel asked me if I would look after them while they were in the city and help them with their project. The BBC crew were shocked at our level of knowledge and understanding of people's problems and how we were able to cut through some of the red tape and get instant results from whichever agency we contacted. I took them to the advice centres, which were always busy with activists working on residents' problems, and to the SDLP offices at the Embassy Building on the Strand Road. We went to the embassy for four days in a row, but the SDLP office never appeared to be open. Though John Hume didn't know it, when the presenter phoned him to ask for an interview, he was actually calling from the Sinn Féin centre on Cable Street, and Martin, Mitchel and I stood listening as Hume tried to avoid meeting with her. By agreement, she phoned him later that evening from the Everglades Hotel in the Waterside, by which time Hume had had a change of heart and agreed that she could interview him at his 'surgery' the following afternoon.

I picked up the reporter Rosalyn, her cameraman and sound man at lunchtime the next day and took them to the Embassy Building. Sure enough, the SDLP office was open and there, conveniently placed, were four people waiting to be seen by John Hume, who sat next door at his desk, apparently up to his eyes in paperwork. The *Newsnight* team conducted the interview with Hume, without telling him of their four previous failed attempts to gain entry to his office, though they did tell him later. Of course, it wasn't that Hume wasn't in attendance at the SDLP office every day, but that they had no one dedicated enough to go there and work on behalf of the party and the people who had voted for them. Even their local councillors were too busy with their 'day jobs' to deal with their constituents. They just couldn't compete with Sinn Féin.

It didn't matter what the problem was, we were there every day on the ground, ready and able to deal with any issue. Indeed, to prove the point we set up a so-called 'public meeting' to discuss 'petty crime in Derry', to which I took the BBC crew. We had stage-managed the meeting and the audience was stacked with Sinn Féin supporters invited by Mitchel. The idea was to give the general public an insight into Martin's view of crime in the city. We had him and a few other local dignitaries on the platform, which included a priest and a 'friendly' SDLP councillor. It didn't take long before, right on cue, someone raised the subject of 'punishment shootings' or 'kneecapping'. This was something that at the time was causing great concern in both the media and amongst the residents. Over the years there has been a lot of misinformation written on this subject by politicians, journalists, Sinn Féin and the IRA, so it's worth dealing with 'kneecapping' for just a moment.

In the early 1970s, the IRA declared that 'fraternising with the RUC or the British Army would be severely dealt with'. This had the effect that residents of the Creggan, Bogside and Gobnascale were afraid to report criminal activity for fear of being seen entering or leaving an RUC station. To go to a police station, even about motor tax, warranted a visit from 'the boys'. This fear led to the estates having no effective policing or system for the reporting of crime. Initially, to drive home the policy, young girls were 'tarred and feathered' for being friendly with soldiers or RUC men. This led to the next step, young men were beaten up for stealing or breaking into houses. Finally, there was 'kneecapping', where an individual was shot from behind, in the knee pit, with a low velocity gunshot using a handgun. The victims were mostly youths who had been warned about their behaviour, then threatened, then beaten up and finally, as a last resort, kneecapped. Ironically, it was ordinary, normally decent Catholics who demanded that these 'hoods' be kneecapped. 'I'll get yee kneecapped!' or 'I'll see McGuinness about yee!' could often be heard shouted during an argument in Derry.

Martin McGuinness had always been against 'the kneecapping of non-republican members', meaning anyone who was not a member of Sinn Féin or the IRA, despite what some have written. Republicans could be dealt with under the rule of 'bringing the republican movement into disrepute', though some of the more ruthless members of the IRA took it upon themselves to kneecap petty criminals as well. The situation was getting out of hand and eventually reached the stage where young men who stole in order to 'make money' by gambling were being kneecapped and then claiming compensation from the Northern Ireland Office, which resulted in them being paid thousands of pounds. Worse still, some volunteers were even demanding half of the compensation from those they had kneecapped. But as in all societies, there was more in our midst than just young hoods; there was also domestic violence, sexual abuse and rape. Once, during a conversation with Seamus Keenan the discussion moved to a general one about kneecapping, which I also passionately opposed. Mitchel had often advised me not to be so outspoken about kneecapping, suggesting that 'You need to understand the feelings of the victims in some of these very sensitive cases; they're not always black and white.'

But I must admit I was left unclear when I was asked, 'What do you do or say when an ordinary decent mother enters your office in a blind rage and tells you that a 16-year-old babysitter has sexually abused her 11-year-old daughter? Or a young 17-year-old girl, in tears, tells you that two men have just raped her?' They were difficult questions, bearing in mind that the normal route in any other society of complaining to the police was not an option in most of Derry. The fact was that by trying to act as a civil police force, the military wing of the movement had made a rod for the backs of Sinn Féin. It was time to stop the whole process and concentrate on bringing about some kind of normality, because we had moved on from kneecapping being an acceptable solution to republicans to a situation where a man was castrated with a knife and his penis left lying on the street in the Bogside. The whole situation was a nightmare; there were even a few volunteers who clearly enjoyed kneecapping. In my opinion, there were some thugs who, if they hadn't been in the IRA, would probably have been criminals.

Some of the volunteers from the Creggan and Shantallow made ordinary volunteers look like trainee priests in comparison, and their friends now stood in the corner of the room, cringing at the answers McGuinness gave to the local residents whilst being filmed by the *Newsnight* team. Yet despite being watched by other IRA men, Martin dealt with the pressure in a very compassionate and articulate manner, saying at one stage, 'The last resort has to be that you resort to violence.' We had advised him to try to avoid being verbally combative and not to use his favourite saying, 'make no mistake about it', but he did well and we were pleased, as was Mitchel. Martin was learning how to perform in public, though he would never match Gerry Adams's public appearances.

During a separate visit by the BBC, they wanted to film Martin in the 'predominantly Protestant' Waterside, meeting constituents and dealing with their problems. So I took them and Martin to Frank O'Kane's house in Bards Hill. Frank, a staunch republican, had been visiting the centre, demanding two houses for his ever-growing family. They also wanted to interview Martin in our Sinn Féin centre in Gobnascale, but it wasn't available that night so I arranged for an empty flat in Mimosa Court to be dressed up to look like it. We put in a desk and chairs, a telephone that didn't work, a tricolour, and hung a poster of Michael Collins on the wall. Patricia Allen, a local Sinn Féin member, was filmed waiting to see Martin. We had managed, to an extent, to pull the wool over the BBC's eyes, and not for the first time.

That night McGuinness learned a salutary lesson in the art of being interviewed, when the presenter suddenly dropped in a question about Martin's friendship with Dominic McGlinchey, the head of the INLA. 'Mad Dog' McGlinchey was the most sought-after man in Ireland after the attack on an Evensong service in the village of Darkley, County Armagh, in November 1983. During the service, three masked men calling themselves the 'Catholic Reaction Force' burst through the front doors of the little church and shot dead three church elders and wounded seven other worshippers. McGlinchey, an ex-IRA man and long-time friend of McGuinness, initially denied that the murders were the work of the INLA but later admitted that he had provided a weapon to one of the gunmen involved in the attack. In an unrelated event, McGlinchey was later wounded in a shoot-out with the Gardaí in County Clare and arrested on 17 March 1984, Saint Patrick's Day, three days after Gerry Adams was shot by the UDA.

In answer to the question, I thought I heard a cock crow three times as Martin denied that McGlinchey was his friend. Asked about the murders, Martin didn't have time to think and was forced, on camera, to condemn them. The interviewer, the veteran BBC reporter Tom Mangold, then asked about Martin's 'membership of the IRA'. On hearing this I stepped forward and interrupted, 'Okay guys, that's enough.' To my surprise Martin said, 'I don't mind answering that.' On the second take, he was asked again and replied, 'No, I am not a member of the IRA.' The interviewer became aggressive in his questioning and tried to pressure Martin. I was angered by this and we pulled the microphone out of the hands of the sound man and kicked over the white umbrella they had been using for lighting on the ceiling. Tom Mangold, who had bragged about interviewing famous leaders and terrorists, was visibly shaken because he knew that he had overstepped the mark. After some minutes of shouting everyone calmed down and the crew packed up. I never saw them again, but they got what they came for. This was no longer an in-depth report on Sinn Féin and its workers, but on Martin McGuinness denying his membership of the IRA and his friendship with Dominic McGlinchey. Martin's last two sentences out of a whole week of filming became headlines on the BBC news and were shown around the UK. The documentary was eventually broadcast in July 1984, and some of the footage they shot which wasn't shown would later turn up in the controversial documentary 'At the Edge of the Union' as a part of the *Real Lives* series.

The day after the piece was shown I thought I would be in trouble with Mitchel for not managing the interview in the Waterside properly. But just when I thought I was in trouble, Mitchel congratulated me on the way I had organised the BBC's visit and the interview itself. He had left me to my own devices and was very pleased with what he'd seen. As we travelled to Creggan one day, he did make one comment. During the filming on Cable Street there was a shot of me on the telephone and several others in the background. The voiceover stated, 'This

Centre is open every day to deal with citizens' problems, and is permanently manned by two secretaries, two ex-prisoners and an ex-British soldier.' Ironically, Mitchel was slightly miffed at the fact that I had let them know that I had been in the army. 'It's not a problem for me, Willie, but there are those who didn't know and I would rather it had stayed that way. I'm not sure of your politics but I do know you're articulate, organised and you're a bit of a leader, as well as being well liked by Martin, Seamus and the people at the Top of the Hill. You could even be a sound candidate for either the city council one day or some other Sinn Féin post. But don't be too free with your background to journalists, no matter how friendly they appear to be. It might come back to haunt you one day. Don't worry, I'm not getting at you, just be careful with what you say. Anyway, I don't know why I'm advising you, because you frighten the shit out of me every time you start to speak.'

* * *

A new departure for me, and one that delighted my army intelligence handlers, was that occasionally I drove Martin McGuinness about. On one of the first occasions with him in the car, he appeared very depressed about the news coming from the south. In September 1984, a huge IRA arms shipment on board the trawler *Marita Ann* was intercepted off the southern coast, and one of his closest friends in the movement, Martin Ferris, had been arrested at Fenit port in County Kerry. It later turned out that the then southern IRA military commander, Sean O'Callaghan, had betrayed the arms shipment and Ferris. By the mid-1980s, O'Callaghan was arguably the Garda Síochána and the Irish state's most important agent inside the IRA.

Ferris's arrest and the discovery of the weapons on the *Marita Ann* was a big loss at the time. As it had been all over the news, I said to Martin, 'That was bad news about the ship in Kerry.'

'Not half,' he said, as if not wanting to talk about it, and shifted position in his seat. 'Over a million pounds worth of bad news,' he said, rubbing his neck as he spoke.

'Well don't look at me, I haven't got that kind of money.'

Martin just smiled and went back to writing in the reporter's notebook he always had with him.

As we travelled towards Strabane we discussed Raymond Gilmour, his father Patrick, and the issues surrounding the forthcoming 'supergrass' trial. Gilmour's statements to the RUC had brought charges against other volunteers, involving everything from conspiracy to murder, to membership of the IRA. Though Martin wouldn't admit it, Gilmour's action had devastated the IRA in Derry and left him scared witless as he tried daily to remember what he'd said or done in the presence of those now in jail. As we talked it became clear that he regarded Gilmour with contempt, calling him a 'slabber' and a 'scumbag'. Martin's big worry was that some of those arrested might crack under pressure and drop him in it. There had been several 'supergrass' trials in the province affecting both the IRA and the UVF. In August the previous year, under the same Diplock process – non-jury trials used for political and terrorism-related cases – IRA man Christopher Black saw to it that twenty-two volunteers were jailed for a total of more than 4,000 years, with one of their leaders receiving 963 years. Unlike Black's trial, Gilmour's evidence not only affected volunteers but also the leadership of the Derry Brigade itself.

The thirty-five members of the IRA that had been taken out of 'Martin's struggle' were just about all that there was in Derry. As we spoke about the supergrass we went on to talk about Gilmour's father, whom the IRA had kidnapped and then released. Martin agreed with me that had anything happened to Patrick Gilmour, the people of Derry would never have forgiven Sinn Féin, let alone McGuinness. 'It was a bad idea to lift him in the first place,' he said. That answer gives you an idea of how careful Martin was. It was well known that it was his idea, but here he was agreeing with me that it was a bad idea.

As we were nearing Strabane we came up against a checkpoint manned by the RUC. We slowed and waited in the queue. When it was our turn I wound down the window and handed over my licence. 'Boot and bonnet please,' said the RUC officer, walking away towards the Land Rover parked on the bend. He never spoke again, and after searching the empty boot and looking at the engine he just nodded and motioned me to go on.

As we drove off, I must have been smiling because Martin was looking at me. 'What are you laughing at?'

'Oh, I was just laughing at your favourite weapon.' I was referring to the Sterling submachine guns the RUC carried back at the checkpoint.

'Don't mention those bloody things,' said McGuinness. 'I got into trouble the last time you brought that subject up in Cable Street.' I took this to mean that either Joe McColgan or Mitchell had had a go at him for once mentioning in front of me that when he fired a submachine for the first time in the early 1970s it had made a 'terrible rattle'.

As we drove on towards Omagh, we discussed politics and the city council debate. I told him that during my travels around Creggan, some people wanted to know what a Sinn Féin-led council would do about raising the issue of Bloody Sunday.

He agreed it was an issue but didn't think there would ever be another enquiry. I reminded him that I had not been there, but was a bit confused about what had happened. After all, the Bishop of Derry, Edward Daly, had said there were guns in the Bogside on the day of the march. 'There was, but the situation was very confusing and hectic,' Martin said.

'So we did nothing to defend the marchers?' I asked him.

'At the time I wished we had but I suppose it was good job we didn't, or there would have been a lot more dead, mostly us, and we would have got the blame for all of it.'

'So who owned the guns?' I asked. Martin was getting a bit fidgety, he clearly didn't like this line of questioning but answered all the same.

'The Stickies [Official IRA]. They had issued two revolvers in Creggan after the shooting started but we managed to step in and get them off-side. We gave our word to John Hume and Ivan Copper the day before that we would move all weapons out of the Bogside, which wasn't much in them days.' Martin stopped talking as we travelled on. Bloody Sunday was a turning point in his life and it obviously still had an effect on him.

We eventually reached our destination, which turned out to be the Killyhevlin Hotel, near Ennsikillen. This was the third time I'd been there; I once played there with my country and western band, and the other time was when I met my MI5 handler Alan over my concerns about Ben. Martin took out an envelope and went inside. Shortly after, two men got out of a blue Ford Cortina which was parked a short distance away and followed him into the hotel. I didn't know who they were at the time. Two hours later, we were on our way back to Derry; he never spoke about his meeting or who the two men were. I decided that I wasn't going to ask any more questions about politics or the war and soon it was McGuinness who broke the silence, asking me about my hobbies.

He knew that I had written a few songs and told me he enjoyed writing poetry. His poetry was very deep Celtic stuff, whereas mine was more traditional. Then he asked me about the poem I had delivered at the H-Block rally at The Diamond. 'That bit about "not with a gun". What was all that about?'

It was a tricky question, so I said that I was simply remarking that these two young men, who no one had ever really heard of, died in peace without a shot being fired and their deaths became world news for weeks. 'Why did you ask that?' I enquired.

'Ah nothing really,' he replied. 'It's just that some people wondered what you were getting at and if it was a veiled remark about "peaceful protest".'

I panicked a bit and stressed it wasn't. He then began to tell me about his love for fly-fishing, the bright colours of the flies, the best way to tie them and the right time to use a particular fly. 'Trout are very intelligent, they can often spot the fly and know not to go for it,' he told me. 'You can spend a whole day standing in waders with trout all around you and not catch a thing.'

'That sounds a bit boring to me, just waiting around to pull in a fish once you've hooked it,' I commented.

'It's not, Willie. It's a good way to get away from deep thinking and just relax. Mind you, it's still a bit of a battle trying to catch a trout. The anticipation that any minute now you'll have a fight on your hands as you try to out-think the fish.

'You see, once you have a bite, only then does the struggle begin. You have to draw the fish towards you on the rod. The trick is to stop and let it swim away, thinking it's safe. Then just when it thinks it's free, you jerk it back towards you. This sudden, unexpected action embeds the hook deeper into its mouth and causes it to struggle and panic. Then, depending on how strong it is, you let it swim away again. This battle of wits and strength can continue for up to twenty minutes, and even then you can lose the trout, as it out-thinks you or your line snaps, which can happen.'

'So,' I asked, 'it can be a real fight between you and the trout?'

'Absolutely, you see the only reason you end up with the trout on the bank is because it gets exhausted and eventually gives up.'

Apart from his childhood in Donegal, I'd never heard Martin speak so passionately about anything like this. I was telling him about my childhood in Donegal when he suddenly asked, 'where did you go?' I explained about my Granda's farm in Convoy and the great times we had there on our summer holidays. To which McGuinness said, 'Convoy! Sure, when I first got involved with the movement that's were me and another guy went to hear more about the movement.' We just laughed at the fact that we could have been in Convoy at the same time.

As we drove I remember thinking that Martin had just told me how and where he had joined the IRA, in Convoy. This was the real Martin McGuinness; he wasn't making a speech, he was totally himself and he obviously loved it. He obviously loved the chase and the tactics needed to win. In my mind, I suddenly saw the similarity between his description of how to catch a trout and his own strategy for dealing with the British government. 'It sounds a bit like us and the Brits,' I said, jokingly.

He smiled back at first. Then, as he turned and looked at me sternly, his blue eyes caught the lights of an oncoming car. 'Ah, but the difference is we're the trout and we're never going to give up. The Brits'll get tired of the fight before we do.' His voice was less relaxed than it had been.

We then got talking about my relatives who had emigrated to Glasgow and the long-standing connections between Derry/Donegal and Scotland. It was during this part of our conversation on the way back to Derry that he made an interesting revelation about IRA tactics and its bombing campaign across the Irish Sea. As we talked about our links to Scotland, I asked him a question, 'Is it the movement's policy, no action in Scotland?'

He shifted position in the passenger seat, as if he was uncomfortable. 'Well, I don't know about policy but it would certainly go against the grain. The Scots were disenfranchised, just the same as the Irish. The English took away their language and killed off their culture, so I think it's more a principle than a policy. After all, they're a Celtic nation just like the Irish, except they haven't got the balls that we have to fight for self-determination.'

So, there it was. The IRA's unstated position was that there were to be no bombs exploding in Scotland during the armed struggle. Even though loyalists such as the UVF had bombed Catholic pubs in Glasgow in the 1970s, the IRA would not extend their bombing campaign into any part of Scotland.

Shortly after revealing this, Martin turned on the radio to listen to the five o'clock news on BBC Radio Ulster. This was his way of telling me that he didn't want to talk anymore. As we drove back to Derry on the Prehen Road, we both realised we were hungry. However, the problem driving with Martin was that you couldn't just stop off somewhere and have a coffee or a sandwich. Not in the North anyway. He was impatient to get home and I couldn't wait either, not just to get something to eat but I would have to head straight out again; I had a meeting with Ginger at 7pm along the very road we were now on. I remember thinking that if Martin knew that, he would have me shot dead as quick as look at me. Though I still couldn't help thinking about the time I saw him leave that MI5 safe house in Limavady. I was still perplexed over that sight.

Just after six, I dropped Martin off on Cable Street and headed back to the Waterside to get ready for my meeting with Ginger. I parked at the Prehen Golf Club just after seven and waited in the rain to be picked up. Within minutes, the blue van pulled in beside me and I was soon on my way to Ebrington Barracks. Night-time meetings with Ginger were more relaxed because neither of us was in any hurry to go anywhere. I reported on the usual Sinn Féin meetings over the last fortnight, their plans and motions, who voted for what and who voted against. I also gave him my thoughts and opinions on the way things were going and the state of Sinn Féin's finances. We chatted for over two hours, and then I got to the 'McGuinness half-hour'. Suddenly Ginger was more focussed than ever, and it was clear to me that this handler was fixated on all things McGuinness. Where had I seen him? What day was it? What time was it? Who was he with? Had I spoken to him? What did he talk about? It was the usual stuff of placing Martin in a certain place, at a certain time.

When I arrived for our meeting Ginger had said, 'Before you start, hang on a minute.' With that he left the room, returning a few minutes later carrying an envelope. He sat down opposite and handed me a hazy looking photograph. It was a black and white picture of me sitting in my car outside the Killyhevlin Hotel that very day. I didn't know whether to be happy or angry, because I didn't like being followed.

'Don't worry, kid, they didn't follow you. The boys up the country were following these two gentlemen.' He then handed me another photograph of the two men from the blue Ford Cortina who followed Martin into the hotel. 'Do you know who they are?' he asked.

'I haven't a clue.'

He just smiled and put both photographs back in the envelope. 'Who are they, Ginger?'

'Better you don't know, but they're both very senior IRA men.' He smiled again and added, 'I'll leave you to work it out for yourself.' (It would be years later before I would know the identity of one of the men. When Barry Penrose of *The Sunday Times* asked me at a meeting in London if I knew who the man was in a photo he had, I remember telling him that I'd seen him but didn't know his name. It emerged during the meeting that the man was Thomas 'Slab' Murphy, who was a Senior IRA man who owned a farm near the border. *The Sunday Times* was involved in some sort of libel action against him.)

Ginger ended our meeting by talking about our conversation about fishing and Martin's view on the Celts of Scotland. He asked me if I was sure of what Martin had said about Bloody Sunday and the Scottish question. He seemed puzzled and left the room again. I could hear him on the phone in the next room but couldn't make out what he was saying. As we finished up he said, 'There will probably be a need to see you in again next week or so because I heard on the grapevine that a civvies guy from London was asking to see you.'

'No problem,' I replied. And with that I was driven back to the golf club, where I picked up my car.

A week later I was back at Ebrington Barracks. Once I had greeted Ginger and Eddie in the debriefing room they both disappeared. As I sat there looking around I thought that this man who had come to meet me must be important, because there was a different coffee table and over on the sideboard sat sandwiches and sausage rolls covered with cellophane, as well as a tea and coffee service laid out on a separate tray.

Ginger brought the man in. He was tall, in his early thirties, and dressed in a dark, pinstriped, three-piece suit, blue pinstriped shirt, and blue tie. He said his name was 'Stephen', and after a few minutes of chit-chat Ginger left us alone again. Stephen was interested in quite a few things, mostly my opinion on the elections for the city council and the debate at the Bogside Inn. He showed me a photograph of Lord Gifford, to make sure we were talking about the same person. It seemed that this man's office did not think the peer should have been there. Then he produced a small tape machine and replayed my conversation with Ginger the week before. ('So, it's all taped in here when I come in,' I said to myself.)

He pressed play and there I was, talking about my conversation with Martin about fly-fishing and the Celts from Scotland. He stopped the tape and looked at me. 'Are you sure McGuinness also said that "we're not giving up"?'

'Definitely,' I said. 'You don't think he'd say anything else, do you?'

He screwed up his face a little bit and nodded. 'Well, who knows?' I remember thinking, surely this man hasn't come from London just to ask me about fuckin' fly-fishing! We then talked about Bloody Sunday and the fact that Martin had said the IRA had no weapons in the Bogside that day. He asked, 'Do you believe him?'

'Why not? He was there, I wasn't.'

Stephen also asked me about the conversation with Martin way back in March over the submachine gun, and was I sure he said SMG and not a Thompson. No, I told him, it was me who had been talking about it in the first place. He just shrugged his shoulders and we moved on to discuss the state of Sinn Féin's finances. I briefed him on the fact the hunger strike had cost us nearly a million pounds. The 1983 elections had cost over £300,000 and we were now running advice centres all over the province at a cost of over £200,000. 'You'll soon need more money than the IRA,' he said with a smile. We then got on to Martin's view on Scotland. 'That's a real gem of a piece of information you know, Willie,' said Stephen, as he ate his sandwich and poured more tea.

'What's good about it?' I asked.

'Well, it's the first time it's ever been confirmed,' he said, surprised by my attitude.

'I thought everybody knew that the IRA doesn't attack targets in Scotland?'

'You're wrong, Willie. We know that apart from a small device in the Shetlands in 1981 they haven't, and the boffins in London assume that they won't, but no IRA leader has ever said it. The fact that McGuinness said it to you confirms for the first time something which until now we could only assume was some sort of policy.' He went on to explain how valuable the information was when it came to military planning and counter-terrorism strategy on the UK mainland. This information, Stephen stressed, would calm the minds of those anti-terrorist commanders in Scotland. He was clearly delighted, and began to ask lots of questions about Martin, mostly about his private thoughts and ideas. Why did I think he was in favour of taking our seats in the councils all over the North? The question of how come the IRA was apparently on board.

What effect was Gilmour having on the movement in Derry? How would Sinn Féin cope when the thirty-five IRA volunteers all get sent away to prison? What would the movement do if we didn't get anybody elected in Derry? These were all tough questions but, as he was only asking for my opinion, I did my best to answer him. Naturally, he taped it all and then put the little recorder away in his briefcase. He asked if he could come back and see me after Christmas to discuss the planning for the 1985 council elections. I agreed. We sat for ages talking about everyday life and he was very interested, especially in how Sinn Féin were preparing – even at this early stage – for the council elections in May.

I liked Stephen, he was well versed in Irish history and was a very educated man. As we chatted about his time at university and my time in the army, Ginger interrupted and pointed at his watch as if to tell Stephen his transport was waiting. Ginger was also getting anxious about how long I'd been there and wanted me back out on the streets by tea-time. To be honest, at the time I had not understood the significance of what I was telling him but Stephen clearly saw this political intelligence as important. In hindsight, it would enable British strategists to work out the best way to entice and cajole the movement deeper into political activity at the expense of the military struggle. And what I would next reveal to them about the internal struggles within the movement at the very highest level would become vital in the British plan to promote the Adams–McGuinness axis and its evolving path towards the peace process.

* * *

The Sinn Féin centre at Sandville Terrace was now open full-time and I was very busy taking care of the issues that arose every single day. Life was now more orderly; I had given up being the local Sinn Féin secretary in order to concentrate on running the centre and preparing for the May 1985 elections. While I had managed the Sinn Féin finances well, I ran into some difficulty with the ACE scheme when a Department of Environment audit of our books revealed a shortfall of £2,750. At first I was suspected by the local IRA 'fuck-up squad', who were just waiting to get at me, of embezzlement. I had used some money from the scheme to put towards my car payments instead of claiming petrol expenses, plus the typewriter for Cable Street and other small bits and pieces. This didn't marry up to the overall shortfall but it was something they couldn't get their heads around. They believed that because they were in the IRA, I had to be accountable to them. I have to admit, for two weeks I still couldn't account for over £1,900 of the missing money and the situation became so serious that Mitchel McLaughlin was called in to make a judgement on the whole affair. Things didn't look good for me at all, even though it was the local tenants' association money and really had nothing to do with the movement. Mitchel reminded me of something he had said a year earlier, 'If anything goes wrong here, we'll get the blame. Remember, Willie?' However, Mitchel couldn't understand it either so he ordered a complete check of everything before any action was taken against me.

I was at home two nights later when Mitchel phoned and asked if I was in bed. 'No, why, what's up?'

'I'd like a word with you but I don't want to discuss it over the phone. Can you come over here to the house?'

This is it, I thought. 'Of course, when?'

'Come over now, it won't take long. Oh, and by the way, don't bring your car, the RUC's floating about here and I don't want any trouble outside my house with your car.'

I put the phone down and broke into a cold sweat. Fuck me, I thought, you're for the high jump now. I didn't know what to do. I was in a complete panic and picked up the phone to my handler. Then I put it down again. After twenty minutes I decided to leave and walk over to Mitchel's house. After what seemed like ages and with my head in a spin, I was walking down the flyover heading for the Bogside. Walking up Westland Street I stopped dead. There in the distance, leaning against the gable wall at the end of Mitchel's street, were two men, just standing there as if they were waiting for someone. I knew there and then that it had to be me. I turned quickly and headed back towards the Bogside Inn. I was in a real panic and began talking to myself to get a grip and calm down. I turned and walked back towards Mitchel's house. The two men were still there and they moved forward as I approached. I took a deep breath and crossed over to their side of the road by the gable wall. Then one of them said, 'Bout yee?'

'Not bad,' I replied and began to walk past them towards Mitchel's front door. Shaking, I knocked at the door, not daring to look back. Mitchel opened the door, ushered me in and showed me into his living room. Standing by the door which led to the kitchen was a tough-looking young man, and sat on a chair was a man whose photo ID I had seen before in one of my earlier meetings with agent-handler Frank, but I didn't know his name. He was introduced to me as 'Sean', and he was obviously one of the men who had got off-side as the raids over Gilmour started. Clearly, Sean was up from over the border for something or other. I became very nervous again, but just as I moved to sit down Sean said, 'Right Mitchel, we'd better head on but I'll deal with that matter later.'

'Okay guys,' Mitchel replied. 'I'll speak to Martin and he'll probably get back to you.' Within seconds of my arrival, Sean and the other guy were gone. Mitchel opened a drawer and produced three plates. They were the small commemoration type of plate made for anniversaries and celebrations, with photographs embossed on them. He showed them to me. 'I was thinking that we might be able to sell these types of plates in the Sinn Féin centres, with photographs of the hunger strikers on them or prints of volunteers.' I'd seen this type of plate before but hadn't made the connection.

I looked at the plates. 'It all depends on the cost of the raw material, the production cost and the selling price. But I'm sure the Americans would buy them.' I was still wondering why I was there, although I was relieved that Sean and his mates had left, and this aimless chit-chat quite threw me

'Alright, Willie,' he said, 'I'll leave it with you. Let me know if it's worth buying the kit to produce them.' Within a few minutes I was on my way out of his door and walking back towards the Bogside Inn. Feeling relieved, I berated myself for being scared and foolish, then as I started to walk up the flyover it dawned on me as to the real reason for the visit. This wasn't about any fucking plates, Mitchel could have told me that at any time. It certainly didn't need a midnight visit to his house. I was convinced that I had been asked over to his house in order that this guy, Sean, could get sight of me and know what I looked like. I concluded that Mitchel's inquiry must have ended and I was to be shot for embezzlement and bringing the republican movement into disrepute. Very clever, I thought. It took me ages to get home, because every time a car came alongside me or someone came up behind me I stopped and either crossed over or turned back from where I had just come.

I reached home in one piece and fell into bed, a nervous wreck, and tried to get some sleep. At lunchtime the next day

Paddy McNaught called at my door and told me to be at the Sinn Féin centre for half past seven that night. I was to stay away until then. I walked into the Sinn Féin centre at dead on 7.30pm only to be met by Eddy McGowan, who told me that the meeting was cancelled. Then he smiled and said, 'Willie you're in the clear, the boys found out what happened to the money from the site.' I would have to account for the money I'd drawn out for the two car payments and the typewriter, but fortunately for me, Isobel, who worked with me in the office, had found the answer and saved my bacon. She had been asked by the IRA to go through all the books and receipts and try to figure out what had happened to the monies. And leave it to her, God bless her, she did.

It transpired that the brother of a senior IRA man in the Waterside had been helping himself to cheques from the backs of two of the ACE scheme accounts. He had been doing this when I wasn't there, cashing them and keeping the money. Once this was discovered the IRA planned to 'kneecap' him. However, his brother, who was serving a prison sentence for IRA membership, heard about the planned 'punishment' shooting and sent word out of Long Kesh jail that his brother wasn't to be touched. The irony of this sordid episode did not escape me. I had been close to being shot, not for being an informer but by being falsely accused of embezzling Sinn Féin funds. Although my name was cleared, I started to believe that I was no longer trusted by the republican leadership in the city. I had left the office open to swindlers and, as Sinn Féin treasurer, the security lapse was all my fault.

Mitchel McLaughlin said he was pleased and relieved that I had been cleared and was very impressed by the way I had conducted myself during the investigation. Of course, as I had thought, there were those who felt that my judgement wasn't to be trusted when it came to managing Sinn Féin's finances and Mitchel suggested I should step down as Sinn Féin treasurer. 'However, I think it would be good for you if you took over the running of the centre in the Waterside and used your skills to work for us and the community over here'. 'This', he continued, 'is something I was going to suggest to you anyway because it will up your profile in time for the council elections in May. Because Willie, even though the plan is for mostly IRA volunteers to stand all over the North, it's not that clear-cut over there and I think given a clear run you could win a seat.'

Whilst I was a bit embarrassed about the whole affair, I resigned as party treasurer and started working full-time managing the Sinn Féin centre at Waterside. For a few days I hadn't twigged about the reality of what he said about volunteers standing in the election, but I made a mental note to tell Ginger the next time I would see him ... only IRA volunteers need apply!

A few weeks later, on 12 October 1984, my son – who had been up late playing with his computer – woke me at 3.30am to tell me there had been a bomb at 'Mrs Thatcher's hotel in England'. I got up and went downstairs to see for myself and sure enough, there it was on television. Thirty minutes earlier, a bomb had gone off at the Grand Hotel in Brighton, where most of the Conservative Party were staying during their annual conference. The emergency services were frantically trying to rescue the guests and there were reports that there were many casualties. By daylight it was clear that the IRA had tried to blow up Margaret Thatcher and her entire Cabinet.

CHAPTER 7

GILMOUR DROPPED AND DING-A-LING DITCHED

At the end of 1984, my life was turned upside down when my father died of a stroke in the early hours of 1 December. Family and friends came from near and far to say goodbye to my dad, including a Protestant woman from across the border in County Donegal who had brought us up as children. After the trauma of burying my father we were hit with another major shock just four days later, when Eddy McGowan and Paddy McNaught called at our door to tell me that young Willie Fleming had been shot dead in an ambush at Gransha Hospital. Willie had been at my father's funeral only a few days before and shook my hand beside dad's coffin. The young lad had been a regular in the office and was very interested in politics. I hadn't a clue that he was deeply involved in IRA activity and I looked upon his death as yet another terrible, futile waste of life.

Fleming, nineteen, and Danny Doherty, twenty-three, had travelled from Derry on a motorcycle and made their way to Gransha Hospital, where they tracked a bus taking nurses and workers to the hospital. They pulled up alongside the bus and waited for their target to get off but he/she didn't emerge. They aborted their mission and headed back towards Derry. As they approached the roundabout leaving the hospital grounds, an undercover SAS unit rammed their bike from behind and opened fire. Willie fell from the back of the pillion seat and hit the ground first. A few yards further on, Danny fell from the bike as it travelled on and smashed into the roundabout. No attempt was made to arrest them and the SAS unit shot them both, killing both boys instantly.

Willie and Danny were savagely and deliberately 'taken out' on the anniversary of the Ballykelly bomb. To my mind, and to this day, I still believe this was a revenge killing. One of the mortuary workers at Altnagelvin Hospital was able to tell us that Willie's remains lay on a slab before him covered in at least thirty bullet holes, most of them to his back and the back of his head. He said that there were at least two bullet holes in the back of his head fired at point-blank range, and it looked like his helmet had been removed before he was shot. Danny Doherty lay beside Willie with just as many bullet holes in his body. Most of his wounds were from the right-hand side and the back of his head was partially missing. Danny also had two bullet holes fired at point-blank range to the back of his head and his helmet had obviously been removed as well. Two loaded revolvers were recovered from each of their bodies, which the RUC later confirmed had not been fired. Such was the ferocity of their injuries, we were told, that when preparing the remains there was very little blood to extract. Their bodies had lain on the ground for over three hours before the RUC allowed them to be taken away. We were advised to collect Willie's remains as soon as possible. It was decided that some of us would stay with the family and his remains were released shortly after 6.30pm and brought to Rose Court, where the RUC and the Brits had already gathered.

There were over forty Land Rovers belonging to the RUC and over twenty belonging to the British Army on the Gobnascale estate that evening. Every road leading in and out of the area was blocked and there were two helicopters in the air. As we set up the trestles, candles and crucifix, two of the IRA honour guard in full dress uniform came into the room, took up positions on either side of the coffin, and stood at ease. The RUC, who were standing in riot gear in the gardens of the surrounding houses, attempted to break into the house to arrest them. Seeing this, we removed the honour guard from the room.

By now, Seamus Keenan and Mitchel McLaughlin had arrived and we sat in the kitchen and planned the funeral. Willie would be taken straight to City Cemetery in two days' time, where he would be buried at the same time as Danny. Willie's remains had to arrive on time at the top end of the cemetery, where both he and Danny Doherty would receive their salute (a volley of shots over the coffins). Martin McGuinness wouldn't be coming over to the Waterside but would meet up with us on the city side with Gerry Adams.

For two days and two nights we were completely hemmed in by the RUC. No one was allowed in or out except a few priests and some relatives. We took it in shifts to stay awake, fearing the RUC would attempt to arrest the honour guard, which was now back in place on either side of Willie's remains. Willie Fleming lay in his coffin with a cold-looking, drained white face. During a decade of the rosary in the early hours of the second morning, the RUC came under attack from young republicans in Gobnascale. I asked Sean Doherty to take photographs of Willie's remains, the honour guard, various visitors and the RUC men standing in their hundreds in the neighbours' gardens. The tension mounted as the hours went by.

The next morning the hearse arrived, bedecked with wreaths of green, white and gold. The undertaker asked us to leave the room while he carried out the formalities required in preparing the remains for burial. The biers were lifted away and Mickey and the boys moved in to carry Willie out. At the sight of the tricolour in the doorway the RUC baton-charged the mourners and attempted to pull the emblem from the coffin. We moved quickly back into the hallway and closed the door. We were surrounded and unable to get out.

After intense negotiations with two RUC inspectors, we agreed that if they backed off we would remove the tricolour and place Willie in the hearse. No sooner had we agreed to this than we received a message from Mitchel McLaughlin. It was miles to City Cemetery but he had received instruction from the IRA that Willie was to be carried all the way. I informed the undertaker, who turned the hearse around in the car park at Rose Court. As we left the house through the front door a second time, we again came under attack from the RUC, this time insisting that Willie's beret and gloves be removed from the coffin. These antics were repeated before we were finally allowed to leave the house.

As I walked on that cold wet December day behind Willie's body with the rest of the mourners, I remembered with fondness the times he had come to see us all for a chat and a warm cup of tea by the fire. I bowed my head and caught sight of the bullet hole in the wall from where other undercover SAS men had once attempted to kill me. We marched down the Trench Road and onto Strabane Old Road, people joining in as we went. Approaching Annie's Bar and the waste ground I caught site of more RUC vehicles, which were trying to form a barricade between us and a loyalist crowd from the nearby Irish Street. All they managed to achieve was to give protection to the loyalists, who threw stones and bottles at us from behind the safety of the RUC vehicles and were gleefully chanting, 'We wish you a Merry Christmas and a Happy New Year.' As the missiles rained down and people fell injured to the ground we began running, carrying Willie's remains all the while.

In an effort to calm the situation I instructed Eddy to place Willie's remains in the hearse so that we might move out of harm's way of the loyalists a little faster. We walked down Fountain Hill onto Spencer Road and across the lower deck of Craigavon Bridge. All the while we were surrounded by RUC Land Rovers, which moved along, two abreast either side of us. There were approximately eight Land Rovers at the front of the cortège and over twelve behind us. As we turned onto the Foyle Road there were yet more RUC Land Rovers, and there seemed to be helicopters everywhere. Along the quarter-mile stretch of the Foyle Road next to the river there were over 300 RUC men lined up on the wall waiting for us. As we continued to change the pallbearers it became evident that the RUC was going to try to thwart our attempt to take Willie through the Bogside. On we marched in the pouring rain and up the long walk of Southway, where 'Pop' and George had been shot in May 1982. Eventually, two hours after leaving Willie's house we arrived in Creggan to the applause of hundreds of mourners, who had patiently waited with Danny Doherty's remains while we fought our way from the Waterside. Gerry Adams and Martin McGuinness pinned tricolours and berets to both coffins. Shortly afterwards, four volunteers (two from the Waterside and two from the Derry side), comrades of Willie and Danny, stepped out of the crowd and fired a volley of shots over their coffins.

With helicopters deliberately hovering very low above us in an effort to drown out the speeches, and the RUC now in the cemetery, we carried on with the task of burying Danny and Willie. Pat Coyle was in charge of the proceedings and led the order of merit. McGuinness gave his usual speech, as he did on occasions such as this. Within an hour it was all over. Willie Fleming and Danny Doherty were buried with honour and dignity despite the efforts of the RUC and the British Army air corps. As the young men's families, still in shock, left the cemetery trying to come to terms with what had happened to them over the last three days, Martin and Mitchel left to prepare for more days of politics and war.

Two days later I was picked up by the FRU and went to see Ginger. This was a lengthy meeting, as we went through the video of the funeral and there were many questions about what went on and the identities of the mourners. I really wasn't up to it, but I did my best. Knowing that the tape was running next door I told him all that had happened: the missing money, the call from Mitchel, meeting Sean from the White House (the safe house in Buncrana) and the commemorative plates, the investigation and me being cleared, and being moved on from being Sinn Féin treasurer to running the Waterside centre full-time. Ginger was particularly animated about my conversation with Mitchel McLaughlin about volunteers standing in the forthcoming city council elections and the problems that it would throw up in Derry.

A few days after that meeting, Ginger called again to ask if I could come and meet Stephen. When we entered the debriefing room at Ebrington Barracks, Stephen was already there – with his cup of tea and sandwiches – and we discussed the events once again. After chatting for over an hour, Ginger left the room to take a call, leaving Stephen and I alone. Silently, he pushed a note over to me, which read, 'Can you come down to the White

Horse Inn after we leave here for a quick chat?' I looked at him and said nothing. He knew the tape was running and he hadn't wanted this request to be recorded. After the meeting, to be sure I wasn't followed, I drove back towards Chapel Road, then turned and headed out of the Waterside towards Eglinton and the White Horse Inn. I walked into the pub and looked around to see Stephen sat on his own with a glass of red wine. 'Thanks for coming, Willie.'

As I sat down, I explained to him that this place was a favourite haunt of RUC men and that I might be spotted.

'We'll be fine.'

Stephen went to the bar and ordered me a glass of white wine. We went over the revelation that IRA 'volunteers' all over the North would be standing for the city council elections in May. His office had originally thought otherwise, and that it would be run-of-the-mill Sinn Féin workers like me who were candidates, but I assured him this was not the case. It would be mostly IRA men because that was the only way Martin McGuinness could placate the IRA leadership, and at the same time it demonstrated they weren't going soft. Then we talked about Raymond Gilmour, the trial's effect on us in Derry, and the obvious impact it would have when the boys were sentenced. Stephen lowered his voice, and what he said next left me flabbergasted, 'Well, you never know.'

I looked at him, 'Stephen, you must be joking.'

'The judge might not see it the way you all think,' was all he said.

'You mean he's been threatened by the IRA?'

'Now, now, Willie,' Stephen shook his head and smiled. 'Look, all the judges that sit in these "Diplock" situations [non-jury trials] carry a heavy burden and more often than not seek legal guidance from Lord Lowry as the Chief Justice. But in this case, with a delicate matter like Gilmour's, he'll seek guidance from the judiciary and in some cases it'll go right up through the Northern Ireland Office and even on up to the Home Office. The questions he asks are considered and legal guidance is passed back down.'

'And?' I asked.

'Well, I have it on very good authority that Lord Chief Justice Lowry has sought and been given such guidance. Apparently, there are or have been a few flaws in the prosecution's case. It's not a game-changer but Lord Lowry will now have to reflect on that guidance before he comes to a decision.'

'You mean they might get off?' I was dumbstruck.

'I'm not saying that, Willie. But it will be interesting to see if he is swayed by the guidance he received.' Stephen paused. 'Don't forget, his query, questions and the guidance he's received have all been noted, so he'll be cautious about the judgement he hands down.' He looked at me, leaned over and smiled. 'Of course, in this case his legal guidance comes with some private political guidance, too.'

'What do you mean, Stephen?'

'It might not be in the public interest, long term, to convict. If, as you've said to us, IRA volunteers are being prepared all over the North for the May council elections, then that's a huge step towards some semblance of peace further down the road. Because it's our guess that those volunteers will effectively and eventually be "de-commissioned" and that's got to be a massive first step! However, as I judge it, Gilmour is the fly in the ointment for Derry and it won't help your friend Martin McGuinness if his volunteers-cum-democrats are all locked up in Long Kesh.' In that instant I remember thinking, fuck me, if Martin was here right now he would kiss this guy.

As Stephen left, he gave me an envelope containing £300, a personal Christmas present from him. I remember driving back to Derry wondering what might happen if everybody was released and the RUC was forced to dump Gilmour. It would open the way for (at least some) Derry volunteers to be free to stand in the council elections and would save Martin and the Derry movement any embarrassment. Being privy to this information was a bit like winning the lottery and not being able to tell anyone. Lord Lowry was known as a right bastard, and he had stopped various pieces of evidence being introduced on behalf of the defence. Mind you, republicans regarded all judges as bastards, so he was no different. The import of what I had just heard from Stephen had not yet fully sunk in.

* * *

It was close to Christmas 1984, and the day had arrived for the sentencing of the Derry Brigade suspects. Martin McGuinness, Mitchel McLaughlin and most of the families affected by Gilmour's accusations had gone to Belfast for the judgement, while I remained in Derry. This would surely be a bad day for the organisation, I thought, as I sat in Cable Street having a chat. Suddenly, a young woman burst in through the front door shouting, 'Bernie! Gilmour's trial's collapsed, the ol' judge called him a fuckin' liar.'

I nearly had a heart attack, it appeared Stephen had not been exaggerating after all. I remember thinking Martin McGuinness is one lucky man and he should buy a racehorse. Within an hour, as the news spread, it seemed as if the whole of the Bogside was out on the streets. By late afternoon, cars were being made ready for a victory cavalcade through the city that night. The word was that most of the prisoners had expected to be sent away and sat in total shock as Lord Lowry delivered his finding. Now many had been released and were on their way back to Derry.

Lord Chief Justice Lowry directly addressed the supergrass Gilmour, 'You are a selfish and self-regarding man to whose lips a lie invariably comes more naturally than the truth.' Gilmour had been caught out under cross-examination and wasn't convincing. He had even started to lie and boast about IRA operations he was never involved in. So Lowry had acted on his doubt, and the 'political guidance' he had received, and the case against the thirty-six was unexpectedly thrown out. Some of the accused were still held over on other charges, but twenty-six of the IRA volunteers were released immediately, much to the disgust of the RUC who, it has to be said, hadn't helped their case when they introduced evidence that Gilmour clearly knew nothing about and had tried to lie his way around. Of course, Martin McGuinness was delighted, not least because he now had his more experienced IRA men back in Derry. This also meant that many of them could stand as Sinn Féin candidates in the upcoming local government elections. Soon some of the freed prisoners would become familiar faces behind the desks of Sinn Féin advice centres in the city, as their profiles were built up ahead of the council elections. McGuinness had got his way, and I had received the heaviest of hints from Stephen that this 'political guidance' handed down from the top of the British government regarding Gilmour's reliability as the State's witness was central to the collapse of the trial.

Some of those released became involved with the business of war once more. Eddie McSheffrey from Creggan was highly regarded by Martin, and it didn't take him long to get back to the armed struggle. However, had he known what lay ahead of him, McSheffrey might have wished that he had been sent to prison. Three years after the collapse of the Gilmour trial, he was blown up whilst transporting his own bomb on an IRA mission. Meanwhile, elation over the collapse of the trial was soon to be replaced by sombre news from the border. The very next day I was summoned by Mitchel McLaughlin to the Sinn Féin Derry HQ on Cable Street, and on entering the office it was immediately obvious something serious had happened. I was informed that Ciarán Fleming's body had been recovered from the River Bannagh and was on its way to Derry.

Ciarán Fleming was one of the IRA volunteers who had escaped from the Maze prison in the mass breakout of September 1983. He had returned to active duty and in December 1984 was involved in a two-man operation to blow up an RUC patrol near Kesh in County Fermanagh. Instead, the ASU was ambushed by the SAS and Ciarán's colleague killed, along with an SAS soldier. Following the operation, Martin McGuinness and other IRA volunteers had searched the area for two days, looking for Ciarán. It turned out that he hadn't been shot dead in the SAS ambush after all but had drowned. Although he couldn't swim, Ciarán had jumped into the river in a last-ditch effort to escape a hail of bullets. Once again on the Waterside we had to prepare for another republican funeral.

Ciarán didn't live in Gobnascale but instead stayed with his mum in the Clooney area of the Waterside. However, it was decided that his remains should lie in his Aunt Betty's house (Willie Fleming's mum) instead. So began another period of mourners and organisers being baton-charged by the RUC and beaten constantly for forty-eight hours. I was one of the pallbearers at Ciarán's funeral on Christmas Eve in 1984 and was nearly killed. Just as I was lowering the coffin to allow another pallbearer to carry it, an RUC officer fired a plastic bullet at me. It hit another mourner instead, right on the left side of his temple. He collapsed and the coffin nearly fell over onto me. Just then a riot broke out behind us, and when I got to the front of the cortège Micky said, 'When we get to that lane up ahead on the right, we're going to wheel right and run up it as fast as we can.' It happened just like clockwork, with the RUC caught by surprise. The mourners piled in behind us and blocked the RUC from trying to follow us. We ran up the hill with the coffin until we reached Bishop Street, where we were met by a hundred or so republicans who cheered us on. At this point we slowed to catch our breaths and eventually made our way down the flyover and into the Bogside. From there we took Ciarán to the cemetery where Martin, an IRA firing party and others were waiting. December had been a very rough month for all of us, me in particular, but I tried my best to enter into the Christmas spirit with Mary and the children.

* * *

In early January 1985 I travelled across the Foyle to the Cable Street headquarters, expecting to link up with Seamus Keenan for a meeting later in the day with the editor of the *Derry Journal*. By pure coincidence, I happened to walk into an unholy row between Martin McGuinness and someone who, unknown to me, was one of his most dangerous opponents within the republican movement.

Before we left the office, I told Seamus I needed to go upstairs and get some files, including press releases, to hand over to the *Journal* as part of our ongoing publicity campaign. Keenan already had a panicked expression on his face, 'For fuck sake, hurry up and get it. And don't go into Mitchel McLaughlin's room,' he warned me.

'Why, what's wrong?'

'Martin McGuinness is up there with Ding-A-Ling, and there's going to be blood spilt, so fuckin' hurry up.'

I ran up the stairs and went into Seamus's office to get my files and I could clearly hear Martin shouting at someone. 'You!' I heard him roar, 'Aye, you! Who was it that covered for you, eh? Me, that's who. I went out on a limb for you. It took fucking weeks to get Gerry Adams to come around. Such was the outrage caused by those deaths that we were forced to admit that it hadn't been authorised.' This was the first time I'd ever heard Martin McGuinness in a full-blown rage. By 'we' he was obviously referring to the IRA's Army Council. It was also very, very rare to ever hear Martin swear in anger. It went quiet for a few seconds and then I heard the man shout, 'Fuck Hegarty!'

Jesus, I thought. I'd better get out of here!

Just then Joe McColgan ran upstairs past the open door and before long he had joined in the shouting match. The man Martin was having a go at wasn't from Derry. Then I heard him shouting at Joe, 'And you!! You bastard, you stay away from my wife with your fuckin' slick talk.' Martin then began shouting at Joe who, though separated, was still married to Martin's sister, Geraldine. It sounded like Joe was being blamed for trying to chat up this guy's wife, who was now using it as an excuse to deflect from the argument he was clearly losing with McGuinness. Things got worse and there was the sound of a scuffle. I heard the door open and somebody stormed down the stairs. Then the shouting in the office started again. It was obvious that Joe had left, as Martin was yelling at the other man, 'How dare you accuse me of that, I can't defend you over the things you've been saying and planning because you're dead wrong. You're bang out of order and if this gets out even Adams won't be able to save you! Make no mistake about it, you could be court-martialled over what you've been doing.' Then the man said something about Kevin and Danny, to which Martin responded, 'Fuck McKenna and McCann.' As soon as I heard this, I was gone. Interesting as it was, I knew that I shouldn't be there, although I tried to remember everything from that fascinating exchange.

I headed downstairs to find a very agitated Seamus Keenan waiting for me in the car. 'Hurry up for fuck sake and let's get out of here before Mitchel gets back.' As we drove away I asked him, 'Who's the poor bastard getting the fifth degree from Martin?'

'You shouldn't have been fuckin' listenin',' he roared.

'Jesus, Seamus, it was hard not to. Martin's going fuckin' mental.'

'I know,' he replied. 'There'll be a murder before Mitchel gets there.'

As we drove out the Northland Road past the fire station, I asked him again who the man was because he certainly wasn't from Derry. 'Do you not know? That's Ding-A-Ling from Belfast.'

'Who the fuck's Ding-A-Ling?'

'Ivor Bell, Martin's buddy. Well he was, but I think he's in a bit of a soapy bubble now. He'll be lucky to get back to Belfast in one piece.'

To be honest, at the time I had never heard of Ivor Bell and didn't understand the significance of his stand-up row with Martin McGuinness and the way he was shouted down. Instinct told me I should inform the handlers and later that same day I connected with Ginger, who sounded equally shocked and fascinated as I relayed the highlights of the spat inside Cable Street over the phone. Three hours later I was picked up and taken to the barracks, where Ginger and another man were waiting. The other man didn't introduce himself but just leaned against the wall and listened. I went over and over what I'd heard in the Sinn Féin office, and as I was repeating myself for the umpteenth time the other man just left. He had clearly heard enough.

Then Ginger left and a few minutes later came back with some cans of lager. In all the time I'd been coming into Ebrington Barracks this was the first time anyone had ever offered me a beer. It turned out that Ivor Bell was one of the most senior IRA men in Belfast. He was a personal friend of Adams and had helped McGuinness restructure the IRA from the 'old Company-based' system to the current 'Cell' system based on independent active service units which were smaller, tighter and supposedly harder for the security forces to penetrate.

The word from Ginger was that there was a rumour Bell was upset about the IRA's dwindling finances. He had been trying to drum up support for some motion or other about halting money being redirected to Sinn Féin. Bell was angry that there was less money for the IRA as resources were being concentrated on Sinn Féin's political machine. Ginger stressed that up until now there were only rumours about Bell's growing anger over the way the movement's finances were being transformed. Now, however, my information appeared to confirm those rumours, which Ginger emphasised was a priceless piece of internal IRA intelligence. Bell was effectively accusing both McGuinness and Adams of strangling the IRA war chest while building up the Sinn Féin campaign fund. The Protestant-born IRA veteran, who also had the nickname 'The Heathen', suspected this double-act was starting to run down the IRA's armed struggle. This information also confirmed in the FRU's mind the power McGuinness continued to wield within the IRA leadership, given that it was he who had summoned Bell to travel seventy-two miles from Belfast essentially for a bollocking, and it underlined an assumption among the FRU and other security-intelligence agencies that Adams and McGuinness were an unbreakable duo who looked out for each other. McGuinness would stand by Adams against Bell and vice versa.

McGuinness might not have had complete control of the IRA but he was engineering his own men, some of them his relatives, into most of the top jobs. They could continue to act on their own but they would always be answerable to him. This was a delicate time for McGuinness, but the collapse of the Gilmour case and the ability to face down Bell indicated to the FRU that he was slowly winning the struggle for power within the movement.

Ivor Bell's complaint, and his later removal from power, signalled the beginning of the end for those IRA leaders who might dare to speak out or question the journey McGuinness and Adams were taking the movement. I like to think that the political intelligence I was supplying my handlers at this critical time in Sinn Féin's development played a role in their strategic thinking. Bell was eventually isolated, court-martialled and warned he would be executed if he tried to set up a rival IRA in defiance of Adams–McGuinness. 'Ding-A-Ling' recognised that those who had promised to join his internal rebellion were melting away, and he opted for the quiet life, walking his greyhound dogs in West Belfast, drinking and occasionally bitching about how McGuinness had betrayed him. I am certain the politico-military strategists of the FRU, RUC and MI5 engineered scenarios to undermine Bell's authority in those crucial weeks and months in the mid-1980s, just as I am sure their 'advice', sent up to the heart of Mrs Thatcher's government, in turn resulted in the collapse of the Gilmour trial.

***

By February 1985, I was up to my eyes in Sinn Féin work in Gobnascale. The local council elections were due in May and everyone was working flat out in their own areas. The IRA, mostly 'Gilmour's men', were making noises about the candidates Sinn Féin were promoting.

Meanwhile, Mitchel McLaughlin was concerned that some of the volunteers who were now out of prison just didn't have what it took to get elected. With that in mind, we all gathered at a special meeting on Cable Street to nominate candidates for each area of the city, including the Waterside. The atmosphere was tense as Mitchel went through the agenda that Tuesday night, eventually arriving at the 'Nominations for the City Council Elections'.

Most of the other volunteers had sat through the meeting waiting for this moment. One by one the nominations of IRA personnel were proposed, seconded and carried. To be fair to Mitchel, he did his job as chairman and didn't engage the meeting in too much discussion or debate, nor did anyone else for that matter. The majority of Sinn Féin members just sat there as things moved smoothly along. Mitchel had obviously negotiated his way to recruit a fair number of the right people who could win if properly supported. I had mixed feelings about it all. On the one hand, I felt sorry for those Sinn Féin workers who had done all the groundwork over the years to establish themselves in the party and now had to move aside for a few IRA volunteers, most of whom it must be said were quite acceptable. On the other, I was delighted that in their arrogance and desire for respectability, volunteers like Hugh Brady had marched straight through the political door like pigs going to a poisoned trough. Even Barney McFadden allowed himself a wee smile when the Creggan cumann proposed Brady. As I walked along Cable Street with Mitchel later that evening, it became obvious that he had engineered the whole thing and had been only too willing to allow the IRA to think that they might not get their way. They had always been told by Martin McGuinness that it would be volunteers first. When he appeared to question some of their nominations, they got angry and turned up for a fight. A fight they didn't get. No one could ever say they were coerced into it, but these guys were taking the very first steps away from the war. It would take just over four years, but there would be no going back for the IRA in Derry. Influenced by McGuinness, his relatives and Mitchel, by 1990 the IRA would be put on a virtual ceasefire in the city.

As for my political aspirations, John Carlin, my old adversary in the Waterside, had been nominated by the IRA instead of me and was to be given a chance at the council seat in our area. To be fair, he was very competent but I didn't believe he could get elected. The residents in our area wouldn't vote for just anyone Sinn Féin put up, unlike say Creggen or the Bogside; plus there was the fact that the 'fuck-up squad', the IRA unit on the Waterside, had caused a lot of hatred in our area over the years. As weeks passed, John would take the occasional verbal swipe at me as he swaggered around the area as the 'prospective candidate for the Clondermot Ward'.

Then, out of the blue one day, Seamus Keenan called to tell me that John had withdrawn his nomination and there was a strong possibility that I would be nominated. I was shocked. Why would John Carlin walk away from the glory that he had sought for years? There were rumours of a family row that had got out of hand, and the negative publicity surrounding John was detrimental to the party. He was removed from the Sinn Féin list of candidates and I was chuffed. With Carlin out of the way, I looked forward to meeting up with Stephen from London again to brief him on the entire goings on in Sinn Féin. Stephen seemed delighted with the direction the movement now appeared to be travelling. However, my secret euphoria over my rising status in Sinn Féin and the way the organisation was inching further towards political activities was short lived, and the sickening violence of the Troubles returned to haunt our family once more.

***

Evelyn McElhinny sat on the sofa looking tense as I entered my mother's living room. Evelyn was my young cousin from Ballykelly and had been brought up by my Aunt Mary and Uncle Davey. The last time I saw her was when she sat with my mother round the bedside of my other cousin, Priscilla White, who had been maimed in the Ballykelly bomb. Evelyn now lived with her husband Dougie and three children on the neighbouring, mainly Protestant, Irish Street estate. She told me that Dougie had been in the Ulster Defence Regiment but had left it some months earlier. This was something I didn't know but she went on to ask me if the amnesty for ex-UDR men was still in place? Martin McGuinness had recently stated that civilians who had worked for or even had once been members of the security forces should come forward to Sinn Féin. McGuinness 'advised' them to give their details to the party, who in turn would pass on the information to the IRA, principally to say that they were no longer involved with the British Army or the RUC. In doing so, McGuinness promised they would be immune from IRA attacks.

Evelyn explained that her husband believed he had been followed by two IRA men for a couple of nights. I could see her problem and promised that I would see someone about it. The next night I asked an IRA volunteer who had recently been released after the collapse of the Gilmour trial to see if he could help me out. This guy was a bit of a nutter but he knew the right people and I knew he would keep me right. He sent word to me a few days later that as far as he could establish no one in the IRA was targeting Dougie and that he had passed the information of his discharge from the UDR over to the right people. That evening I visited Evelyn and Dougie at their home on Bann Drive in Irish Street. It was not the safest place in the world for me, but I felt that it would be good to ease their minds as well as my mother's, who liked Evelyn. Dougie, who I'd never met, turned out to be a pleasant man, well-spoken and in his forties. He was quite a bit older than Evelyn, but they had a lovely home and I spent a pleasant few hours with them in general conversation as Evelyn recalled the times we used to play as children on the shingly beach near her home during the 1950s. Before leading me to the door, Dougie shook my hand and thanked me for the news I had brought him. He was much at ease now and glad that he wasn't a target anymore. As I drove out of Irish Street I felt good that I had been able to help and I called in to my mother's on the way back to give her the news: Dougie was no longer on any IRA hit list.

Yet just eighteen hours later, on 24 February 1985, Dougie McElhinny was shot dead as he dropped off a friend on the

Glenvale estate on the Derry side. Two masked gunmen jumped from a Toyota van and pumped bullets into him as he was about to drive off. I was totally dumbfounded. My mother was so angry with me that I decided to go and see the IRA volunteer and ask him why he'd lied to me. But before I got to his house I received word that Dougie had been shot dead by the INLA, who claimed that he was a spy. Of course, the truth was they were wrong; Dougie McElhinny was just another innocent man who had paid for what he used to be. The INLA had twice brought death and injury to my mother and her family, once with their bomb at the Droppin' Well bar and now with Evelyn's husband. I was sorry for her and my aunts and uncles as they tried to come to terms with it all. Little did I know that Dougie's murder would have potentially lethal consequences for me.

Two days later I was standing in the hallway of Cable Street when a Sinn Féin official approached me and whispered, 'Listen kid, you need to step up your security over there in the Waterside, especially now that you don't live in the Gob anymore. When word gets out that you might be standing in the council election for Sinn Féin, you'll be in danger.' Then he leaned closer to me and whispered. 'I have it on good authority that the UVF in the Waterside are blaming you for setting up Dougie McElhinny. His wife told them that you visited their house the night before he was done and assured them that he was safe enough to travel over to this side of the bridge. Make no mistake about it, they'll fuckin' do you if they take the notion, so you be careful. You need to go down to Keys in the Strand and buy some large bolts and a fisheye viewer to fit onto your door. You might even consider some steel or heavy plate at the back of your front door.' I was shocked at this turn of events. I had done my utmost to give Dougie an assurance from the IRA that he was not on their hit list and I had no idea that the INLA were targeting him. Now I was being blamed for setting him up, the UVF were on my tail and I was at risk of assassination myself.

It didn't take long for the 'hunters' to start stalking their quarry. I was driving down the Trench Road when a blue Ford Escort screeched out of the Holymount estate and tried to overtake me. It swerved back in behind me to avoid a bus, which had just turned out of Rose Court, and as the bus passed and its lights shone on me, I could see in my mirror that the driver and passenger in the Escort were masked. In a panic, I threw the car into gear and drove like a bat out of hell into Gobnascale, with the UVF hit team still behind me. I swung the car left and headed up Corrody Road and out into the countryside, deciding that keeping on the move gave me a better chance than trying to stop and make a run for it. On and on we drove, in and out of the tiny twisting road. By now the UVF unit was having difficulty in keeping up with me as I threw the car around the bendy road. As I swung down into Tullyally and drove past the car breaker's yard I heard a shot and a thwack as a bullet hit the boot of my car. I swung out onto the main Derry Road and started to drive back towards the city.

When I was about half-way up the road, heading towards Altnagelvin Hospital, I became stuck behind a lorry. The UVF car caught up and was behind me again. Just then I spotted a bus and a long line of traffic coming down the road towards me. I moved out to overtake the slow-moving lorry and waited until the bus was very nearly on top of me, then I swung out into its path, threw the car into gear and floored it. I just managed to get past the lorry and narrowly missed the bus as the driver braked in order to avoid hitting me. The Ford Escort was trapped behind the lorry and prevented from overtaking it by the oncoming cars as I sped up the hill. When I reached the roundabout I swung right into the hospital and into the main car park, where I parked and ran into the trees to await the arrival of the two gunmen. After about fifteen minutes it was obvious that I had lost them, and an hour later I drove the short distance to Riverview. I parked the car in Dunfield Terrace and walked back home through the lanes so as not to be seen. Once home I thought of phoning Mitchel McLaughlin and telling him about my narrow brush with death at the hands of loyalists. But as it was after midnight, I decided to leave it until the next day.

The next morning (Friday, 1 March 1985), I drove to Strabane for a pre-arranged meeting with some of the relatives of the Devine family. The Devine brothers, David and Michael, had been shot dead by soldiers in an undercover operation as they approached an arms dump in the dark of night. The army had been tipped off by a local man who was an agent for the RUC. Their joint funeral had been a very emotional affair and Gerry Adams criticised the security forces' use of fire power. Given the deployment of camouflaged soldiers surrounding the dump, the use of a helicopter and sophisticated technology, Adams pointed out that the two brothers should have been given the opportunity to surrender to be questioned. However, with the killing of Willie Fleming, Danny Doherty and now David and Michael Devine, it was clear to me that there had been a shift in the British Army's military thinking. These weren't just deaths, these were messages to the IRA that the gloves were off and from now on no prisoners would be taken. After completing my meeting in Strabane, I drove on to Omagh for a meeting with Francie Molloy, which, as it turned out, was cancelled. When I got back to Derry I decided to hold off contacting Mitchel McLaughlin and Seamus Keenan about the UVF attempt on my life. It was a fateful decision, because I was totally unaware that my life was in double-danger; not only from the UVF but from another source, too. The IRA's counter-intelligence unit, commonly known as the 'Nutting Squad', were on my trail.

CHAPTER 8

MY COVER IS BLOWN

I faced a stark choice at the emergency meeting at Ebrington Barracks that evening: either be extracted or executed. I had been called out of the blue by Ginger and ordered to go to Ebrington Barracks. There I was thinking that my handlers and the team of FRU officers around them were about to warn me I was a prime target for the UVF in Derry, but instead they came with an even more chilling piece of news. The IRA's internal security department were onto me, thanks to a tangled web of betrayal and Cold War intrigue, and Ginger, Karen and an agent only known as 'the Boss' assured me I would be dead within twenty-four hours unless I did what I was told, which was to flee Derry and enter into a witness protection programme somewhere in Britain. My eleven-year career as an agent burrowing inside the republican movement in my native city was over.

In the gravest of tones, the Boss relayed how close they had come to losing me, 'Look Willie, you have no idea how lucky we were to get this intelligence. I know that you'll find this all hard to believe but this is not our fault, nor is it yours. You did nothing wrong. If anything, it's my view that given time you were going all the way to the top. Our people are livid and as we speak there's a hell of a row going on in London.'

'Whose fault is it, then?'

The Boss asked everyone to leave the room. When we were alone, he turned to me and said, 'Look, I'll deny this if it ever comes out but you deserve to know. Your ex-contact from MI5, Michael Bettaney, or Ben, as you knew him, passed your details to an IRA prisoner in a prison in England and dropped you in it.' I sat in silence as he explained about Michael Bettaney's treachery, his arrest and imprisonment, and how Bettaney was left alone with an IRA prisoner where he divulged information about me. 'He couldn't remember your surname but he did say that your name was Willie, you were ex-army and that you were one of McGuinness's trusted allies when it came to politics. He also said that you'd been down here since 1974. That's how your name came up. McGuinness had already been asked about you earlier but didn't believe a word of it. However, two days ago the IRA's "Nutting Squad" from Belfast took the decision to travel to Derry tonight and lift you anyway.'

In shock, I asked the Boss how he knew this stuff about a 'nuttin' squad'. He paused for a moment, leaned even closer and whispered, 'Willie, I'm not from this end of the province, I'm I/C of the Belfast office. I only heard about you again two years ago when I was over in London. I knew that you'd walked in here five years ago having already spent six years with MI5. Willie, that's never happened before and never will again. I was gobsmacked when the boss here told me you were back and everybody was very excited. But then I never heard very much about you again until I was told that I needed to start reading your intel because it was very important. Your stuff had been bypassing me and going direct to the Home Office because it was more about politics. But when I started to get your recent stuff I was very impressed. Your info about The IRA's attitude towards the Celts of Scotland was passed to me and it was just amazing. Straight from Martin McGuinness's mouth. That's just gold dust, Willie, and then of course there was the amazing stuff you gave us about Ivor Bell.

'You will never know how valuable that was to me and the guys in the Security Service. I had to fly to London with it, that's how important it was. You're an amazing find, Willie. That's how I know your Sinn Féin career was on the up and up. You really do need to trust me because one of my teams in Belfast handles the very man in charge of that squad and he's on his way right now to lift you, and that's how we know.'

I was speechless as he continued. 'What I want you to do is go home now, tell your wife and give her the choice of coming with you. But you must emphasise to her that her life will be in danger if you disappear on your own. I can have you and your family out of here in a couple of hours and I'll take you all up to Belfast tonight where you'll be safe, but we must move fast because I don't know who else knows or who might move against you. I can't tell you what will happen after that because we've not had this happen before and we're sort of making this up as we go along. You can be sure of one thing though, the Prime Minister already knows and is said to be livid, so you can bet she will be asking questions. You don't have to worry about being abandoned, you'll be well looked after.' He vowed that someone would pay for this treachery, although my old handler-turned-traitor to the Soviets, Ben, was already ready paying the price for his betrayal in jail across the Irish Sea. I could not believe that I had been rumbled due to bigger Cold War power-play politics.

As he was leaving, one of the handlers turned to me and said in a regretful tone, 'Willie, you were going all the way to the top and the political chiefs in London are just as gutted as we are. You know son, when you first turned up here in Derry all those years ago the boss here wasn't sure what to do with you. You see, our job is watching the IRA, INLA and UVF twenty-four seven, so you were a bit of an enigma. But when the bods in London wanted to know more about your intelligence and your opinion, I knew you were what we call "a nugget". You've actually changed some of our military aims and objectives with the political information you've been gathering. No one's ever going to top your achievements here on that front. So, you should be very proud.'

As I travelled back to the house with Ginger, he tried to put a brave face on things. 'You'll look back on this moment and thank God for our man in Belfast because he just saved your life.' Who was this mystery man whose intelligence thwarted the IRA's plans to abduct, interrogate and kill me? What Ginger said next made the whole bizarre evening even more uncanny. 'Willie, the IRA man in Belfast who passed this information to us is one of ours, just like you, only on the other side. He is unaware of who you are and doesn't even know that we're doing this, but he'll find out in a few hours and he'll be able to put two and two together. He's the one that would've nutted you if you'd cracked and Willie, you would have. So, get into the house now and get your family. This whole area is covertly sealed so take your time and, by the way, just one suitcase, leave everything else. It's a complete new start for you, Mary and the kids.' It was barely sinking in that the man who had passed on the information about my imminent demise was also the man tasked by the IRA to shoot me dead after interrogating me. I tried to get this concept straight in my already capsized brain. The head of the IRA 'Nutting Squad', the operative who would pull the trigger, was the agent whose intelligence had saved my life.

With my head spinning I left the car and walked down the hill towards my house, trying to think what to tell Mary. Over the next twenty minutes I tried to explain things to her and also reminded her about the car and the UVF. God bless her, she said right there and then we should wake up the children and pack. We took the decision to stay together and gamble that this whole nightmare would blow over. I promised her that if things could be sorted out over the weekend, we could possibly come home again on Sunday and no one would be any the wiser. Of course, as she woke the children I knew that we wouldn't ever be coming home again.

At 2.20am Ginger rang and within minutes we were in two cars heading out of the street. We spent the next four hours in Ebrington Barracks as the Boss tried to explain things to Mary, telling her how brave I was and how Mrs Thatcher had personally contacted MI5's Stella Rimington in London to express her regret. I just sat there in another world, I wasn't feeling very brave or much of a husband or father for that matter. What the hell had I been thinking of? I should have known that this would happen one day. We left Derry in a convoy of bullet-proof cars just as daylight was dawning. The children slept most of the way, completely unaware that they would never see their friends again, and Mary slept fitfully and quietly sobbed. I was exhausted, but too much in shock to sleep. I wasn't sure why I was being taken away like this and was beginning to question the whole thing. We spent the next week in a house in Palace Barracks just outside Belfast, and by Thursday afternoon found ourselves boarding Mrs Thatcher's ministerial jet at RAF Aldergrove, beside Belfast's main airport. The RAF crew had no idea who we were, they just knew that we were VIPs. We were accompanied by Eddie and Karen, who tried their best to engage us in positive conversation during the flight.

On arrival at RAF Northolt we were shown into the area normally reserved for the royal family or visiting dignitaries. Desi, my old contact from Derry, was in charge of the operation and greeted us on arrival. After a short briefing we left the airfield in another convoy of cars and were taken to a safe house near Brighton. From the moment we walked into our temporary sanctuary we were impressed. We were met at the door by a young man called Trevor, who was part of the team and had been getting the property ready for us. It was obvious to me that this house belonged to the Ministry of Defence. We spent the next few weeks there and Desi, Bill, Kevin, and Karen were now the team looking after our needs. Two days after our arrival I was given a tour of the bombed-out Grand Hotel, which the IRA had blown up during the Tory Party conference in 1984. For the children, passing the time was easy: going to the beach and of course shopping for new clothes. Mary, being the mother that she was, was determined that all this would have as little effect on the children as possible.

As for me, every day seemed to bring someone from London or Belfast who wanted to talk to me. Mark from the Northern Ireland Office and my old friend Stephen from London were regular visitors to our home. Mark was able to tell me that thanks to my evidence about personating and vote stealing amongst all parties in Northern Ireland, legislation was being passed through parliament which would ensure that it couldn't happen again. Though the British government had been aware of personating for years, I was, apparently, the first person to get the evidence to the right people at the right time. I told him that I did it to help Sinn Féin, because from now on they would have to physically get their vote out and do what they had to do to bring about an end to abstentionism in the minds of a lot of nationalists and republicans. If that helped the government, then so be it.

Mark was a good man and he took everything that I said without being offended. Before he left he said, 'You know, Willie. There are MPs, Lords and MEPs who spend their whole lives involved in politics and legislation but there aren't many of them who can claim to have been responsible for getting the law changed. You did and you should be very proud of your achievement. The system used by us back then is still used on the UK mainland today. It has never been changed and I often wonder why the government hasn't changed it. There are marginal seats all over that are just rife for the taking using personation and stealing. Living in Scotland and being an SNP sympathiser often tempts me to approach some local activists and show them how to achieve this feat. Mind you, London would be the easiest of places to run such an operation. London is like a big melting pot where nobody knows anybody and voters just wander in and out of stations with just a polling card. There are a lot of foreign people with little or no understanding of what to do on such occasions. Being stupid or acting as such goes a long way to being assisted by a friendly electoral officer, but I'm too old for that these days.'

While I was with Mark I also walked him through the system of obtaining grants and how I had set a lot of them up. He took that information away with him and passed it to his boss, who discussed it with Douglas Hurd, the Secretary of State for Northern Ireland. Consequently, on 27 June 1985 Douglas Hurd announced, 'In future, no government funds will be provided to some local community groups, because of their "close links" with paramilitary organisations.' One day, Desi brought me notes of thanks from both the home secretary's office and the Northern Ireland secretary's office. I was also personally thanked for my work and advice to the Electoral Commission. I smiled as I thought what Mitchel might say if he knew that it was me who was responsible for both laws being passed. Especially the voting legislation, because he had often agonised over how to overcome personating and 'get these bastards off their arses to go and vote themselves, instead of us having to risk Sinn Féin personnel doing it for them.' Now he could simply tell them that it couldn't be done anymore and that they would have to go themselves. I knew it would help them in the long run, and so it did.

As for the legislation on government grants, I didn't really care because the groups I'd set up already had their money and it couldn't be taken back. Stephen from London was more of a friend than an official. He and I would discuss everything from the Army Council down to the basic cumann in Strabane. He was shocked when I told him that Sinn Féin hoped to take more than fifty seats in the forthcoming Northern Ireland local elections; the officials at Stormont were estimating just over thirty seats. He smiled when I showed him on the map where and how, and indeed that some councils would actually end up being controlled by Sinn Féin, like Omagh and a few others. They hadn't thought that Sinn Féin would take up mayor and deputy mayor offices on local councils.

* * *

One day, the man in charge of the security team, James, asked if I could meet two RUC officers the following day. I refused point-blank because I hated the RUC and he knew it. But he put pressure on Mary to speak to me, telling her that non-co-operation at this stage could affect our resettlement. After two more days of saying 'no', I eventually agreed. They had been staying in a hotel nearby and were finally called forward on the Friday morning. They arrived in plainclothes just after 10am and were shown into the dining room. I joined them alone shortly afterwards and began to listen to their questions, which it has to be said were mostly about the finances of Sinn Féin and account estimates. I had brought the Sinn Féin account books with me and they were amazed when I showed them the photocopies. We had been chatting for about an hour or so when one of them suggested a short break so that he could nip to the next room to collect some documents for me to view. While he was away the other RUC officer opened a briefcase and took out a handful of photographs. He passed them to me and asked, 'I was wondering if you could help me in identifying some of the people in these photos?' I started to look through them and recognised them instantly. They were my photographs! The same ones I'd organised Sean Doherty to take at Willie Fleming's funeral.

I stayed as calm as I could. 'This is Fleming's funeral, where did you get them?'

As his colleague returned and took his seat, the RUC man said, 'One of our patrols stopped the Sinn Féin minibus on the Glenshane Pass and took them from the driver; we think they were on the way to Belfast to be used for publicity purposes.'

I stood and called James, who was sat in the next room. 'What's up, Willie?' he asked.

'The meetings over, get these two out of here.' I walked past him and into the kitchen, where Desi was having a coffee. Within minutes, James came out and asked me to go back and explain to the RUC officers what they had done wrong. I was going to tell James what, but I felt so angry and used that I decided I would give it to them in front of him. I walked back into the dining room with James and picked up the photographs, which still lay spread out on the highly polished table. 'Tell me again in front of James where you got these, and don't lie to me?'

'I told you, from a van on its way to Belfast.'

I turned to James, 'He's a fuckin' liar.'

'Look, Willie,' interrupted the other officer. 'We weren't actually there on the VCP (vehicle checkpoint) but that's what we were told.'

James was looking confused, 'Willie, what's the problem with where they got them?'

I walked back to the table and picked up the photographs. 'These photographs are mine. They were taken by a member of Sinn Féin. They were not being taken to Belfast, because Seamus Keenan and I already saw to that and two were chosen by Danny Morrison for the newspapers. I had these photographs in my house until a few weeks ago, when I loaned them to another Sinn Féin member.'

There was a pause as the two officers looked at one another. Then one of them said, 'And?'

I put my hands on the table and leaned into his face. 'I'll tell you fuckin' "And?" I loaned these photographs to someone from Sinn Féin while I was still in Derry and it occurs to me that he just happens to work at Gransha Hospital, where Willie Fleming was murdered by the SAS. That's fuckin' "And?".' I banged the table at the word 'And'. There was a long silence as the two officers stared at the photographs. James's eyes were bulging in his head as he shook it in disbelief.

It was as if they had all been struck by lightning. This certainly wasn't what they had in mind when they came to talk to me. I was still seething, so I leaned across the table again and hissed, 'I'm not sure which of the three of you I should be most angry at. You two for just blowing his cover, or you James, for authorising these two cunts to come here in the first place.' With that I opened the door to leave the room and bumped into Desi and Bill, who had been standing outside listening to the shouting match. 'I'm going for a walk now. So somebody better get fuckin' ready and come with me, because as sure as God I'll go to a phone box and get him stiffed.'

I stormed out of the front door, Desi following after me and he spent the next two hours talking to me as we walked on the stones of Brighton beach. He couldn't believe what had just happened, though he smiled at one point and said, 'These things just turn up at your door, don't they Willie? Having the luck that you've got is probably why you were so successful.' But he added, 'It's probably a good thing, because there's a few doubts about your loyalty in the camp.'

'How do you work that one out?' I asked.

'Well,' he said, 'if you were really one of them, you wouldn't have reacted the way you did. You would have bluffed your way through the meeting and told them nothing of your suspicions. Instead, sometime in the future you would have passed the lad's name to Martin McGuinness and got him taken out, which would have earned you brownie points with the movement. You see, Willie, you haven't got what it takes to have that kind of thing on your conscience; that's what separates you from McGuinness and the rest of them. I don't know, but I suspect you're right. However, I'll tell you this much: we didn't know and we exchange this kind of thing all the time. This was either his first run out as an RUC agent or somebody has got some serious explaining to do to.'

We went on to talk about Willie Fleming and how I felt about his murder. Desi said, 'Look, Willie, you're going to have to deal with all of this and put it to bed, otherwise it will just eat away at you like a cancer and we'll never get anywhere with your resettlement. No one's going to let you go anywhere until you're clear about everything. You say Willie Fleming was murdered and that's your view, but let me paint this picture for you. There was obviously a tip-off. Now, that tip-off saved a man's life, just as that man in Belfast just saved yours. To that young UDR guy, that agent is a fucking hero! As for the SAS, maybe it was a hammer to crack a nut, but Willie, when they're stood up they're not there to ask for names and addresses. They are sent to take out targets, to kill them. That is their job, nothing else. Just like Willie Fleming, who was an IRA volunteer on a job to take out a target. He didn't go down there to arrest the UDR man as he got off the bus. He went down there to kill him, and if he had managed to pull it off a young wife would today be wandering around Stewart's Supermarket in the Waterside, grieving and desperately trying to focus on everyday life now that her husband was dead. You really must get all this in perspective.' I knew he was right but I just couldn't handle the betrayal. Then he said, 'We'd better get back before they come looking for us.'

'Desi, I'm not talking to those cops again.'

He laughed out loud. 'You must be fucking joking. Those two are on their way back to police headquarters at Gough Barracks to find out who the fuck had the idea about the photographs, because it certainly wasn't theirs. As for James, he'll be getting on to the chief constable's office for a few answers. He's a new broom in our organisation over here but he carries a lot of weight over there. He'll sweep whoever is responsible into the fucking dustbin.'

As we walked past the Grand Hotel he laughed as he told me how every agent in Northern Ireland has a number. Their names are never used at meetings, just their file numbers. It's usually a four-digit number, which gives his identity to his handlers. Your identity was 3007. But you were always referred to as 007 at meetings.'

What? 007! I thought he was joking. 'Fuck off, Desi, you're winding me up.'

'No, honestly.' He laughed. 'You were 007. The chief constable and the people at the Northern Ireland Office always called you 007. They didn't know who you were; not even Mrs Thatcher knew your personal details, though she often asked, "How's 007 getting on in Londonderry?" to the amusement of the high bosses in London.'

Apparently, I was the only British agent ever to have had this number. Now, the thing that I found fascinating is that I have been identified by this very same number since the day I was born: 30 July, 30/07. How's that for coincidence? Or was it fate? Of course, I never had a gun, or a blonde on my arm, or a car that fired rockets out of its headlights, and in those days I had to memorise everything, which I became really good at, and it's an ability that has stayed with me to this very day.

Back at the house Mary, the children and the three other minders sat in the lounge waiting for us to return. After a bit of ribbing about me verbally abusing the two inspectors of the RUC, we all settled down again.

***

After a few days in Brighton Mary was allowed a phone call to her mother. She had spent weeks asking for this treat and she finally got her wish. It was very emotional to watch, even Bill and Desi had tears in their eyes. During the twenty-minute call, her mother asked to speak to me. I took a deep breath and went on the phone. She sounded very understanding and cared only that we were all okay. 'Martin McGuinness and Mitchel McLaughlin have been to see us,' she said. Martin told her, 'I just can't figure out why Willie left. Tell him that whatever he's been told, it's not true, tell him to come back and I'll do everything in my power to see to it that he's safe.'

I'd heard this sort of carefully worded 'come hither' language before during Gilmour's defection and I wasn't playing. I whispered to Mary not to take it too seriously; to go back to Derry now would mean certain death. Her mum and I chatted for a few minutes and then she said, 'You know that fella who collects the PDF [Prisoners Dependants Fund] money?' Though she didn't know it, she was talking about the very same person I was talking to the RUC about a few days earlier. 'Well, he and his wife disappeared in the middle of the night last week and they haven't been seen since.'

I was right, he was a fuckin' RUC tout! I didn't know whether to jump for joy or cry. Afterwards I spoke to Desi, who seemed to know all about it. 'You were obviously right in your deductions and I don't suppose the RUC were going to take the chance, given what had happened here, that you wouldn't blow his cover, so they've moved him out. James was the one who influenced them to do it.'

'Why? Doesn't he trust me?' I said, with a wry smile.

'He thinks you got "divided loyalties" and told the RUC not to take any chances.'

I don't know why but that confirmation seemed to lift my spirits and I entered into this resettlement thing with a much more positive attitude. I even went shopping and bought a whole new wardrobe of clothes and a guitar as I tried to move on with my life, which seemed to be looking up.

Then, one night just after 11 all hell broke loose in the house. The children were asleep and Desi, Mary and I sat in the living room chatting when James and Geordie, James's sidekick, turned up. Geordie shook his head and rolled his eyes at Desi as he sat down as if to say, 'Don't ask'. James on the other hand was worse for wear with drink. I had never seen him like this before. He asked Desi to leave us for a minute and then started shouting at Mary! He was very, very angry. 'You,' he snarled. 'You have a loose mouth! You were warned not to say anything to your mother about where you and Willie are living. Yet you undermined me and the team here by telling how you went shopping in Brighton. Have you any idea what you've done?

'Your mother is no doubt very vulnerable at the moment. She's had the visit from McGuinness and here you are telling her where we all are. Does it not occur to you that McGuinness will be back to talk to your mother again? You're just so fuckin' stupid!'

I felt really sorry for Mary, but I was also angered by this sudden tirade against my wife. Admittedly James had a point, but in fairness, all that Mary had done was try to ease her mother's anxiety and let her know that we were all happy and being well looked after. James went on and on and wouldn't let up as Mary began to cry. I shouted at James to stop but he wouldn't, and at that point I lost it and made a lunge for him. As James put his hands up to avoid me, he fell off the chair he had been sitting on. I was just about to punch him in the face when Geordie grabbed me and held me back, but I did manage to kick James as I was being pulled away. Then Desi rushed in, followed by Bill and Trevor who had obviously heard all the shouting. James and Geordie left and the next thing I knew we were moving to another house, away from Brighton. James came around the next day with a huge bouquet of flowers for Mary, apologised and it was never mentioned again.

***

We were moved to a safe house in Kent, and by now the children were getting bored sitting around doing nothing. Mary resisted taking them out all the time, but it was time for them to go back to school, which in our current situation wasn't possible. People were still haggling over who was to blame for my demise, where we should go to live and who should pay for it. We were originally told that we would be going to British Columbia in Canada, but had put in a special request to stay in the UK so that we could be close to Mary's parents. All of this had a knock-on effect on the children's schooling, so James came up with a compromise. He had a friend who used to be a schoolteacher; what's more she was Irish. Anna was a nice young lady who befriended Mary. She would arrive every morning around 10.30 and spend until 2.30pm working with Michael and Maria in the dining room. Things were very relaxed and we all seemed to get on well. By now Mary was savvier than at first and she was allowed regular phone calls with her mother, and her birthday on 14 May 1985 was no exception.

That night the boys gathered in our house with a huge cake and lots of presents for Mary. Andy brought his guitar, amplifier, microphone and stand and we all had a great night, culminating with me playing and all the handlers singing republican songs. As the night went on Mary and the children went to bed and we all sat talking. They were all very drunk, but as I couldn't handle that rate of drinking I had spent most of the last few hours just drinking ginger ale. As I was getting more drinks for everyone, I heard Karen say in a whisper, 'Does Willie know who tipped off the Office about him?'

'I doubt it very much,' I heard Desi say, 'because even I don't know for sure. Peter handles him and says his number is 6126 or something. They say he's a right bastard on big bucks. So figure that one out.'

Then Martin said, 'I heard in the office that he's an Italian who the boss calls Stakeknife. They say if he turns up at your house in the early hours, he's likely to be the last man you'll ever see. He's supposed to be very high in IRA's intel unit, which the boss calls the "Nutting Squad" and he's maybe even the boss. The guys say he's ruthless and they don't trust him.'

'I heard that he sells ice cream as a cover,' said Andy.

Desi replied, 'Naw, that's not true. He's a brickie.'

'So if he's an agent, how come he's allowed to stiff people? Surely that's not right?' responded Andy.

I'm not sure who said what to whom next but time was pressing and I needed to go back in. As I walked back with the drinks, I heard Martin say, 'Search me mate, but I suppose as long as he's stiffing IRA guys and leaving us alone then that suits me.'

So, I thought, the Boss back in Belfast was right: Ginger hadn't been lying to me after all. It was all true. There was a soldier the same as me, and as Ginger had said, 'Stakeknife' had saved my life.

As the months went by, everyone settled into a routine. We were still in Kent in September when Ian Hurst turned up. Ian was the van driver who would pick me up at various locations between Derry and Limavady and then transport me on a circuitous route back to Ebrington Barracks for debriefings. We used to talk a lot in the van and I found him to be very friendly. It was good to see him again and we would walk and talk about all sorts of issues. We became friends and he advised me not to let my guard down because the IRA was all out to find me. Indeed, it was Ian who explained to me how risky life really was, 'You see, Willie, British soldiers are not allowed to carry arms loaded with live rounds in public in the UK unless a special act is passed – civil disorder or some other state of emergency. So here you are all living in a leafy cul-de-sac with only one way out. If the IRA came down the road tomorrow with weapons to attack your two houses, all you have are four unarmed soldiers. Apparently, we are supposed to phone the police!' laughed Ian.

Ian and I had many discussions during those weeks. I remember asking him, 'Do you know of the solider in Belfast who saved my life?' But he didn't, saying he had only been 'at the Derry end of things, Willie, and as far as I know that's a well-guarded secret'. He didn't stay next door with the rest of the team but he did visit nearly every day, so I guessed he must have lived quite close to us in Chatham. A few weeks later Ian told me that he would be moving on. I knew his father wasn't well, which concerned him greatly, but he sighed and said it was 'just a bit of a "predicament" across the water and I might need to be away for a while "just in case".' By early November he was gone, and I wouldn't see Ian Hurst again until May 2000.

* * *

Towards the end of the 1980s, Mary was given permission for a visit from her mum and dad, although we all had to go all the way to Loch Lomond to meet them. Mary was happy to see her parents again and they were delighted to see how well we were all keeping. Maria was just chuffed, and she sat on her nanny's knee as often as she could. The weekend reunion just flew by and after they had left we returned to Kent with a new determination to see this thing through. I was the first one through the door of the house on our return when I spotted a boot mark on one of the armchairs, which had been moved from where it normally sat. Someone had stood on it for some reason, and I quickly reached the conclusion that whoever it was had been doing something to the light bulb holder. I put my finger to my mouth for Mary to be silent, because I suspected the house had been bugged while we were away. I walked around the house looking for more signs of intrusion, and up in our bedroom I found another boot print on the duvet cover. 'Intelligence Corps, my arse,' I thought as I stood there. I became angry at the thought of them doing this. This was not any Provisional IRA revenge squad that had broken into our house but British spymasters now eavesdropping on one of their own. Yet I decided to keep my cool and wait for the right moment to do something about this. Mary and I spent the next few days acting innocently and whispering occasionally if we had anything personal to say to each other.

The following Monday night the boys, our handlers, came around with a takeaway and a load of drink. I decided that if I could get them drunk, perhaps I could go next door and have a look around. At that time I drank Bacardi and Canada Dry ginger ale, so it was easy for me to drink mostly ginger ale all night without them suspecting a thing. I made sure that they drank doubles and trebles, and as the night went on, the drunker they became – but these guys could certainly drink. Andy had brought his guitar, and we played together until late, and at around 3am first Desi dozed off in his chair, then Martin, followed sometime later by Andy. I must have sat there for about twenty minutes as they snored and moved around in their chairs, trying to decide what to do next. I gently opened the bureau and took out our camera, which still had some film left in it from Mary's parents' visit, and quietly photographed them all asleep. Then I left the lounge, closing the door quietly behind me, and went out into the back garden and across the fence to the house next door. They had left the patio doors unlocked, so in I went. I was shaking and really didn't have much time, so I went straight to the bureau that sat against the wall which separated our house from theirs. There was nothing suspicious in their quarters except for three wallets. Inside the wallets were various bits and pieces, including their MOD90s (the British Army identification card).

Desi was a WO 2 (Warrant Officer 2nd class) and there on the card was his real name, rank and number. Martin was a corporal, and his name was indeed Martin. The same was true of Andy, who was a sergeant, but there was no sign of Karen's ID. Also inside the bureau was a brown envelope containing about £4,000 in £20 notes, a few hundred in £10s and some £5s. I lifted the wallets, ID cards, and the money and spread them out on the coffee table. Removing the camera from my pocket I took photographs of everything from different angles. Then I quickly replaced the wallets and money back in the bureau exactly as I had found them. As I moved round their living room I heard Karen upstairs, so not wanting to be caught I slipped back next door and went up to our bedroom, leaving our 'minders' asleep downstairs. Lying in bed, I wasn't sure what I had done or what

I would do with the photographs, but I knew they might come in handy one day.

The next morning the boys were gone and Mary and I tidied up. Martin passed by the window and waved at us as he went off to collect Anna. An hour or so later she arrived, grabbed a coffee from the kitchen and went into the dining room to begin the children's schooling. I decided that I wanted to know who she was as well, so while she was teaching I sat on the chair where she had been and reached down for her handbag, which she had left on the floor. After searching nervously through it I found a Child Benefit book. Her name was Anna Godfrey and she lived at an address in Ashford, in Kent. I felt a bit guilty at this point and put the book back, deciding that I didn't really want to know. Anna was doing her best and had never offended any of us, indeed she used to spend a lot of her time talking with Mary and keeping her spirits up. But I decided there and then to try to find out where she was coming from each day. I walked out to the car and looked in through the window at the dashboard. I noted the mileage and wrote it down; the car was always parked outside until she was taken home. The next day she was back but this time the handler parked the car next door. It was pouring with rain so I went next door and asked if Paul would nip me up to the shops. As we drove I checked the mileage again. The mileometer had an extra twenty-five miles on it.

Just as we came around the corner to turn off a side street, Paul hit another car. It wasn't that serious but the other driver insisted on calling the police, so I immediately got out of the car and casually walked away. Everything turned out okay for Paul but a few days later he brought me an FMT3 form (an army document used when there's been an accident). Paul had obviously reported the accident and he asked me to help him complete the form. As I handed back the completed form to him I noticed a stamp on the front of it. FMT forms are blank so this stamp was placed there by the MTO (military transport officer) from wherever the car was based. 'Templar Barracks, Ashford, Kent', was the answer: the headquarters of the Intelligence Corps. Later, I checked the mileage of the car against a map and it was the same within three miles. So that was where Anna lived, and I figured James too.

A week later, James came to visit next door as usual. Mary and I were home with the children, as Anna had phoned to say that she couldn't make it that day. James came over, and after a brief friendly chat with Mary and the children he asked if I could pop up to the spare bedroom for a chat. This was nothing unusual, but just before he went to go upstairs his driver called to him through the patio door, 'James, your wife's on the dog and bone.' As James went next door to take the call, Andy came in and said to Mary, 'Anna wants to know if you need anything by way of books and things for Michael?' She wasn't sure, so I said to Andy, 'Let me talk to her because there are a few things I believe Mark needs.' As I went to go next door he replied, 'She's on the phone at the minute with James.' Fuck me! James is Anna's husband. Jesus! So, all that friendly chat with Mary was merely her spying on us for more information. She was obviously reporting every little dream or aspiration that Mary had, not to mention anything she knew that I hadn't told James. I was livid but kept calm. Within minutes James was back, and we both went upstairs to the spare room. He told me he was leaving for another job and wanted to say goodbye. He was very frank as he reviewed the circumstances that had led to my cover being blown and was even more cutting about my attitude towards him. Then he said, 'We've had approval from the Treasury regarding the budget for your family's resettlement. You'll be staying in the UK, though Mary's request to go and live in Glasgow has been rejected. You'll have to wait until the officers from the Box (MI5) are satisfied that you're suitable for resettlement and being left to your own devices. I have to tell you that I have made my reservations known to them.'

Reservations? 'What would they be then?' I asked, still inwardly seething.

'Well, Willie, the incident with the RUC officers, our relationship, your overall anti-British attitude and your sometimes belief in the bullshit trotted out by McGuinness and Sinn Féin. You see Willie, I believe you're a good guy but dangerous and I think you have "divided loyalties", and given the right set of circumstances you'd make a run for it, which is why I've had to keep some of my best men here longer than needed and not leave you alone for a minute.'

I couldn't believe what he was saying. After all my family and I had put up with and gone through. I stood up and raised my voice, 'Now just hold on a minute, James. I was sent to Derry before you ever knew where it was. I was asked to go there and "become one of them". It took me twelve years and now you're holding it against me because I was successful?' I was about to lose control, especially now that I knew about Anna, when it suddenly dawned on me that this man had a lot of influence and I needed him to change his attitude towards me. It was time to negotiate. I leaned forward and lowered my voice to a whisper, 'Look James, if I could prove to you that I'm not about to do anything to cause you grief would that change your mind about me?'

'Go on then, impress me,' he sighed cynically. I left him and went to get the developed photographs.

I returned quickly and sat opposite him. 'Okay. See if this impresses you. Your name is Godfrey and you're probably a major in the Intelligence Corps based in Ashford, in Kent. The schoolteacher, Anna, is your wife and it's my guess that you used her to get close to Mary and report it all to you. I'm also figuring that if you're moving on, then so is she.' He went bright red and was clearly very embarrassed but nodded for me to continue. I then produced four photographs of the boys lying drunk and asleep in our lounge and handed them to him. He nearly died and stood up, throwing the photographs onto the coffee table. Clearly very annoyed, he loosened his red tie and sat down again. I picked up the photographs from where he'd thrown them and waved them at him, 'Your *best* men, eh? James, I was fucking good at my job and these piss artists wouldn't last twelve days undercover in Derry, never mind twelve years.' Then I handed him the other photographs showing the living room next door, the wallets, ID cards and the money. 'What you're looking at here is the billet of your "best men"; their names, ranks and numbers, together with around £4,350. So you see, James, you're wrong about me. I could have taken that money and fucked off out of here. I might not share your negative views on Martin, Sinn Féin or your lack of understanding about the politics of the North of Ireland. You probably still believe that the RUC are good guys and on your side. You're basically a soldier and all you believe is the bullshit trotted out by the Ministry of Defence and the British government. You're just another Brit in a big system and when you're finished and start to live in the real world you'll realise that I was a good man who was just a wee bit mixed up. I'm not disloyal, and just because I don't get pissed every night, live on takeaways and sing fuckin' rugby songs doesn't make me dangerous. You should respect what I did for the last twelve years. So why don't you put your clouded judgement to one side and do all you can to get me out of here as quickly as possible. Then I can move on with my life, and as for you, you can take your "best men" back to Ashford, detoxify them and send them off to be retrained.'

He was a different man now and I was enjoying pulling him off his pedestal, not just for verbally abusing my wife but for authorising our home to be bugged and using his own wife in the process. Just for good measure I picked up the photographs and laid them out neatly in front of him. 'Now James, these are for you to take with you. But you're not stupid and I know that you'll figure out I've probably got copies, and you'd be right. You should also know I have knowledge that I've not shared with you and never will.'

He sat there in silence, clearly shocked at my attack on him and his men. I could feel my legs shaking and my heart thumping in my ears. However, even though I was trembling with fear I held my ground and waited to see which of us would blink first. He got up, picked up his blue cashmere overcoat – which lay where he had left it over the arm of the chair – took the photos off the coffee table and walked out of the bedroom door without a word; I never saw him or his wife ever again.

I sat down and tried to take in all that had happened in the last two hours. I was still trembling, because I wasn't sure what James would say or do now that he was next door again. I knew the handlers would be in trouble but I figured James might keep it between them. Men like James are survivors, I thought, and he wasn't the type to report this kind of 'breach of security' amongst his own unit. Not to mention how he had compromised himself and, worse still, his own wife. He might also be wondering if I would speak to someone – his boss or maybe the IRA – about his Irish wife. That's the thought I hoped would eat away at him and force him to be rid of us as quickly as possible. I felt sure that he would value his own career and his wife's safety over a few drunken men. All the people next door were good soldiers just doing their best, and they never did me any harm, but I was fighting for my life and a future with my family, which to me justified my actions. As I looked out of the bedroom window I saw James being driven off; he couldn't have been next door very long. That night the boys and Karen came around with more carry-outs and lots of drink. I knew then that they knew nothing of my conversation with James.

After our clash, James got his promotion and returned to Northern Ireland. He was the army intelligence officer who a few years later stood up in court in Belfast under the guise of Colonel J. and gave a glowing reference for Brian Nelson, FRU agent 6137. An ex-soldier and member of the UDA, Nelson was fed information from his handlers about republicans in order that they could be targeted, including two attempts on the life of Gerry Adams. Nelson was implicated in the murder of Belfast solicitor Patrick Finucane and other murders. However, in a behind-the-scenes deal and in an effort to save Colonel J. and Nelson's FRU handlers from prosecution, it was agreed that Nelson's involvement in the murders, including Finucane's, would not be brought into court. Instead, he would plead guilty to five charges of conspiracy to murder and other minor charges. As agreed, Nelson was sentenced to ten years' imprisonment but after only four years he was spirited away by the MOD from an English jail and resettled into a new life, all paid for by the British government.

The MOD let it be rumoured that Nelson had gone to live in New Zealand, and eventually admitted that he was in Canada.

The truth was he never went anywhere. He was actually resettled in a leafy suburban avenue in Great Britain and died of a brain haemorrhage in 2003. Though Nelson had cancer, his death still came as a shock to his family. His death certificate was issued under his new name, though he kept his real date of birth. His death was sudden and would be viewed in certain quarters as more than a coincidence, given that he died shortly before the Police Commissioner, Sir John Stevens, who had pursued Colonel J. for years, officially announced that he was preparing papers for the Director of Public Prosecutions in relation to Colonel J.'s involvement in alleged collusion between his FRU unit, Nelson and loyalist paramilitaries. With Nelson gone and all his secrets buried in Great Britain, the case against Colonel J. and his unit was simply filed away.

CHAPTER 9

HAUNTED BY THE PAST

One of the strangest days in my post-agent life was a trip to London on the pretext of visiting the Passport Office to complete the process of creating our new identities. I don't recall much about the journey, but I do remember the cars driving down cobbled streets as we reached our destination. A lady in her thirties came forward and opened the rear doors of the car to let us out. From the street she led us down four or five steps into a basement; then we turned left and walked up some more steps into a room filled with desks, on which sat the large personal computers that were commonplace in offices in the mid-1980s. I also remember the sight and sound of some very large fans, as they vainly distributed the office's warm air but did little to relieve its general stuffiness. The room itself was very posh, with beautiful paintings hanging on the walls and some easy chairs scattered around.

The next thing I recall is a 'wee' woman entering through the black door to our left. I say 'wee' because she was no taller than I am and I'm only 5 ft 5 in. It was none other than Margaret Thatcher, and yes, she did carry a handbag over her left arm. 'Now, who have we here?' she said as she swept into the room followed by another lady. Mary and I stood up to meet her and I nervously put out my hand to shake hers. She pushed it aside and stroked me on the arm saying, 'You must be William? Can I say that I am extremely proud of what you achieved in the service of your country and apologise sincerely for the way you have been treated.' I opened my mouth to speak but she continued, 'I can assure you that you will be well taken care of and I personally will ensure that everything is done to make life much easier for you from here on in.' The thing I remember most is that she never once spoke to or acknowledged Mary; it was as if she wasn't even there. But she looked down at Maria and said, 'Now young lady, you must be hot after your journey and I'll bet no one has offered you anything to drink or eat?'

'Have you any chips?' Maria replied, God bless her. It was a very strange moment and I remember feeling a little embarrassed, but Mrs Thatcher wasn't fazed in the slightest and insisted that someone was sent to get Maria some fish and chips. As quickly as she had appeared she was gone. We just stood there, staring at the lady who had entered the room with the Prime Minister. It must have been some twenty minutes later that the fish and chips arrived, but by this time all Maria wanted was the can of Coke that came with the food. Within an hour we were led out of the room and taken back to the car. If Maggie had come to pay tribute to my work, it was a whirlwind visit.

* * *

In February 1986, we received word that the government had not approved our demand for resettlement in Scotland. Instead we would be going to live in Wales, though it would be leaked that we had been resettled in Canada. Three weeks later, with new identities, we crossed the toll bridge over the River Severn on our way to a new home. We decided to keep our forenames but opted for the surname 'Gallaher' after Mary's granny. I had a new driving licence, a new date of birth and a new National Insurance (NI) number. At the same time I was advised that from now on, I was to refer to myself as Bill and not Willie. Our new home was 27 Woodland Place, Penarth, just a mile west of Cardiff. The house was ours and the deeds were lodged at our solicitor's office. We refurbished the whole house, built a garage and installed a new patio at the rear. Whilst there, Les continued to look in on us every now and again, but we were very happy and doing well; Michael was in his new school, as was Maria.

One afternoon 'John', a well-dressed man who was definitely not army, called to see us and advised me that a figure had been agreed as to my 'settlement'. He was very apologetic that the process had taken so long and went on to explain that there had been a lot of meetings and deliberations. He looked at Mary – 'Paperwork and receipts,' he said with a smile. It had been agreed that the settlement would come from two different departments, the MOD (army) and the 'Security Service/MI5'. He explained that part of the problem had been to establish which department was responsible for looking after me. I remember saying to him that 'the Boss' in Belfast was adamant that 'somebody would pay for this and it wouldn't be the army'.

John explained that a compromise had been reached regarding the army's share of the settlement based on an estimate of the rank I would have achieved had I stayed in the service. 'So the Intelligence Corps didn't have to pay?' I asked.

'Well, it's really all about pots within a bigger pot if you know what I mean, but they signed off on it.'

'Are you allowed to say a figure?' I said at the thought of all that money coming my way, and that was only the army's bit.

He looked up at the ceiling and around the living room. 'Well, you're sitting in it.' So our house, all the furniture and the renovations were paid for by the army.

Then John walked me through the other part of the settlement and which department would be paying for that. 'Willie, I'm sure I don't need to tell you who that is, do I?'

'MI5,' I thought to myself.

John explained that everything that had happened to us since leaving Derry had to be paid for out of somebody's budget. The rent on the married quarter in Belfast, Mrs Thatcher's ministerial jet, the teams of people who cared for us, their cars and their fuel, all our new clothes, etc., the rents on the different houses we stayed at and all the food and shopping.

'Does that include all their takeaways and their drink?' I asked.

'Afraid so,' said John, with a sigh. So there was no such thing as a free takeaway and what had started off as close to half a million pounds was now greatly reduced. However, it was still a substantial amount of money considering we now owned this beautiful house.

John summarised the financial settlement that was being made to us and started to pack his files into his briefcase. As he stood in the porch and said his goodbyes, I'll never forget his parting words, 'You're the only one who hasn't negotiated and it'll be no surprise to anyone if you stick up for yourself, your wife and children. It's your future. You know Willie, when the files on this episode are closed you'll be on your own with probably just an emergency phone number.' Then he added, 'Besides Willie, I believe you hold more cards than all the players in this game. So think on it and I'll call you next week.'

Over the next few days I thought about the settlement and talked to Mary. Eventually, I concluded that I should say no, so when John phoned I turned the offer down, citing that this money was for the rest of our lives and that he should not underestimate the difficulties I was going to have trying to get a job and earn an annual income. We didn't hear anything for over a month and I was beginning to worry that I might have blown the whole thing. Then John called one day with the news that the settlement had been increased by £70,000. I was also to receive a monthly income of £750 until we all agreed that I didn't need it. Sadly, John was killed in the helicopter crash on the Mull of Kintyre. John had tried to do the decent thing by Mary and me, and I will never forget that.

****

By 1989 I had bought a restaurant in Cardiff as well as four shops in the Windsor Arcade area, employing ten full-time and six part-time staff. Business was booming and I could afford to fly Mary's mother and father over from Derry twice a year for holidays. As for my former 'employers', every six to seven weeks there would be a courtesy call from various handlers to make sure that we were safe and secure. Otherwise, the Gallahers were settling into a conventional middle-class lifestyle, with me even being elected to the local rotary club. The only echo of my former life as a secret agent was a new hobby – I had joined a local gun club. I was introduced to the club by one of our best customers at the restaurant, who was a gunsmith. He invited me to the club and I soon found myself there every Tuesday night, firing a 9 mm Browning. Despite being in the British Army I had never fired a handgun, though I became quite adept at it.

The gunsmith suggested that I apply for a firearm certificate, and occasionally he let me take the gun home to show my sons, Mark and Michael.

One Sunday morning I was watching television and there in the studio was the man who had tipped off the RUC about Willie Fleming and Danny Doherty. The discussion was about the National Health Service and the lack of funds in northwest English hospitals, and he was speaking as a union representative on behalf of nurses. When the credits rolled at the end I could see that the programme had come from Manchester. The death of those lads at the hands of the SAS still filled me with fury, and I don't know why but I decided that I would call the next day and see if I could track this man down. Pretending to be a nurse, it took me the best part of two days to find out at which hospital he was working. I'd forgotten that he probably had a new identity, but by Monday night I had the name of the hospital and his new name, and even the shift he was on. Crazy as it might sound, I decided that I would go there and confront him. That Tuesday night I was in the club, shooting on the range, and I must have fired at least thirty rounds at the target, pretending in my mind that it was him. That was when I decided that if I could steal two rounds of 9 mm ammunition and persuade the gunsmith to let me take the Browning home I would travel up to Manchester and kill him.

I figured out a way to get the gun and a couple of rounds out of the club, and the following morning hid the gun underneath the spare tyre in the boot of the car and drove to Manchester. I remember being very nervous and I kept imagining I was being followed. Shortly before 1pm I pulled into the hospital car park. Of course, now that I was there I didn't really know what to do. I went to reception to make sure that he was starting his shift at

4pm, as I had been told earlier, then returned to the car and took out the pistol. I sat in the back of the car, loaded the two rounds into the clip, and waited for my quarry. I waited, shaking at the thought of what I was about to do, when suddenly there he was, walking with another man, right in front of me. I gripped the pistol in my hand, got out of the car and took aim at the man's back as he walked towards the hospital, completely unaware that his life was in some stranger's hands. At the last minute I froze. My brain was telling my finger to pull the trigger but no matter how hard I tried I just couldn't do it. It was the strangest feeling and I even began to shake. Within seconds he was gone and I was alone in the car park.

I must have been crazy to think that I of all people could shoot anyone, but that's how close I came to killing him. I got back into the car and drove out of the hospital car park. Three hours later I was back home in Penarth and the next night the gun was back in the cabinet where it belonged. I kept hold of the two rounds for over a year, but eventually I threw them into the river. I still cannot fully explain why I came to within seconds of shooting dead the former Derry republican turned informer. I had almost become a murderer, yet something inside had stopped me from going down that dark path.

* * *

After years of living a double life, the pressures of de-stressing took their toll in other ways. In 1991 my marriage started to fall apart, which I want to stress was nobody's fault. Mary and I were working around the clock and we argued all the time. It was clear to both of us that we needed a complete change, so I got in touch with my contact and it was agreed that under the circumstances we could move to Scotland. It was sad leaving Penarth, as the people there had taken us into their hearts, but we resettled in Bishopbriggs just north of Glasgow and I enrolled on a course at Glasgow Polytechnic. Eventually, I got a job with a local company whose main role was training unemployed people to get back into work. It turned out that I was quite good at motivating the unemployed managers of Glasgow, and within two years I was a director in a company that had secured contracts with nearly all of the local enterprise companies.

It was at this time that I met a lovely business couple, who took me into their company and their lives. I spent some of the happiest years of my life whilst working with them. Indeed, when their daughter was born, they asked me to be her godfather. This is a great privilege for any Catholic and I well remember holding her in my arms as the priest asked me to honour my spiritual commitments to her and the Catholic Church. Sadly, I had to leave the beautiful coast town where I lived to start a new life all over again, and I wasn't able to fulfil my obligations to her as a godfather. It saddens me to this very day that she doesn't even know my name. Yet when you have lived as a secret agent for so long, many of those you have met, and the stories and controversies swirling around them, always seem to come back to haunt you.

One particular murder that has haunted me more than any other was that of Frank Hegarty. I hadn't seen Ian Hurst since his visits to me in Kent fifteen years earlier and this time it was my friend the late Liam Clarke, the courageous *Sunday Times* Ireland correspondent, who introduced him to me once again. Ian had left military intelligence, battered and bruised by his experiences fighting the dirty war in Northern Ireland, and in particular the loss of one of his agents in Derry, Frank Hegarty.

Martin McGuinness had cynically lured Hegarty back to the city from a secret hideaway in Britain, and he paid the ultimate price for betraying the IRA – and, in particular, providing intelligence that led to the seizure of a huge arms haul from Libya that McGuinness had secreted in northern Donegal.

Ian was operating under the nom de guerre 'Martin Ingram', and we arranged to meet at the luxurious Shelbourne Hotel in Dublin. At the meeting it became apparent that Ian nurtured a deep hatred of Martin McGuinness. Initially, I wasn't able to work out why Ian had developed such animosity towards him, but later that night Liam confided in me that Ian had been looking after Frank Hegarty, just as Ginger handled me. Ian believed the agent Stakeknife had played a role in the interrogation and killing of Frank Hegarty, and had decided it was time to expose the British superspy running IRA counter-intelligence.

Frank was a senior IRA man from Derry and an FRU agent who was reputed to be in charge of some key arms dumps in the Irish Republic. He had been whisked away by the FRU in January 1986 to be resettled, but after three months in exile Frank absconded from his minders and returned to Derry, only to hand himself over to the IRA at the Donegal border. Frank trusted that after explaining himself he would be back home in Derry but instead he was taken away and shot dead. When I spoke to Ian about it he was still clearly upset and blamed Martin McGuinness. Apparently, Martin had promised Frank that if he came home he wouldn't be touched. I remember the tortured face of Frank's mother, whom McGuinness had conned into helping persuade her son to return to Derry and that all would be forgiven, and thought of Martin and Mitchel McLaughlin's visit to Mary's parents, when they had said the same thing. In a way I could understand Ian's bitterness towards McGuinness.

I knew from my own handlers that a safe house in England had been prepared for Frank between November and December 1985 once he had been 'extracted' from Derry, just as I was. Frank Hegarty's time in the IRA was nearly up after the huge weapons haul from Libya was captured in Donegal. It had been Frank's task to safely store the weapons until they could be taken across the border for IRA operations. Strangely though, these weapons were not officially 'found' until January 1986, which begs the question: why did Hegarty's handlers prepare the ground for his exfiltration four to five months before the arsenal was 'discovered'? The answer, I suspect, lies in the murky world of high politics.

I first met Kevin McNamara, Shadow Secretary of State for Northern Ireland from 1987 to 1994, when I made an appointment to see him back in 2001. I had asked to see him regarding the plight of Kevin Fulton, an MI5 agent who allegedly spied on the Provisional IRA, and we met in his office at Portcullis House (adjacent to the House of Commons) in London. At our meeting, Kevin asked how I was so knowledgeable of the situation in the North. My new identity and name meant nothing to him, but I would later see him away from his office and explain my former situation and new life. That led to a friendship which lasted until he stepped down from politics in 2005. McNamara might have been able to help me justify Fulton's claims, but he also revealed information that was pertinent to the delay in the discovery of Frank Hegarty's arms shipments.

During meetings with Kevin I learned a lot of new information, including the challenges that his predecessors faced with their counterparts in the Irish government. Kevin was a staunch believer in Irish Unity and was puzzled at their lack of vision. He went on to relate the tortured and tangled negotiations leading to the Anglo-Irish Agreement back in 1985. His knowledge and understanding of all that went into the agreement prior to the announcement was extensive. According to Kevin, one of the last-minute glitches was Mrs Thatcher's information about IRA arms shipments and weapons dumps in the Irish Republic. Just prior to the signing of the agreement, the Irish Taoiseach Garret FitzGerald agreed that when these arms dumps were (officially) uncovered, all information about their contents and who was involved (or arrested) would be shared with Thatcher's office. She was assured this could happen within weeks, but she also insisted that from November all persons wanted in the UK should be extradited from the Irish Republic and not blocked, as was then the case. A few months later, Frank's arms dumps were uncovered and taken away for examination. Clearly, the reason for the delay in the operation was that the British military had asked that some of the dumps be let through in order that the weapons could be 'bugged' and 'tagged'.

Following Frank Hegarty's extraction from active service by the FRU, the Intelligence Corps followed standard operating procedures in ensuring his safety from IRA reprisals. As soon as someone is extracted they are transported almost immediately to a safe house in Belfast or they are debriefed in Derry and then flown (with their handler) to England and on to a 'secure safe house'. Where possible, an agent is met by a handler that they know and trust (in Frank's case this was Ian Hurst). Almost immediately Frank would have been asked for his driving licence, passport and any other means of ID. This is standard procedure and is 'not negotiable', simply because it's the beginning of the process which leads to being given a new identity. That can only happen by applying to change a person's name by 'deed poll'; the original ID is needed to acquire the new driving licence, passport, etc. This doesn't happen in a day and it can sometimes take months, but the timeline usually runs in tandem with the process of working out where a former agent will be resettled. That could be Canada, Australia, New Zealand or anywhere in the world, so there is often no rush to get the new ID prior to that decision. Finally, they would have to apply for and receive a budget (resettlement money) before everything could be wrapped up.

Apparently, Frank was staying in England with his handler (Ian Hurst) and absconded while they were visiting a betting shop in Kent. Just twenty-four hours later he turned up in Derry, which in itself raises several questions. Since Frank was in an unfamiliar town with little money and only the clothes he was wearing, how did he get to the airport or ferry that transported him to Ireland? Why wasn't he intercepted before he travelled back to Derry? It's worth remembering that Martin McGuinness had been in contact with Frank for three weeks, and once Frank was back in Derry he stayed out of sight for over two weeks. Then he took a chance on Martin's word and was taken over the border and held for a period at an IRA safe house in Buncrana in County Donegal. Was it possible that McGuinness was pleading for Hegarty's life during this time, but on the insistence of hard-liners in Belfast his pleas were ignored and it was decided their captive had to be killed?

It was clear from the FRU's viewpoint that someone had fatally dropped the ball with Frank Hegarty. There is no suggestion that Ian Hurst played a role in that cock-up, but one thing is for sure: he was haunted over the years by what happened to Hegarty. Ian blamed McGuinness for cynically luring Frank back to Derry using his own mother as bait. He also ran a campaign in the media alleging that McGuinness was himself an agent and was being protected at the highest levels of the British state. He can now certainly point to my sighting of McGuinness coming out of the MI5 safe house outside Derry that Michael Bettaney and I had used in 1980. But Ian has also written material about me that is plainly wrong. In a *Sunday Times* article on 21 December 2011, Ian alleged that he had handled both Frank Hegarty and myself. However, this is not true as Ian was solely the van driver who collected me from secret pick-up points so that I could be driven to my handlers at Ebrington Barracks. He was not my handler in the sense of being the FRU agents who listened to, absorbed and analysed the political intelligence I was giving them.

As for Martin McGuinness informing on his comrades, there was never any evidence that he ever did, though the British state counter-insurgency strategy certainly started to orbit McGuinness from the late 1970s and early 1980s. I think the British became aware sooner than the public imagined that here was a man they could do business with. They certainly went out of their way to undermine his rivals on the IRA Army Council, particularly Ivor Bell, in order to protect the fledgling politicisation of the movement. The capture of the Donegal arms dumps certainly blunted Bell's project to ramp up the IRA's violent campaign in the mid-1980s, which not only prevented Bell, Kevin McKenna and their cohorts from unleashing fresh murder and mayhem in Northern Ireland, it also tipped the balance of power away from them towards the McGuinness–Adams axis. I hold Ian Hurst in high regard and wish him well, but I think his obsession over McGuinness being an agent is misplaced. I think he needs to put a different perspective on Martin's role. He was not so much an agent but an influencer, whom the British could subtly manipulate, promote and protect. Suspicion, rumour, and innuendo morph into a fog and the clear picture is obscured. Unless documentary evidence can be produced to prove McGuinness was a long-term agent, my conclusion is that Ian is looking down the wrong end of the telescope.

* * *

When my family and I were first spirited out of Northern Ireland in the mid-1980s, I imagined that I would be finished with the world of spies, informers, double-agents and spooks. Yet apart from pondering over the actions of 'Stakeknife', I was also plunged into a second agent–handler scandal that turned out to be personally dangerous for me. In early May 2001, I was living alone in a flat in the Scottish borders when I received a call from Liam Clarke. After some pleasantries, Liam told me about a man called 'Kevin' who was claiming to be an ex-soldier, just like me, but unlike me, he had told Liam that he had been left high and dry by his handlers in the FRU. Liam said Kevin had been asking for my number to see if I could somehow help him, but being an ethically-driven journalist, Liam wouldn't give him any details without my permission. After a day or so of thought I called Liam and told him to go ahead and give the spy my number. The next night, he called and told me of his predicament. Apparently, Kevin had taken part in the making of a UTV documentary in April with the working title of *Don't Shoot the Messenger*, which had been 'D-noticed' (banned by the government) at the last minute. The programme had been heavily trailed by UTV and by the time it was 'pulled' it was apparent that 'Kevin Fulton', the cover name of Peter Keeley, an IRA volunteer from Newry, was the interviewee. I was shocked, because according to Liam he was recruited when he was in the Royal Irish Rangers and worked for the army in the North. Kevin told me of his time within the IRA, which was now very suspicious of him, and he was deeply concerned that he would be lifted and shot. I called Liam and asked him what he thought? 'Willie,' Liam said, 'Kevin is a strange wee character but I'm inclined to believe him all the same.'

Kevin must have rung me at least five times over the next two nights as he and his wife sat up keeping watch for the IRA to arrive. I called Liam again the next day and told him I was going to go over to the North of Ireland to bring Kevin out. 'Jesus, Willie, why would you do such a crazy thing?' I explained to him that the way I looked at it, no one would ever suspect that I would have the nerve to return to Ireland, let alone to a republican town like Newry. Besides, I knew that Kevin would be dead within days if he didn't get out of the North. The next morning Liam booked me a flight from Glasgow to Belfast and after a bus journey to Newry I arrived in the town at just after 11am. I had arranged to meet Kevin at the local supermarket, and as I waited for him it started to dawn on me that I must be mad. After all, here I was standing in Newry waiting for an IRA man who could easily get me stiffed into the bargain.

Kevin arrived on time and we walked back to his home, where we were met at the door by his lovely wife and their boxer dog. He was a small man, around 5 ft 4 in tall and slightly porky. After a couple of phone calls to Ulster Television, which had been under pressure to abort the documentary, I managed to secure a flight to London and a hotel for Kevin. A few days later I flew down to London and met up with Kevin, who whilst relieved was now 'a lost wee soul' in the big city with nothing to do. We spent the next few days just walking and talking. He grew to trust me and admired what I had done, and the more I listened to him I thought him to be one of the bravest men I had ever met. His story was amazing, but it soon became clear to me that not only was he a complete nervous wreck but he wasn't going to last too long here in London, either.

While I tried to negotiate deals with UK newspapers, Kevin informed me that he had some startling information he wanted to make public. When I asked him what was it about and was it that serious, he stood up, came very close to where I was sitting, put his face right up against mine, looked sternly at me and said in a rough voice, 'The Omagh bomb!' You could have knocked me down with a feather as he told me what he had done to try and prevent it. The next morning, Kevin and a journalist I admired, Ian Gallagher, got together, and as if to prove his point Kevin phoned his ex-handler, an RUC officer to whom he had given the tip-off. Ian and I just stood there and listened in amazement. The RUC officer on the other end of the phone knew Kevin and immediately said, 'Ah, what about yee Kevin?' When Kevin asked him about the call, the RUC man confirmed that he could recall that day very well but would need to check his notes as to where the information went. We taped the call and Ian was delighted.

I spoke to Kevin again that night, who pulled out a folder and showed me all his stuff. It was all there: his time in the IRA, the jobs he went on, the bombs he had made, and the tip-offs he had given to his handlers. There were even diagrams of how to make bombs, not to mention evidence of his time in America with the CIA and how he had help developed the 'flash bomb' (a second bomb left at an attack site that is triggered by the flashes of the cameras used by the forensic teams who turn up to lift evidence and take photos, killing nearly everyone within twenty yards or so). That night Ian came around and we went off to a local pub for a drink. While we there Ian took a call and went outside. He came back in looking shocked, 'They're pulling my story. I need to go to the office to try to sort this out.' The next morning he came back to tell us that the paper wasn't going ahead with the story and the contract was cancelled. Ian was as gutted as I was, but I mostly felt sorry for Kevin. I'm not clear as to what actually happened but I suspect the paper became frightened at the possibility of being D-noticed by the Ministry of Defence. At that time, the person responsible for issuing D-notices was Rear Admiral Nicholas Wilkinson of the Royal Navy.

A few days after Kevin hit this brick wall of censorship I contacted Imran Khan, the famous human rights lawyer who had handled the Stephen Lawrence case. Imran invited me to his offices where we discussed Kevin's situation, and within days Imran went on TV to question the whole system of young soldiers being used in such a way by their superiors. So respected was Imran that his news went everywhere. He also contacted the office of Nuala O'Loan (the Police Ombudsman) and discussed Kevin's allegations, especially about the Omagh bombing being preventable. I also spoke to Nuala O'Loan in Imran's office and told her that I was in possession of a recording of the RUC officer confirming Kevin's tip-off. Two days later a police inspector from the Ombudsman's office flew to London to meet up with Kevin. I didn't stay, instead I left them to it and waited at a friend's house for Kevin to return. To begin with, Kevin wasn't too sure about the whole Police Ombudsman investigation, but as time would prove, it was one of the best things he did.

It struck me that if I could get on a 'live' news broadcast with Kevin's tape regarding the Omagh bomb, no one could stop it and it would cause a huge stink. After making quite a few calls, the news editor of *The World Tonight,* a British current affairs radio programme on the BBC's Radio 4, invited me onto that evening's broadcast. I remember thinking that although the nightly news on Radio 4 wasn't exactly what I had in mind, it was listened to by over a million people and by anyone who was anyone in politics. That night I was introduced to the presenter, Robin Lustig, who took me into the studio. The programme started at 10pm and, after the main headlines, I was introduced and interviewed. After stating who I was, I explained about Kevin, the FRU, the warning he gave about the Omagh bomb and the Police Ombudsman's interview with him. The sound people behind the glass window played the tape of Kevin and the RUC officer and, unknown to me, the news editor of the programme had managed to track down John Reid, then Labour's Secretary of State for Northern Ireland. He was clearly taken aback by what I had said and he had just heard, and when Reid was asked why he hadn't set up an inquiry about Kevin's allegations all he could say was, 'It wouldn't be right for the Northern Ireland office to hold such an inquiry' and that the Ombudsman's office was probably the right course of action.

After we went off air, Robin Lustig was clearly pleased and wished me well in my endeavour. It turned out that Robin's father had been in the Intelligence Corps during the Second World War, which perhaps was one of the reasons he had pushed for me to appear on the programme. As I left the BBC, I remember thinking how lucky I had been to get hold of Lustig at just the right time and in the right place, and that John Reid had been in the wrong place at the right time. I later discovered that the next day a very angry Reid had contacted Ronnie Flanagan, then the RUC Chief Constable, to ask if there was any truth in my information. That's when Kevin was labelled with the 'Walter Mitty' description, that he exaggerated the importance of his information. Indeed, Ronnie Flanagan later appeared at a press conference repeating the Walter Mitty allegation, stating that he would commit 'hari-kari' if Kevin's information was true.

Nuala O'Loan published her 'damning' report into the whole affair regarding the Omagh bomb in December 2001, and confirmed that Kevin's call to his RUC contact was 'highly significant'. Within days I was contacted by Michael Gallagher and several other families who had lost loved ones during that awful day. Michael and his wife flew to London to meet with me on the understanding that I would introduce them to Kevin. Later that day, I sat in McDonald's at Liverpool Street station listening to Michael and Kevin talking about the bomb. It was very sad hearing this poor man and his wife, who had lost their son, and Kevin was visibly upset that his warning had been ignored.

Shortly after that meeting and interviews with several newspapers, I took Kevin to Glasgow to meet Neil McKay of the Scottish *Sunday Herald*. Though I didn't know it, I was about to meet one of the finest journalists in Britain. As we sat alone in his office, the first thing I noticed was his desk and the paperwork strewn all over it; how he was able to find anything on it was beyond me. Liam Clarke was always well dressed and worked away diligently, but when Neil entered he was the complete opposite and stood out from the rest of the journalists in the main office. Neil was casual, very hip and wearing jeans, trainers and a black short-sleeved top. His black hair was unkempt and he needed a shave. Another thing that I didn't know about him at the time was that he was Irish. McKay was unlike any other journalist I'd met, he was 'ballsy' and had this 'couldn't give a fuck' attitude. I suppose that's how he got the job done and went on to win so many top UK awards.

As an example of the kind of journalist Neil was, when Kevin was telling his story he mentioned a phone number that he still had for his ex-handler. Any other journalist might have continued writing and note the number as he was building the piece for publication. But as soon as Kevin revealed the number Neil grabbed the phone on his desk, flipped the receiver up in the air slightly, caught it with his left hand and dialled the number with his right hand. As I sat there watching, his head suddenly shot up and his eyes rolled. He immediately put the phone down and stared at Kevin, 'Fuck me, you're right!' he exclaimed. Neil was also a decent man, and as it was a beautiful summer's day he suggested that we get out of the office and get some lunch. We sat outside a nice coffee-shop-cum-restaurant in Sauchiehall Street where he continued to record Kevin's remarkable story. By the following week, Kevin's story was front and centre in the *Herald*, and it wasn't long before Radio Clyde and several other media outlets started calling Neil for my number.

While I was in Glasgow I went to see Michael Martin, the Speaker of the House of Commons. He lived just along the road from Springburn Park, and we chatted about all sorts of issues. I was to discover that he had some interesting views. Obviously, as the speaker there wasn't much he could say about Kevin's predicament because he was restrained from getting involved in daily politics, but he did write a good article about my endeavours to help Kevin. I was on a roll, and when I got back to London I tried to get the Pope on our side.

I went to see a young journalist from the *Catholic Herald*, which is handed out every Sunday in all churches after mass. He approached Cardinal Cormac Murphy-O'Connor, who agreed to see me. You can imagine how nervous I was as I waited in the room on Francis Street, just beside Westminster Cathedral.

When Cardinal Murphy-O'Connor entered the room I was surprised at how tall he was. Dressed in normal priest's attire, he shook my hand and we dispensed of me kissing his ecclesiastical signet ring. 'Well young man, it's a real privilege to meet you.' This took me by surprise because I had thought I would have to speak first and explain myself; I even had a few well-rehearsed lines. It turned out he was an avid *Sunday Times* reader and had been taken by Liam Clarke's piece about me in May 2000. We also talked about my time in Derry, Mrs Thatcher, Bishop Daly, Bloody Sunday, Martin McGuinness and the Pope's visit to Ireland in 1979. He told me how sad it was that 'John Paul' never got to visit Armagh when he visited. Like me, he was a bit of a raconteur and it took over forty minutes for us to get to talk about Kevin's plight. It soon became clear that he was reluctant to get involved because protocol and church politics didn't give him much of a choice. My attempt to win over the Catholic Church had failed, but Cardinal Murphy-O'Connor produced a tiny relic from St Oliver Plunkett's casket in Drogheda and placed it in my palm saying, 'Keep that on your person, Willie, and pray for him; he's the patron saint of peace and reconciliation in Ireland, something that must be dear to your heart too.' With that, and right on cue, there was a knock at the door and he was informed of his next meeting. This time he did offer me to bow and kiss his signet ring, a huge piece with an oblong crucifix on it, and with that he was gone. I still have the relic to this very day and always carry it with me. I have twice been to the church in Drogheda to visit the main relic, the head of Oliver Plunkett, and I am always consumed with sadness when I pray beneath it.

While I was attempting to get Kevin Fulton some exposure, he did himself, nor me, no favours. He had managed to contact several other ex-soldiers, all claiming to be former spies who had been left high and dry by the Brits. He and his friend 'Tommy' started posting stuff on the internet using my name as their 'spokesperson', and whilst some of it was true, a lot of it was just plain lies, such was his mind-set, which I fully understood. That weekend, now back at my friend's apartment, it was my turn to feel the cold hand of officialdom on my shoulder. I was obviously causing a great deal of embarrassment in Belfast, Glasgow and in London because a few days after the *Herald* ran Kevin's story, two men in plainclothes claiming to be Special Branch came to the apartment to arrest me. I knew what they were up to because they were using my old name, but I put them at ease and kept them chatting while I got ready in the bedroom. As it was a basement flat they assumed there was only one way in and one way out, so I kept chatting to them on and off as I got dressed. During one of my pauses I climbed out of the window and jumped over the 6-foot wall at the back of the apartment. As luck would have it, the patio door of the next-door basement flat was open. This basement was different to that of my friend; whereas my friend's back room was a bedroom, theirs was a sitting room, and as I stepped into the room I could see a young Chinese couple with a baby on the girl's knee. The young man jumped up off the sofa and started yelling something in Chinese. I'll never forget the look on his face. 'Excuse me,' I said and ran past them. It was a crazy moment and it was like something you might see in a movie as the hero escapes his would-be captors. I ran out of the front door and up the stairs onto the street. I surreptitiously checked my friend's flat, now one door away on my left, and sure enough the two men were still waiting for me in the lounge. I calmly but speedily walked out of the street and phoned Kevin, who was by now staying at a B&B in Earl's Court with some money his wife had sent him. I stayed with him for a few days before venturing back to the apartment. Some weeks later Kevin moved on; he left one afternoon and I've not seen him since. A week later I returned home to Scotland.

Over the years I've heard and read a lot about Kevin, from descriptions of him being a hero to accusations of him being a liar and someone of bad character. But the man I knew was really a good guy and all he ever wanted was to be a 'soldier'. He was simply caught up in the whole 'dog-eat-dog' affair of the dirty war in the North. As for Kevin ever being recompensed for his service? I doubt it very much.

It's my understanding that anyone who is, or was, a member of a 'terrorist' organisation (IRA, UVF, etc.) cannot get compensation from the British government irrespective of who asked them to join, because technically they break the law when joining such an organisation. The only exception is when a member of a so-called terrorist organisation turns Queen's evidence and this results in the conviction of other terrorists. In that case it is deemed that the informant's life would be in danger and the government then allows monies for what's called a 'Duty of Care' programme. As Kevin never named names or turned Queen's evidence, he had never fitted into that category. However, I hope he sticks at it because I'm sure the powers that be will eventually relent, give in a little and see him housed and safe, if nothing else. Wherever he is these days, I wish him well and trust that he and his wife are safe.

* * *

Martin McGuinness, Derry and the Troubles were never far away even in my years of exile across the Irish Sea. In 2001, I was summoned to speak at the Saville Inquiry into the events of Bloody Sunday. This was mainly prompted by the urgings of MI5 handler 'Stephen', one of my most trusted associates. He came to visit me shortly after a phone call telling me that he was in retirement and owned a little vineyard in Italy. But old MI5 agents such as myself never seem to retire completely, and Stephen was on a mission that concerned the fate of none other than Martin McGuinness.

'Willie, Lord Saville is heading up the inquiry into all that happened on Bloody Sunday in Derry back in January 1972,' said Stephen. 'It's becoming abundantly clear to him and his team that the Paras ran amok that day and it's possible that charges could eventually be brought against some of the soldiers. My contact tells me that in order to counterbalance the blame there is to be evidence by a so-called informer they are calling "Infliction". "Infliction" will claim that McGuinness admitted firing the first shots that caused the confusion that led to the soldiers returning fire on Bloody Sunday. Willie, you have the key to that and can prove that's not true because you reported it to us in the 1980s.'

I was absolutely stunned by this as Stephen had clearly remembered a conversation between myself and McGuinness in the presence of another senior republican back in the 1980s in which Martin denied he was armed or had any involvement in shooting against the Brits on the day. Now, here was Stephen asking me to give evidence to Lord Saville's inquiry to knock down what could be construed as a dirty tricks campaign aimed at McGuinness. The former MI5 handler was clearly under orders to persuade me to counter this allegation at the Bloody Sunday tribunal. After a few days deliberating whether or not I should give evidence to Saville I decided to initially expose 'Infliction' in the international press. I contacted Henry McDonald of *The*

Observer, and forty-eight hours later I was back in Belfast for a meeting with Henry in the Europa Hotel to pass on that an agent called 'Infliction' was trying to link Martin McGuinness to the opening shots on that terrible day.

The following Sunday, Henry's story was published in *The Observer* and all hell broke loose. As soon as I got back to London I was served with a notice banning me from naming 'Infliction' because it could endanger his life. Following the story, Lord Saville's legal team issued me with a summons to appear before the tribunal, which I had no problem in doing. Worryingly, however, Henry had a visit from the RUC, who demanded that all his interview notes, along with the laptop on which he allegedly wrote my story, be handed over to them. Henry refused to break source confidentiality and was arrested. *The Observer*'s management backed Henry, providing one of the sharpest legal minds in Northern Ireland to defend him, whilst the National Union of Journalists issued a statement condemning his arrest and the pressure he was under to hand over the interview notes. Clearly, he and I had hit a raw nerve.

Once Henry was freed, having resolutely refused to hand over his notes and his computer, it was my time to go under the spotlight of the Saville inquiry. My appearance was quite eventful because it took place in London rather than Derry. I was to be interviewed in the offices of Imran Khan, the human rights lawyer, where I would give evidence on video tape. This was witnessed by two men, one a member of the Saville legal team and the other, I later discovered, was a member of the security service who had served notice on the tribunal for access to my evidence prior to it being given to the chairman. Two weeks later a heavily edited copy of my evidence arrived at Imran's office. The written statement I had given in conjunction with the tape had also been redacted, and when Imran asked about this he was informed that the redactions were for 'security reasons' and even Lord Saville wasn't cleared to read those segments of my evidence.

Although this experience was surreal, it did afford me the chance to punch a hole in the 'Infliction' theory over McGuinness firing the first shots at Bloody Sunday. I recall using the words 'bogus and erroneous' to describe that allegation. Why? Because the lie grew out of something I overheard McGuinness saying many years earlier when he described firing a submachine gun for the first time in the early 1970s. I later learnt that 'Infliction' had also been party to that conversation, and he must have relayed the information to his own handlers. That juicy titbit of McGuinness gossip had lain dormant in military intelligence files until it was unearthed again when it became politically expedient to do so as the British state prepared for the Bloody Sunday tribunal. It remains a mystery to me that while a branch of the British security forces was prepared to bend and twist the intelligence from an informer, another wing of the deep state was urging me to do what I could to damage the validity of that allegation. Perhaps the latter faction of the security apparatus was looking at the wider political picture and recognised how important Martin McGuinness remained in terms of guiding the republican movement away from the cul de sac of armed struggle and towards peaceful politics.

I recall something I said to Henry McDonald a few weeks before giving evidence to the Saville Inquiry, and I stand by it to this day: 'Before I die, I want to give evidence to the inquiry. McGuinness should fry for some of the things he has done, but I can't stand by and see an inquiry that is trying its best to get at the truth about the murder of those people on Bloody Sunday be muddied by the Ministry of Defence. The statement from "Infliction" about McGuinness's involvement is bogus. I am not prepared to keep silent while I see the law abused.' Of course, I didn't get any thanks from republicans for undermining this crude British attempt to link McGuinness to the first shots on that dreadful day in 1972. In fact, in the midst of the inquiry my lawyer received a tip-off from the security service that two men with thick Irish accents and fake journalist identity cards had turned up in London. They were trying to find where I was about to give evidence, so naturally we made a quick exit from the office in central London and changed our security arrangements. As we were whisked away I remember something Martin McGuinness once said regarding the IRA's treatment of informers, 'You know the rules!' It was a warning that I have never forgotten.

A NIGHT AT THE BOXING

It was 2001, and I was sitting at a table in the plush ballroom of the Europa Hotel in Belfast with the tenacious *Sunday World* investigative reporter Hugh Jordan when he told me to turn around and see who was standing directly behind me. When I swivelled around in my chair there was Sir Ronnie Flanagan, then the Chief Constable of the Royal Ulster Constabulary, planted just two feet away. Jordan pointed at me and asked Sir Ronnie, 'Do you know who this is?' Flanagan looked at me for a second, then exclaimed, 'Jesus! Willie Carlin!' He leaned across to shake my hand and asked if we could have a private chat outside.

I had flown back to Belfast, ostensibly to work with Channel 4 News on a report about my role as an agent, as well as comment on a number of scandals that were breaking all around the security forces in Northern Ireland. Jordan had heard that I had quietly slipped into the city and contacted me. He asked if I would like to attend a charity boxing match organised by the RUC at the Europa. Although I had a long-running antipathy towards the Northern Ireland police force, I thought that at least I would be safe amidst the tight security around the event, and it was a chance to catch up with Jordan and share a few 'war stories' with him.

While the RUC boxers took on all comers in the makeshift ring, I left the arena to verbally spar with Sir Ronnie. We had previously had a major disagreement over Kevin Fulton's testimony to the Omagh bomb inquiry headed up by the redoubtable Police Ombudsman Nuala O'Loan, who had taken Fulton's claims very seriously that intelligence he passed on to the RUC about a planned attack on Omagh in August 1998 had been ignored. Her criticism of the RUC's handling of the intelligence, and thus its failure to intercept the Real IRA bomb, was based partly on Fulton's evidence. Even though I had stood by Fulton, and Baroness O'Loan's report had singled Sir Ronnie out for explicit criticism, Sir Ronnie said he bore me no malice. 'You know Willie, I used to read about you and although I didn't know your name I knew you were a very brave man. You did a lot of good here and I am personally very proud to be standing here talking to you.'

Touched by his generous attitude, I imposed on the goodwill of the last Chief Constable of the RUC with one more question, something that had been consuming me since my extraction from Derry fifteen years earlier: what about the 'soldier' way back in the mid-80s who had saved my life. The informer who had tipped off the FRU that I was about to be lifted by the IRA 'Nutting Squad' for interrogation and execution? Wasn't he called 'Stakeknife'? Suddenly, Sir Ronnie's relaxed attitude changed. Stiffening, he came close to me and whispered, 'Listen, son, you stay well clear of that. He was no soldier and that's all going to go bad. You have nothing to do with it, do you hear me?' As he turned away I slipped outside the Europa for a quick cigarette and wondered why Sir Ronnie was so adamant that I should 'stay away' from Stakeknife. I was perplexed, because this man had passed information on to his handler that the

IRA was about to 'lift' me after they had discovered I had been working first for MI5 and latterly the FRU. Why should I avoid him at all costs, I wondered?

After my extraction by the FRU, I had learned from my handlers that none of them knew who Stakeknife was apart from some unsubstantiated rumours that he was either an ice cream salesman or a builder, but that he was certainly ruthless and not to be trusted. The first hints of the existence of 'Steak Knife' emerged as far back as 1999, when my good friend the late Liam Clarke disclosed in *The Sunday Times* that there was a high-level spy in the IRA who earned £60,000 and was described as the 'jewel in the crown' of British intelligence in Northern Ireland. Stakeknife even had his own dedicated group of handlers and agents, and it was suggested that the British government allowed up to forty people to be killed by the IRA's Internal Security Unit – the 'Nutting Squad' – in order to protect his cover. Yet it was Stakeknife who saved me from a bullet in the back of the head, which might seem strange given that he stands personally accused of more than two dozen murders, the overwhelming majority of them alleged informers from within the IRA. But why did he pass on information to his handlers in my case? Why spare me instead of going ahead with his deadly deceit of being a loyal spy-catcher for the IRA and using my death to enhance his reputation inside the organisation's most ruthless killing unit?

I knew that my 'political' intelligence eventually overtook the usefulness of some military information, and as a result it had been given a very high priority. It was thanks to me that electoral law was changed in the North, and I had passed strategically vital intelligence about the bust-up between McGuinness and Ivor Bell that cemented the British state's determination that the former triumph over the latter in that internal IRA battle. My guess, albeit an educated one, is that I was extracted simply because of bigger power play politics. If Stakeknife had made it to my door and 'lifted' me it is certain that under his lethal glare and vigorous interrogation I would have broken and talked quite quickly. I would have confessed to getting close to McGuinness while all the time spying for MI5 and then the FRU, all under Martin's nose, and this could have been used against him by his opponents on the Army Council and other highly placed echelons of the IRA.

Clearly, Ivor Bell would have had a field day with the material on any Willie Carlin confession tape. Bell and his allies could have used this information to undermine McGuinness's authority and perhaps in doing so set back movement towards the peace process by decades. After all, Bell was correct in his assessment that money was being diverted away from the IRA's war chest to Sinn Féin's coffers as the party expanded and elections put a huge strain on the entire movement's finances. In the event, Bell never did get the chance to derail McGuinness. In 1984 he was court-martialled and dismissed from the IRA. He was later to be arrested by the police in 2014 and was charged with aiding and abetting murder and membership of the IRA. It is said that Bell is awaiting trial but suffers from dementia and is a sad shadow of his former self. However, I can only conclude that it was essential for British politico-military strategy to keep me out of the hands of Stakeknife and his team of 'head-hunters'.

Michael Oatley, a former MI6 officer, was posted to Belfast in 1973 and became convinced of the need to develop dialogue with the leadership of the Provisional IRA with a view to influencing it in a political direction. He succeeded in establishing secure lines of communication with the IRA leadership, though back then the talks between McGuinness and Oatley were at a very early stage. This secret channel, facilitated by the likes of Brendan Duddy and former priest Denis Bradley, ultimately delivered an IRA cessation of violence in 1994. The 'Nutting Squad' could have winkled many secrets out of me, including my sighting in the 1970s of Martin McGuinness leaving the same MI5 safe house that Michael Bettaney used. What might have happened to McGuinness if this had been exposed on tape, or if I had been paraded by the IRA at a press conference in Belfast admitting to having been a British spy in Derry for nearly twelve years?

It is worth remembering that both MI5 and MI6 were tracking Ivor Bell's Libyan arms shipment, due to arrive in Ireland a few months after my extraction, in August 1985. After the realisation of my 'betrayal' of Sinn Féin, the Security Service knew that McGuinness was going to have to go some to survive Frank Hegarty's subsequent 'treachery' and his own judgement in bringing 'Franko' into the movement in the first place, even though Hegarty had originally been in the Official IRA and left under a cloud of suspicion. McGuinness was already under savage pressure, and the last thing he needed was any Carlin confessions being deployed against him. For all of these reasons I contend that I was actually spared to save Martin McGuinness.

Given the intense interest my handlers placed on the evolution of McGuinness's political thinking, it is clear they saw in him someone they believed could, alongside Adams, bring about an end to the IRA's armed struggle. Their assessment was that Martin had to be protected from the hard-liners as much as possible. My guess is that the British recognised these dangers and acted rapidly to rescue me from the IRA's internal security team. In the end it all turned out benign, as the McGuinness–

Adams axis won through and pulled a masterful trick on the Irish republican base and pushed it, slowly at first and then with surprising haste, towards ending armed action and fully embracing democratic methods.

* * *

In May 2003 it was alleged in the press, partly as a result of information posted online by Kevin Fulton, that Stakeknife was a builder from Belfast by the name of Alfredo 'Freddie' Scappaticci. The grandson of an Italian ice cream salesman, Scappaticci was said to have been recruited by the FRU and given the number 6126, and eventually the codename 'Stakeknife'. Scappaticci denied that he was ever Stakeknife, but it continues to be a conundrum: he was allegedly killing IRA informers, and it was reported that he was sometimes given the 'green light' to do so by the FRU. Why then, when he was eventually 'outed', was Scappaticci allowed to turn up in Belfast and give a now famous and much choreographed press conference in the west of the city and then simply walk away? Tellingly, there were no significant Sinn Féin figures present at the press conference, and it was clearly obvious that senior members of Sinn Féin didn't want him saying anything about what he did for them when they were leaders of the IRA, and neither did the British Army.

The word 'scandal' is still appropriate when describing the work of Stakeknife and what his own spymasters allowed him to get away with. It all centres on claims that while he worked as a top spy inside the IRA's 'head-hunters'/counter-intelligence unit he was directly linked to the deaths of numerous IRA members. But why was Scappaticci allowed to commit crimes up to and including murder whilst working as a paid state agent, and why did no one in the IRA ever act against him? As someone who has spent decades living in the shadows and practising the art of survival on a daily basis, I feel there is great credibility to the claims that Scappaticci has an insurance policy that protects him (for now) from his former comrades. The allegations are that he has voluminous tape recordings stashed away as his 'get out of jail' card, detailing his life in the IRA, including the actions of those around him, some of them currently holding very senior leadership positions in the republican movement on its military and political wings. What might happen if these tapes are publicly released on to the internet or to a major news organisation? What might happen to the peace process if such tapes reveal that senior IRA men who are now Sinn Féin officials were complicit in murder or major criminal activity? How would that information affect issues ranging from Brexit, the Irish border question and the Good Friday Agreement?

This is surely an issue that not only haunts some of my old comrades in the republican movement but also the British state, as it ponders on the endgame of Operation Kenova, an independent investigation launched in 2016 into 'a range of activities surrounding an individual codenamed Stakeknife' and also whether 'there is evidence of criminal offences having been committed by members of the British Army, the Security Services or other government personnel'. Led by former counter-terrorism detective Jon Boutcher, Operation Kenova has a budget of around thirty million pounds and allegedly an assurance from the former British Prime Minister Theresa May that the operation's officers will be allowed to poke and probe into every dark corner that Stakeknife and his handlers cast their shadows. In January 2018, Freddie Scappaticci ('Scap') was arrested by officers from Operation Kenova 'in connection with the investigation into allegations of murder, kidnap and torture'.

The families of the men (and at least one woman) who were dispatched by Scap and his 'nutting squad' demand justice and truth. Yet I was left with a huge dilemma of my own. I could certainly help prove he was an agent of the FRU, because he had saved my life by tipping off his handler about my fate. However, that would mean flying against the established narrative of Stakeknife as an angel of death instead of the saviour of life that he had been in my case. Nonetheless, I decided I would still talk to Operation Kenova detectives and tell them the truth. On Ash Wednesday 2019, I met with two of Chief Constable Boutcher's team, detectives I will call 'Robert' and 'Bernie'. By now I had been working with this pair for over a year. I understand that they have also spoken to some of the handlers who were looking after me when I was living in Kent, and who were aware of that night in March 1985, in the early days of my exile, when they started to open up about the man who had saved my life – the agent from Belfast, the FRU's 'jewel in the crown'.

Working with Robert and Bernie has certainly spooked someone in the security establishment, because in April 2019 I discovered that my new home was covertly entered while I was out and someone had rifled through my belongings. They found a briefcase containing private papers and my redacted evidence, not only to the Bloody Sunday Inquiry but also my notes on Stakeknife. The latter would make good reading for senior members of military intelligence, whom I believe would dearly love to thwart the efforts of Robert, Bernie, and the rest of the Kenova team. At the very least it would give the FRU a chance to prepare for questions from the Kenova detectives based on notes that I had made about the scandal. Weirdly, perhaps, the full manuscript of this book was sitting right in front of them but they totally disregarded it. Whoever was in my house knew what they were after.

On one level Sir Ronnie was right that night at the Europa Hotel in warning me against getting too deeply immersed in the Stakeknife saga. But even now, I have to look back on the events at Ebrington Barracks in March 1985 and our subsequent flight from Derry, and wonder that if Scappaticci had not acted quickly enough in warning his handlers about the target of the IRA 'Nutting Squad' I would be dead. If Scap ever does end up in court, the question remains: Do I give evidence against the man who saved my life? I don't know, but I will continue to work with Boutcher's detectives to get to the truth. The only thing of which I can be certain, as I observe the events of the Stakeknife story taking ever more serpentine twists and turns, is that this man unquestionably saved my life and probably, in the long run, kept the momentum within the movement that I first infiltrated way back in 1974 in the direction of peace.

AN AFTERLIFE – OF SORTS

A secret agent never really retires; you are doomed to live a lie for the rest of your time on this earth. You may have a new identity, a new passport, a new driving licence and a National Insurance number in the name of someone you weren't supposed to be, but the truth is there is no such thing as a new identity. You will always be you.

In this weird afterlife such things are mild burdens compared to forever looking over your shoulder, protecting your loved ones and being in exile from your family back home in Ireland. For instance, how do you explain to your 6-year-old daughter that she will never see her granny again, or tell your 10-year-old son that he has to learn a new name? There's also the whole issue of relocating and your children going off to school with this new cover story. Your whole world becomes one big lie, and you can't reveal who you really are to anyone. After a few months, you realise that you've been an addict living on adrenaline for years, and you're now going cold turkey. This is when you crave the drug and take risks with your life just to get a fix. If you're not careful, you can spiral out of control and start looking for a replacement drug, which usually comes in the form of a vodka bottle, and you can end up an alcoholic like Raymond Gilmour. Fortunately, because you have your family to care for, you have to fight the temptation daily and concentrate on the task of this new life.

I remember Stephen saying to me one day, 'If you ever tell anyone about being Mrs Thatcher's spy and that you're a real 007, no one will ever believe you.' Yet in situations where I would sometimes overhear people in Britain talking utter nonsense about the Troubles or Derry I wanted to scream out that I was once on the inside track; I had been party to intelligence that reached 10 Downing Street and inside an organisation that the British state had fought against for a quarter of a century. The frustration at having to listen to the ill-informed comments and opinions of people, including English politicians, many of whom could barely locate the north of Ireland on a map, was nerve-shredding.

Of course, this was nothing compared to the whole question of the loved ones we had to leave behind. The guilt of leaving parents and cousins to cope with the wreckage I had caused in the republican movement in Derry was and ever will be a terrible burden. I have personal experience of receiving information about the death of loved ones, which each time was devastating. I was at home one night when I received a call to tell me that my mother was in a really bad way and probably wouldn't make it through the night. I was bereft and just sobbed, but worse still was being told that I couldn't go to her funeral because of the ongoing danger that the IRA would try to exact revenge – even though this was long after ceasefires and decommissioning. Five years ago, I received a call to tell me that my daughter Maria had been killed in a tragic car accident. It is the worst piece of news that I have ever received. My little girl, who left Ireland with us all those years ago, now lay in a morgue that I was not allowed to visit.

After a troubled marriage, Maria had left Scotland with her two sons to be with her mother. She had settled down and was attending college in Letterkenny, County Donegal. On the first day of the new academic year, she and a friend were leaving college when her friend's boyfriend offered them a lift back into town. As soon as he started driving it became clear to Maria that he was drunk. She screamed to be let out of the car but the young man just kept driving. Eventually, he lost control of the vehicle and hit a telegraph pole head on. Maria's friend, who wasn't wearing a seat belt, was sent flying through the windscreen and was killed almost instantly. The car then spun across the road, rolled over three times and came to rest in a lorry park. Maria climbed out of the back seat and tried to stand up, but instead of trying to help her the driver abandoned them and ran off back into town. Cars screamed to a halt and a young woman ran to help Maria. The ambulance arrived within minutes and took her to Letterkenny hospital. And as the doctor tried to keep Maria alive she was heard to say, 'Please tell my mammy.' Maria is buried beside her friend and lies in a grave with a headstone which carries the inscription: 'Maria, beloved daughter of Mary'. It was felt that to put my name on the headstone might lead to the grave being vandalised. The driver of the car could only be charged with manslaughter and is now serving an eight-year jail sentence in Dublin.

Earlier this year my son Mark, who was only fourteen when we left Ireland, developed sepsis after a short illness and though the doctors tried in vain to save him he died in a hospital in Galway and is now buried beside his sister. Once again, I couldn't go to the funeral or even send flowers in case I was traced to my secret address via the florist. Only a few weeks ago at the time of writing, in the spring of 2019, my dear brother Robert, who grew up with me in Derry and joined the army alongside me, died of cancer. Robert was a good man who kept himself to himself and was dearly loved by his partner, Valerie. I spoke to him a few months ago when he told me that he was finding it difficult to swallow. It was a total shock and again he was buried without me being there. Last year my sister Doreen was diagnosed with terminal cancer and she and I talked every day as she fought her way through her illness and the chemotherapy. It saddens me to tell you that she passed away a few weeks before publishing this book. It's ironic that, all those years ago, Alan Rees-Morgan mentioned her in an effort to persuade me to work for MI5. I've never mentioned it before to anyone, but Doreen was a member of Cumann na mBan (women's IRA). She joined in 1974 at the age of 16, the same year that I joined MI5. She and I never discussed it but just before she died, we had a long, happy conversation about those years when we were both on opposite sides of the divide and neither of us knew. Her last words to me were 'I love you, Bro.' I loved my wee sister dearly and it broke my heart that I wasn't able to go to her funeral. Yet another death that I'll mourn in silence.

For many of those who murdered and maimed for their respective causes in the conflict, their war is long over and they can settle down to as normal a life as possible. The painful paradox for me is that for those like myself who worked to undermine the armed struggle and help nudge mainstream republicanism towards politics and peace, this war never ends. Mine is a war of nerves for the rest of my life; a war of survival and avoiding the traps that might allow someone to exact revenge. Whenever I become complacent about my security or get caught up in the fantasy of returning to Derry for good I think of the fates of Eamon Collins and Denis Donaldson, two IRA figures who took their chances and ended up losing their lives at the hands of former comrades who never forgave them for their betrayal. Collins suffered a horrific death near his home, savagely beaten and stabbed by the IRA in Newry. Donaldson retreated to the life of a hermit in a squalid little cottage in Donegal after being 'outed' as a high-ranking informer within both the IRA and Sinn Féin. He was blasted with a shotgun by associates of the legendary IRA East Tyrone Brigade commander Jim Lynagh, who also personally exacted revenge on an informer before being killed by the SAS in May 1987 during an attack on an isolated rural police station. Despite everything that happened to me as an agent working for MI5, and latterly as an activist working to defend those agents wronged by the British government and the innocents who lost their lives during the Troubles, I often fall asleep wondering what is it that I'm supposed to know that I still don't know. But I have no doubt in my mind that a similar fate awaits me if I ever openly returned to Derry.

Even my dead are not safe from the designs of those who would harm me. I cannot and will not publicly disclose the locations of their resting places. After all, they could be the target of hate mongers and avengers for years to come, their headstones vandalised, their burial grounds violated. So I exist to the end in the world of the unforgiven, even though I firmly believe that I did my bit to help bring peace to the land that I love.